D0984054

JAMES JOYCE'S *FINNEGANS WAKE*

GARLAND REFERENCE LIBRARY
OF THE HUMANITIES
(VOL. 1003)

JAMES JOYCE'S *FINNEGANS WAKE*
A Casebook

edited by
John Harty III

GARLAND PUBLISHING, INC. • NEW YORK & LONDON
1991

Library of Congress Cataloging-in-Publication Data

James Joyce's Finnegans wake : a casebook / edited by John Harty, III.
    p.   cm. — (Garland reference library of the humanities; vol.
1003)
    Includes index.
    ISBN 0-8240-1211-9
    1. Joyce, James, 1882–1941. Finnegans wake. I. Harty, John,
1945– . II. Series.
PR6019.09F59354   1991
823'.912—dc20
                                         90–48730
                                             CIP

Printed on acid-free, 250-year-life paper
Manufactured in the United States of America

For

Adaline Glasheen

CONTENTS

Part II: Joyce's Textual Self-
Referentiality

Part III: Performance

Contents

Acknowledgments

To the essayists. To the staff at Garland Publishing, especially my editor Phyllis Korper. To Lisa Gibilisco for excellent assistance. To all librarians at Northern Michigan University and the University of Florida, especially Dolores Jenkins and Pam Pasak. To Patricia Craddock, Chair of the English Department at the University of Florida, and to Leonard Heldreth, Head of the English Department at Northern Michigan University, and to the faculty and staff at both. To my dedicated typists : Lynn Johnson, Danielle Davis, Kim Gosset, Brian Roberts, and to their supervisor Bob Stillwell. To the National Endowment for the Humanities and Professor Michael Seidel for Professor Seidel's 1987 summer seminar on James Joyce. To the Northeast Modern Language Association for a grant to attend Fritz Senn's James Joyce Center in Zurich in 1987. To Adaline Glasheen.

Editor's Note

Quotations from *Finnegans Wake* are designated as follows. Book and chapter numbers are given in roman and arabic numerals—for example, I.6 for book one, chapter six. Page and line numbers (for example, 293.31) are given in parentheses. The letters L, R, and F indicate left- and right-margin notes and footnotes in II.2 (for example, 290.F2 for the second footnote on page 290 .

Page references to *Ulysses* (New York: Random House, 1961) are preceded by a *U*. References to *Ulysses*, ed. Hans Walter Gabler, et al. (New York: Random House, 1986) are by chapter and line number. Thus, for example, *U* 8.258 refers to chapter eight ("Lestrygonians"), line 258.

Abbreviations

D	Joyce, James. *Dubliners*, ed. Robert Scholes in consultation with Richard Ellmann. New York: Viking Press, 1967. Joyce, James. *"Dubliners": Text, Criticism, and Notes*, ed. Robert Scholes and A. Walton Litz. New York: Viking Press, 1969.
FW	Joyce, James. *Finnegans Wake*. New York: Viking Press, 1939; London: Faber and Faber, 1939. These two editions have identical pagination.
JJI	Ellmann, Richard. *James Joyce*. New York: Oxford University Press, 1959.
JJII	Ellmann, Richard. *James Joyce*. New York: Oxford University Press, 1982.
JJA	*The James Joyce Archive*, ed. David Hayman, et al. New York and London: Garland Publishing, 1978.
Letters I,II, III	Joyce, James. *Letters of James Joyce*. Vol. I, ed. Stuart Gilbert. New York: Viking Press, 1957; reissued with corrections 1966. Vols. II and III, ed. Richard Ellmann. New York: Viking Press, 1966.
P	Joyce, James. *A Portrait of the Artist as a Young Man.* The definitive text corrected from Dublin Holograph by Chester G. Anderson and edited by Richard Ellmann. New York: Viking Press, 1964. Joyce, James. *"A Portrait of the Artist as a Young Man": Text, Criticism, and Notes,* ed. Chester G. Anderson. New York: Viking Press, 1968.
SH	Joyce, James. *Stephen Hero*, ed. John J. Slocum and Herbert Cahoon. New York: New Directions, 1944, 1963.
SL	Joyce, James. *Selected Letters of James Joyce*, ed. Richard Ellmann. New York: Viking Press, 1975.
U	+episode and line number. Joyce, James. *Ulysses*, ed. Hans Walter Gabler, et al. New York and London: Garland Publishing, 1984, 1986. In paperback by Garland, Random House, Bodley Head, and Penguin.
U	+page number. Joyce, James. *Ulysses*. New York: Random House, 1934, reset and corrected 1961.

Introduction

John Harty

"MY WARM THANKS TO ALL CONCERNED FOR PATIENCE
PROMPTITUDE WHICH I GREATLY APPRECIATE."

So read the telegram James Joyce sent to Faber & Faber on January 30, 1939, upon receiving the first copy of *Finnegans Wake*, a title he had withheld from all including Faber & Faber until publication was imminent.[1] The first copy had arrived in time to celebrate Joyce's birthday on February 2, a tradition Joyce had set for the publication of his works, with the implication perhaps being that miracles of birth, especially his own, and the production of miraculous art have a certain similarity.

One wonders how the printers for Faber & Faber must have felt about *Finnegans Wake* as they first began their task. What about misprints? Who beyond Joyce and his proofers would notice errors?

Richard Ellmann describes the details and the drama leading up to the publication of *Finnegans Wake*. Initially Joyce had hoped to publish the *Wake* on February 2, 1938. As February 2, 1938, became impossible, Joyce asked Herbert Gorman to withhold publication of Joyce's biography until March 1938. Gorman agreed, stating to his publisher: "I will never write another biography of a living man. It is too difficult and thankless a task."[2]

Joyce now hoped to publish *Finnegans Wake* on another date—July 4, his father's birthday. Faber & Faber objected because of the possibility of weak summer sales. Joyce had been overly optimistic again and July 4, 1938, passed without publication. Finally, what Nora had labelled "chop suey" was published after a series of harrowing proofings by Joyce's devoted team of friends. Paul Leon supplied some last minute drama as he left a section of revised proofs in a taxi. He rushed to Joyce to inform him of the mishap. Joyce, who had to be exhausted at this point, did not reproach Leon but took the ill omen in stride. The taxi driver later returned the proofs.[3]

To dismiss *Finnegans Wake* is an easy but erroneous solution to the problem of what to do with it. The preponderance of available information on its value now makes it unavoidable as a work to contend with. Had someone else written it, it might have languished unread. But James Joyce was the author.

Rather than give an annotated bibliography of critical movements here, I refer the reader to Bernard Benstock's *James Joyce: The Augmented Ninth* which overviews the Ninth International James Joyce Symposium held in Frankfurt, West Germany, in June 1984.[4] That collection of essays surveys the new critical perspectives on Joyce's works and includes essays on the influence of deconstruction, Lacan, feminism, Marxism, and so forth. For the reader just beginning work on *Finnegans Wake* or in need of a helpful reference, I would suggest Adaline Glasheen's *Third Census* and Patrick McCarthy's "The Structures and Meanings of *Finnegans Wake*."[5] Arguably the most important book to have at hand while reading the *Wake* is Roland McHugh's *Annotations to Finnegans*

Wake, a page by page listing of explications.[6] This book is certainly valuable, but it must be used with caution.

Clive Hart warned *Wake* enthusiasts in his *A Concordance to Finnegans Wake*: "The student of *Finnegans Wake* needs to be a humble person."[7] Problems begin with the title *Finnegans Wake*, as publishers, editors, and others assume that it should be *Finnegan's Wake*.

Joyce often employs misprints. One of the most significant of these in *Ulysses* concerns Martha Clifford's mistyping "world" for "word" in a letter to Bloom.[8] Joyce magnifies this process many times in *Finnegans Wake* and the chance for textual misprints was also thus increased.

Perhaps because of his desire "to keep the professors busy for centuries", and his death in 1941, Joyce gave us little help in deciphering *Finnegans Wake*, misleading the reader as often as not. As with *Ulysses*, he was very careful about comments on the *Wake*.

It has been suggested that what Joyce was attempting in *Finnegans Wake* was a work that could be placed third alongside the collected works of Shakespeare and the Bible. Narrowing the focus, Bernard Benstock has stated that the specific Ur-text for the *Wake* is the Book of Genesis. This idea links up Earwicker's "sin" with Adam's fall (and thus man's) in the Garden of Eden, transformed in the *Wake* into Dublin's Phoenix Park.[9]

This volume contains one outline of the *Wake* and fifteen essays. The outline plus four of the essays are reprints, but the authors in most cases have made changes to their original work. Many of the other essays were originally conference papers at various James Joyce symposia including the June 1987 conference in Milwaukee, the Zurich conference in August 1987, the June 1988 conference in Venice, and the February 1989 conference in Miami, Florida. The rest of the essays here were composed especially for this volume.

I have divided this casebook up into three sections—Part I: Assessments, Part II: Joyce's Textual Self-Referentiality, and Part III: Performance. The essays have been arranged in an order that might allow them to be read in sequence. Since Joyce made it so difficult for readers to understand where they are at any given page in the *Wake*, I have included Bernard Benstock's "A Working Outline of *Finnegans Wake*." Although such an aid cannot be definitive, it does offer needed guidance for a text with no chapter titles, characters who merge into other characters and thus whose identities are ambiguous or unknown, speakers who are not identified, and a host of other problems confusing the reader.

Part I: Assessments

In "Dreaming Up the *Wake*" David Hayman analyses four cryptic dreams recorded in the *Wake* notebooks between 1923 and 1927, speculating about their possible contributions to the evolution of the book. His essay is designed to show how the enormous mass of genetic materials can illuminate both the life and the work. Colin MacCabe's "An Introduction to *Finnegans Wake*" examines book I.7 (*FW* 169-195), the portrait of Shem the Penman. MacCabe discusses

Shem's method of writing as described in the well-known passage (*FW* 185.27-186.8) and examines it against earlier versions from Joyce's notebooks. Beginning with the title, Hugh Kenner's "SHEM THE TEXT MAN" examines certain "words," the language of *Finnegans Wake*, and Joyce's linguistic arrangement of the text. Sheldon Brivic's "The Femasculine Obsubject: A Lacanian Reading of *FW* 606-607" demonstrates that the cited passage, primarily a description of landscape, becomes an object of desire that looks back to the viewer and elicits his or her being. Bernard Benstock's "Quinet in the *Wake*: The Proof or the Pudding" notes that Joyce's use of a sentence from Quinet (*FW* 281.3-13) "stands undistorted in the middle of the Night Lessons chapter." Benstock provides possible reasons for its inclusion and its relationship to the *Wake* as a whole. Vincent Cheng's "*Finnegans Wake*: All the World's a Stage" shows how Joyce conceived the *Wake* essentially as a drama, performed on the "worldstage" by a stock company, and how this theme underlies all the "action" of *Finnegans Wake*. The members of the HCE family-cast perform countless variations of the all-play, the archetypal family drama. John Gordon's "The Convertshems of the Tchoose: Judaism and Jewishness in *Finnegans Wake*" concentrates on the antisemitic attacks that Shem undergoes and argues that Shem seeks assimilation, one reason for his overtures to Shaun. Gordon suggests the possibility of a correspondence between the Bible and the *Wake*, much like the one between the *Odyssey* and *Ulysses*. Al Montesi's "Joyce's 'Blue Guitar': Wallace Stevens and *Finnegans Wake*" discovers that both Joyce and Wallace Stevens were aesthetically attempting similar modern sensibilities. Wallace Stevens, three years older than Joyce, created several poems, including "The Man With The Blue Guitar" and "Thirteen Ways of Looking at a Blackbird," that can be directly compared to thematic concerns in *Finnegans Wake*.

Part II: Joyce's Textual Self-Referentiality

Each of the essays in this section makes connections between Joyce's earlier works and *Finnegans Wake*. Alan Loxterman's "Every Man His Own God: From *Ulysses* to *Finnegans Wake*" argues that the "*Wake* can provide its readers with a more unified reading experience than *Ulysses* because the discontinuity between the *Wake*'s characters and plot and its overall argumentative design is more uniform—in fact, more comprehensive—than in any previous work of literature." Its language is more self-referential than that of *Ulysses*; by comparison, the *Wake* seems unique in expressing "more about itself than about people or ideas." David Robinson's "Joyce's Nonce-Symbolic Calculus: A *Finnegans Wake* Trajectory" outlines the HCE saga found in *FW* I.4 and traces Joyce's use and distortion of "Grace" and "Hades" within *Finnegans Wake*. And finally Kimberly Devlin's "The Female Word" compares ALP's language, especially in her letters, with Molly's various musings in *Ulysses*. The forced coyness of both Martha Clifford and Molly in *Ulysses* becomes ALP's mysterious letter with its official and repressed text. Joyce's male characters often believe that women have an "other" language, one that is not comprehensible to men.

Part III: Performance

The essays in Part III discuss the *Wake* and adaptations of the *Wake* in such a way that an audience becomes a necessary corollary to the experience. One of the best ways to read and study the *Wake* is as a group reading experience, much like an academic class, except that there are no grades. There are at present several groups that meet on a regular basis throughout the United States and

Europe. At the various Joyce symposia each year these groups often attend and share their processes with those at the conventions. David Borodin details the experiences of one such group, The Philadelphia *Wake* Circle, in "'Group drinkards maaks grope thinkards or how reads rotary' (*FW* 312.31): *Finnegans Wake* and the Group Reading Experience." Borodin traces the history of such groups, beginning in the United States with William York Tindall at Columbia University in 1940. He includes the results of a session at Venice in which The Philadelphia *Wake* Circle discussed the Muta and Juva passage (*FW* 609-610) before an audience which was allowed to voice readings also. David Hayman's "Notes for the Staging of *Finnegans Wake*" critiques the early stagings of *Finnegans Wake*, finding them variously inadequate—including the best one, Mary Manning's *Passages from Finnegans Wake*—in that each production through 1962 has attempted to encompass the whole of *Finnegans Wake*. Hayman elaborates a possible stage scenario from II.3 which concentrates on the dramatic situation of HCE in his pub, confronted with his life as projected by the pub clients, through four theatrical sketches. To his early essay Hayman has added a postscript updating his conclusion. Kit Basquin's "Mary Ellen/ Bute's Film Adaptation of *Finnegans Wake*" discusses Bute's adaptation of Mary Manning's *Passages from Finnegans Wake*. Bute claimed in an interview that her film was not a translation of *Finnegans Wake* but a reaction to it. This "reaction" departs a great deal from the novel and omits Joyce's explicitly sexual material. Margaret Rogers' "Thoughts on Making Music From the Hundred-Letter Words in *Finnegans Wake*" imparts her methods of composing her chorale *A Babble of Earwigs or Sinnegan with Finnegan*. The work is based on the ten multilingual portmanteau words (the Hundred-Letter Words) spread throughout *Finnegans Wake*. This chorale has been performed at the University of Wisconsin-Milwaukee and the University of Arizona.

Notes

1. Richard Ellmann, *James Joyce* (Oxford: Oxford University Press, 1982), 714-715. *Finnegans Wake* was not officially published until 4 May 1939. Faber & Faber managed to assemble an unbound copy (really a set of final proofs) from the printer, R. MacLehose and Company, in time for Joyce's birthday (James Joyce, *Selected Letters of James Joyce*, Richard Ellmann, ed. [New York: Viking Press, 1975], 394n).

2. Ellmann, *James Joyce*, 705-706.

3. Ellmann, *James Joyce*, 707, 710, 714.

4. Bernard Benstock, ed. *James Joyce: The Augmented Ninth* (Syracuse: Syracuse University Press, 1988).

5. Adaline Glasheen, *Third Census of Finnegans Wake* (Berkeley: University of California Press, 1977); Patrick McCarthy, "The Structures and Meanings of *Finnegans Wake*," in Zack R. Bowen and James F. Carens, eds. *A Companion to Joyce Studies* (Westport, CT: Greenwood, 1984), 559-632.

6. Roland McHugh, *Annotations to Finnegans Wake* (Baltimore: Johns Hopkins University Press, 1980).

7. Clive Hart, *A Concordance to Finnegans Wake* (Mamaroneck, N.Y.: Paul P. Appel, 1973), n.p.

8. James Joyce, *Ulysses*, ed. Hans Walter Gabler, et al. (New York: Random House, 1986), 8.326-328.

9. Bernard Benstock, *James Joyce* (New York: Frederick Ungar, 1985), 158.

James Joyce's *Finnegans Wake*

A Working Outline of *Finnegans Wake***

Bernard Benstock

CHAPTER 1 (pp. 3-29)

3:	Statement of themes
4:	Battle in Heaven and introduction of Finnegan
5:	Finnegan's fall and promise of resurrection
5-6:	The City
6-7:	The Wake
7-8:	Landscape foreshadows H.C.E. and A.L.P.
8-10:	Visit to Willingdone Museyroom
10:	The Earwicker house
10-12:	Biddy the hen finds the letter in the midden heap
12-13:	Dublin landscape
13-15:	Pre-history of Ireland—the invaders (including the birth of Shem and Shaun, p. 14)
15-18:	Mutt and Jute recount the Battle of Clontarf
18-20:	The development of the Alphabet and Numbers
21-23:	The Tale of Jarl van Hoother and the Prankquean
23-24:	The Fall
25:	Finnegan's Wake revisited
25-29:	Restless Finnegan is told about the present age
29:	H.C.E. introduced

CHAPTER 2 (pp. 30-47)

30-32:	The genesis and naming of Humphrey Chimpden Earwicker
32-33:	Gaiety Theatre production of *A Royal Divorce*
33-35:	Rumors about H.C.E.'s indiscretion
35-36:	The Encounter with the Cad
36-38:	The Cad dines and drinks
38-42:	The Cad's story is spread
42-44:	The making of the Ballad by Hosty
44-47:	The Ballad of Persse O'Reilly

CHAPTER 3 (pp. 48-74)

48-50:	The balladeer and all involved come to bad ends as Time Passes
50-52:	Earwicker asked to tell the old story
52-55:	Earwicker's "innocent" version is filmed, televised, and aired

**   This outline originally appeared in Bernard Benstock, *Joyce-Again's Wake: An Analysis of Finnegans Wake* (Seattle: University of Washington Press, 1965), xv-xxiv.   Permission for use granted by the University of Washington Press.

CHAPTER 4 (pp. 75-103)

CHAPTER 5 (pp. 104-25)

CHAPTER 6 (pp. 126-68)

CHAPTER 7 (pp. 169-95)

CHAPTER 8 (pp. 196-216)

6   James Joyce's *Finnegans Wake*

CHAPTER 11 (Book II, chap. 3, pp. 309-82)

CHAPTER 12 (Book II, chap. 4, pp. 383-99)

CHAPTER 13 (Book III, chap. 1, pp. 403-28)

CHAPTER 14 (Book III, chap 2, pp. 429-73)

CHAPTER 17 (Book IV, pp. 593-628)

PART I: ASSESSMENTS

Dreaming Up the *Wake* **

David Hayman

In the beginning was the woid and James Joyce was obliged by his writer's conscience to fill it with expandable language. *Ulysses* was published by Sylvia Beach over the Shakespeare and Company trademark in 1922, but the actual composition of Joyce's next book, *Finnegans Wake* did not begin until the spring of 1923. What transpired between those dates is a matter for speculation; clearly, Joyce, who, like Flaubert, never repeated himself, was duty bound to find a fresh and novel approach to the novel itself. The Irish writer never publicly announced any intentions. After all, in an early notebook, he went so far as to list the refusal to give interviews or write letters to the editor among the innovations of which he was particularly proud: "*JJ* abolished preface, dedication, notes, letters to press, interviews, chapter titles, capitals, inverted commas."[1] It is consequently very important that he conserved just about every scrap of paper connected with his last book, inadvertently giving us an intimate if cloudy record of some 18 years of creative activity.

Though still untitled, *Finnegans Wake* began to take shape in 1922 as a curious by-product of all the preceding works.[2] That is, Joyce began by taking notes under headings like "Exiles I" or "The Sisters," notes that dealt not so much with the topic of these writings as with what was left implicit. Thus, under *Exiles*, he did not deal with the characters of that failed drama or even with the problems of an Irish writer returning to face possible and half-willed betrayal at the hands of a trusted friend or even with the deeper problem of doubt. Rather, he developed at length a literary analogue, the seduction of Isolde by King Mark's emissary, Tristan. Under the first of his *Dubliners* titles, "The Sisters" he treats none of the mysteries of that tale but rather the problem of the oral tale convention. Under "An Encounter" he deals with homosexuality and Oscar Wilde. Joyce was in fact probing the underside of his production for its repressed potential, moving through his own creative consciousness toward a sort of literary subconscious. The procedure resembles in a sense that which he must have followed when he took the materials amassed during the daytime of *Ulysses* and reassembled them contrary wise to compile the pantomimic nightmare of his *Walpurgisnacht*, the "Circe" chapter.

It seems that in 1922, consciously or not and almost a year before he actually began to write *Finnegans Wake*, he was already planning the universal dream he was to write. But a study of the early notes suggests that he had yet to fix its structure. As a matter of fact, he did not really establish the book's outline until 1926. His shadowy cast of characters was not fully accounted for until 1923. The famous pun-textured prose was only gradually elaborated. And the final passage was not drafted until 1938! What we witness and begin to map in the early notebooks for the *Wake*, therefore, is the grouping process that

---

** This essay was originally published as "Dreaming Up the *Wake*" in *Lingua e Stile*, 22, No. 3, September 1987, 419-430. Permission for use granted by *Lingua e Stile*. A version of it will appear in my forthcoming *A Wake in Transit* (Cornell, 1990).

13

generated what was to be the most revolutionary book of our century and what
may prove to have been the most influential and liberating.

It is arguable that every line Joyce wrote was in some sense
autobiographical. Like Shem, his Wakean persona, our writer,

> the first till last alshemist wrote over every square inch of the only
> foolscap available, his own body, till by its corrosive sublimation one
> continuous present tense integument slowly unfolded all marryvoising
> moodmoulded cyclewheeling history (thereby, he said, reflecting from his
> own individual person life unlivable, transaccidentated through the slow
> fires of consciousness into a dividual chaos, perilous, potent, common to
> allflesh, human only, mortal).[3]

This rather unfriendly assessment spoken in the *Wake* by Shem's fraternal
opposite and enemy, Shaun the post, could stand as a definition of the operative
creative vision of *Finnegans Wake*. In fact Joyce was using not only Ireland and
the Irish history and people as his microcosm but his family and his own person
as standins for the universal human condition. That was, after all, "the only
foolscap available" to him. Like most artists and throughout his career, he did
little more than draw his own portrait, refining it endlessly to produce a deeper
and more immediate likeness. The evolution of his lifework took him from a
portrait of Dublin behind which he stands to the portrait of a Dublin child's
maturation into manhood to the meticulous evocation of a Dublin day and night
to the universal history/dream of an average Dubliner. Ultimately, it reflects
the essential double spiral of his vision. That is, by going further and further
into the individual psychic machine, he was able to go in ever wider circles,
learning and exhibiting his increasingly universal self.

On the surface of it, *Finnegans Wake*, the dream universe of HCE, which
becomes by osmosis that of the everyman reader, is a monument to Flaubertian
depersonalization. In fact, it began as, and in a profound sense remains, that of
Joyce himself. It can even be shown that the tightly controlled "traumscript" of
the *Wake* comes remarkably close to automatic writing. After all, and for all his
notes and other preparations, this is a text shaped by verbal choices. It is a text
which the author, once he got his machine underway, could never fully control
or rather from which the artist could never fully extricate himself. Jacques
Lacan is right when he speaks of Joyce the *symptôme*.[4]

Of more immediate interest to us is the existence of hard evidence that,
for a period of one or two years, Joyce's last book hung on the fruits of his
actual dreamwork, or at least on a small group of 6-8 dreams told to friends or
jotted down in his notebooks, dreams that accompanied as well as fueled the
creative process. I would maintain that, like Shem, Joyce, who was not above
participating in the general enthusiasm for dreams as keys to unlock the psyche,
actually used his dream life as he had previously used his epiphanies to help
direct his muse. Or perhaps it would be more accurate to see him accepting his
dreamwork as part of that process, using it as an extension in much the same
way Freud saw dreams as encoding the sources of our anxieties. This can be
said despite Joyce's avowed hostility to "jungfraud"s. The author was searching
for the universally available archetypes he felt could be dislodged from his own
dreamlife.

What I am advancing is of course speculative, since my evidence is a handful of frequently obscure notations written in a hand that is often far from clear and, occasionally, in something resembling a personal code. But the mere presence of these carefully isolated sequences, usually labeled "Dream," lends my speculations considerable weight, as does the fact that Joyce continued jotting down epiphany-like sequences (or "epiphanoids") during this same period, sequences that actually helped him develop the personae and action of his new book.

The dreams I refer to are different in treatment, kind and function from the two items recorded by Richard Ellmann in his definitive biography. Indeed, I would suggest that the dreams in Ellmann, the one reprinted from Gorman's early biography and the other taken from Helen Nutting's diary, are more like literary constructs. In the first, Joyce describes a comic encounter with an angry Molly Bloom. I have no doubt its source was an actual dream. We even find a cryptic reference to it in a notebook from early 1923: "*JJ* with MB/must tell someone."[5] In fact, as Ellmann shows us, Joyce told it not once but twice and each time differently. The second dream, an Arabian Night's confection about a criminal at risk, may be in large measure a joke.

Both "dreams" are extremely well focussed and coherent. Both present Joyce as observer/participant rather than pure participant. Significantly, the second was told to Myron and Helen Nutting, whose modish enthusiasm for Freud Joyce liked to mock. The dreamer went so far as to analyse his dream's details for his young friends. It is all the more interesting, therefore, that, as it is reconstituted by Helen Nutting, the dream proper does not square with Joyce's reading, that it lacks important details stressed in his mock-Freudian interpretation.

While questioning the significance of this frustration dream, we should say that Joyce did in fact turn to the *Arabian Nights* when he was writing *Ulysses* and began taking notes for the *Wake* under the heading "The Sisters." We should add that the tales in the original Persian collection are themselves frequently configured as dreams. I do not mean to dismiss the dream narratives in Ellmann as insignificant since they do show how Joyce's mind worked and could even be classified as belated epiphanies, that is, as shaped artifacts derived from actual experience. Still, we are obliged to question their authenticity as dreams, and we have yet to determine their significance for the development of the *Wake*.

This brings us to a brief consideration of the demonstrably genuine, if unfortunately fragmentary, dreams found in notebooks compiled between 1923 and 1927. But before citing and analyzing a sampling, we had better give some account of aspects of the *Wake* to which they may have contributed. The basic situation of that book is very simple: a nuclear family composed of father/mother/twin brothers/sister has fallen on hard times. The father, an upright pub-keeping citizen of Dublin, has been accused of moral turpitude. Gossip has it that he watched two servant maids urinating in Dublin's Phoenix Park. He was seen by three soldiers who seem to claim that he was defecating in response to the girls' activity. Since the girls are identified as avatars of the great man's daughter, seen looking in her mirror, there are incestuous overtones. The soldiers, identified as the sons separated by their shame ("*Shem and Shaun and the shame that sunders em*," [*FW* 526.14]), introduce an oedipal and perhaps a homosexual element. Indeed, if we take into account all the ramifications of the alleged crime, we enter the realm of Krafft-Ebing. I would suggest that it is this aspect of the novel that is crucially dream-generated. The male-oriented half of *Finnegans Wake* appears to have grown from it and another crucial motif: HCE's meeting with a stranger in the park during which our heroic pub-keeper makes the Freudian slip that incriminates him in the eyes of the community. The cast of the *Wake* is as limited as are its actions (the other two major acts being the writing of a letter in HCE's defense by Shem the pen at the dictation of ALP, HCE's wife, and the delivery of that letter by their son Shaun the post). Like the members of a *commedia dell'arte* troupe each of them can take on any number of roles that correspond to their central identities.

At least two of the dreams are found in notebooks compiled while Joyce was preparing to write the six skits that constitute the armature of the novel, passages that were eventually placed at its beginning, middle and end. That is, these dreams were written between April and September 1923. The earliest account of the crime was written in September 1923, shortly before Joyce began drafting his first chapter to which it was appended. The account Joyce actually wrote at that time is very brief:

> Nor have his detractors mended their case by insinuating that he was at one time under the imputation of annoying soldiers in the park . . . Slander, let it do its worst, has never been able to convict that good and great man of any greater misdemeanor than that of an incautious exposure in the presence of certain nursemaids. . .[6]

And this passage was probably derived from a note taken in August 1923:

> It is not true that Pop was homosexual [though] he had been arrested at the request of some nursemaids to whom he had temporarily exposed himself in the Temple gardens.[7]

Without exaggeration, we can say that the conception of this brief episode was the necessary *amorce* for literally one half of the book, the half devoted to a treatment of male behavior. In the completed novel, the crime and its aftermath, the fall and reconstitutions of HCE as father and leader, dominated half the chapters, beginning with chapters 2-4, the earliest to be written. Thus the dreams dreamed prior to the passages' composition may have played an integral part at a crucial moment in the novel's genesis.

After all this priming, the actual evidence I present may seem slight, but in fact nothing that relates to the genesis of this mammoth novel which took up half the writer's creative life is negligible. In March or April 1923, Joyce jotted down the only dream that is not clearly labelled as such. At that time he was working on the first passage actually to be drafted, an account of the aftermath of the last great banquet given by Roderick O'Conor, the "last high king of all Ireland." The dream itself is at once the most questionable and the most tantalizing in my collection, but it does bear witness to a significant cluster of preoccupations. It reads:

> pull m — y behind door
>   sawdust
> wh[ores] toss H[usband] off cart, haggle

Stop singing! Leave the room!
   rubber cunt. Sgt!
   show him album clap!
   tell story — 'my husband'
   purge him, shitcan reek, dairy [?],
      ask leave 3 t[imes] for[?] go WC
      tempt H[usband]
      H[usband] write to B[lazes] B[oylan] [?]
      rod is pickle
      after-inspection
      mixed grill[8]

The uncrossed-through, and hence probably unused, passage is written entirely in an unusually spidery hand and tightly grouped as a single unit. Among the longest of the unified jottings in this very early notebook, it bears witness to hasty transcription, suggesting that Joyce wrote it down under pressure, perhaps fearing to lose some of its details. It appears to follow a narrative line that is subject to irrational shifts. Finally, these lines have been hastily but completely enclosed by a rough circle.[9] If we may judge by its presentation, Joyce was intrigued and disturbed by its contents, which are blatantly masochistic, scatological and genital, to say nothing of absurd.

Any reading of this unit must be tentative and conjectural, but we can fix the major setting as a brothel similar to the one in the "Circe" chapter of *Ulysses* and say that, along with the "Husband" or "H," an early version of the Pop/HCE/Joyce-figure of the *Wake*, the protagonists are a group of unnamed whores and perhaps a persona designated by the letters BB (Blazes Boylan?). The action is best seen as a sequence of loosely connected episodes.

The first sequence reveals someone, perhaps Joyce himself, doing something (suspect?) behind a door. Joyce's reticence here is remarkable, given the language of the remainder of the dream. The whores go into action in the second line, apparently "tossing" the abusable "H off [the] cart" perhaps onto some "sawdust." What follows may be haggling over their price. The two commands may have been addressed to a man who has regressed to the condition of a child in a nursery or schoolroom. They may also be a part of a pantomime sequence similar to the Bella/Bello segment of "Circe." Perhaps the man is then supplied with or teased with a "rubber cunt," but it seems likely that that house is also raided by a police "sergeant." After a break or scene change, the whores show H an album (of pornographic pictures?) and someone applauds. Then someone, perhaps one of the whores, tells a story about her "husband." The next two lines are once again violently masochistic. The man submits to a purge, filling a can before he asks leave, again like a child, to go to the water closet. This is followed by a scene of unspecified temptation and what appears to be the public composition of a letter to BB. The next two lines may refer to H's genitals, which are perhaps displayed and inspected. The last item refers to a meal.

Any assessment of the *Wake*'s first months must take into consideration the fact that even after he had finished *Ulysses*, Joyce continued to mediate about changes he would like to make. That is, the completed novel continued to occupy his imagination. It is not strange therefore to find that a chapter like "Circe" on which so much psychic energy was spent can shape the writer's dreamlife in 1923. I would suggest that the complex sexual guilt motif carried over from "Circe" is central to any understanding of the crime of HCE. Beyond that, perhaps even issuing from the impulse that generated "Circe," there is what we perceive as a triple Krafft-Ebing motif of voyeuristic watching, self-pollution, and defecation in the presence of witnesses. Indeed, one half of HCE's crime is already here a good while before Joyce actually wrote down his early HCE sketch.

The remainder is latent in notes concerned with the relation of Pop to his daughter Is[/Issy/Isolde]. Issy, the multiple-personality juvenile heroine of the *Wake*, was from the start a version of Joyce's teen-aged daughter, Lucia. Even more important, she came into being long before Joyce invented ALP as an avatar for the mature Nora Barnacle. The curious shape taken by Issy's personality can be traced in large measure to Lucia's incipient schizophrenia, symptoms of which must have been available as early as 1923.[10] Joyce's emotional investment in this juvenile figure suggests that his attempts to find cultural analogues for her personality and her deteriorating condition constituted a sort of self-help therapy. But before the therapeutic writing came the equally therapeutic dreaming exhibited in the following dream:

> Dream Schwindel . . ., [I] awake in 4 bedded room, A.S[.] & L[ucia?] & other W[oman]. Soli. N[ora] Collapses. I go to theatre [where I] meet O[liver] G[ogarty] and E[ileen Joyce Schaurek?]. 'She has a few drinks in her.' [We] Cross [the] arena to [the] hosp[ital]. [The] Concierge [comes out to stop us]. Finis. I howl oatenmealymouth[ily?].[11]

This dream probably dates from the period when Joyce was writing and revising his early sketches and thinking through his project. It is crowded into a space left at the bottom of a notebook page, as though Joyce wished to eliminate as well as ventilate it. Though, like most such passages, it is written in a relatively clear hand, one senses a curious impulse to confine the most powerful part of the experience. The visual impact is rather like that of a spring under pressure.

After puzzling over the first word, I tentatively concluded that Joyce is using the German word *Schwindel* in its primary sense of "giddyness." If this is true, it motivates the awakening in a room with four beds, three of which appear to be occupied by women. Whatever is meant by "Soli," with its Italian meaning "solitary" or "alone," Joyce's apparent swoon, together with the presence of the women and Lucia in the bedroom, seems to have motivated Nora Barnacle's collapse.

What follows is easier to interpret. Joyce saw Gogarty/Mulligan as a clownish, theatrical, and overpoweringly seductive presence. It is natural that he would dream of encountering him in a theatre and with a woman. Gogarty contributed, along with the Triestine friend Roberto Prezioso, to the portrait of Robert in Joyce's play, *Exiles*. If the initial E does stand for Eileen, it seems fitting that the seducer of this inebriated young woman is none other than Joyce's opposite-equal. The incestuous nature of the seduction would thus be displaced.

The quoted conversation is clearly Gogarty's, probably delivered *sotto voce* to Joyce. And the movement across the "arena" to the hospital probably places the action in Joyce's student days in Dublin, a time when Gogarty and Joyce would have been apt to haunt hospitals and chase skirts. The reference to the concierge, however, suggests that either Joyce has translated the word for doorkeeper or janitor or that the scene has Parisian elements. It is in Paris that a recalcitrant concierge might cut short a romantic escapade: "Finis." We may interpret Joyce's breakfast food/pap/oatmeal "howl" as a cry of atavistic frustration, but it may also function as a displacement of guilt feelings.

The allusions to giddyness, to Nora's collapse, to the profoundly suspicious and doubtless unwelcome presence of an ex-friend, along with the final catastrophe, confirm the impression that this is not only an ominous dream but an absolute nightmare laden with motifs of guilt, frustration and anxiety. There can be no doubt that both halves of the dream are sexual and that Joyce was aware of many of their implications. There is also little doubt that the dream contributed to or reenforced the development of the *Wake*.

If the incest motif is still only latent in the second dream, it is all too overt in one dreamed nine months later in July 1924:

> Dream [I saw] Kathleen [who was complaining about] rats
> O[scar] W[ilde] was there in the guise of a] pontifex maximus
> S[tephen] D[edalus appeared as the] 1st Irish bullfighter L[ucia]
> J[oyce said,] Shame [?] gave me light
> Algrin the blind
> Good God [I? exclaimed with a] cry of shame and horror
> she [is] only 15.[12]

Despite occasional elisions, the exceptional clarity of Joyce's hand and the careful ordering of the events underscore the significance of this complex sequence. Joyce apparently recollected the dream after he had jotted down a bit of behavior signifying Lucia/Issy's sexual maturation: "[Issy] gets rainwater in jug for face." When we consider that the underlying theme of this dream is incest and that the worries of HCE were shared by his creator, the sequence seems to have been tailored for adaptation to the *Wake*, to which it may have contributed several details.

One might qualify the opening lines of this "Circe"-like dream as pantomime, since the first three figures mentioned: Kathleen, Wilde, and Stephen are all either outlandish or outlandishly garbed. In *Finnegans Wake*, Kathleen, a projection of Kathleen ni Houlihan or Ireland, is an avatar of ALP. A late-comer to the *Wake* community, she functions as the ancient, grumbling charwoman, a harpy/banshee. I would suggest that she resembles nothing more than the traditional pantomime "dame," a role generally played by a man, who would be perfectly capable of answering the question, "What are you scrubbing the floor with?" by snarling something like, "*Shite*! will you have a plateful?" (*FW* 142.7). The chapter containing that line (I.6) was written several years after Joyce dreamed his dream, but we find a version of that comic retort in the current notebook. It seems reasonable to assume that Joyce had Kate's role well in hand when he associated rats and Kathleen in his dream.

Oscar Wilde, the very image of the late nineteenth-century decadent, would be a comic chief prelate of the Roman Pontifical College and an even stranger pope. There is evidence of the direct impact of this dream in a note on the bottom of the notebook page, "pawntifox miximost." Joyce was clearly inspired to pun on the term. Though Wilde is identified with Mulligan in *Ulysses*, in the *Wake* he is an aspect of HCE, who speaks of "puntofacts massimus" in the very first line of his longest monologue (*FW* 532.9). Since Joyce was busy writing that passage when he had this dream, we may assume that the Wildean prelate aspect of HCE, of a piece with the citybuilder's sententious hypocrisy, had genuine oneiric roots.

HCE can be seen as a projection of the mature Joyce just as Stephen Dedalus was his youthful self. It follows that Stephen in mock-heroic guise complements a ponderous Wilde/HCE. Among those Joyce met during this period was Ernest Hemingway, whose enthusiasm for bullfighting and bullfighters might have stimulated the image of a bullfighting Stephen/Joyce. Stephen could perhaps have been the first Irish bullfighter had he had better sight and more courage. As it is, the image is pure pantomime fun with an ironic edge on it.

The real surprise is the reference to L. J., clearly Joyce's daughter. Here Lucia's name is ambiguously linked to that of Shaun the post and much more directly with "Shame." If the link is with Shaun, then Lucia straddles the worlds of literature and dream, being at once Joyce's daughter and his creature Issy in ways that she is not in other dreams and in the book. It is to Shaun/Jaun, the hypocritical priest and shame-merchant of *Finnegans Wake* chapter III.2, that she would be referring and specifically to the sermon he delivers to Issy and her classmates. There, Shaun flirtatiously warns the girls away from his brother (Shem/Stephen/Joyce) and her father (HCE/Wilde/Joyce). But the dream "light" is more than a moral illumination, since in that section of the book Shaun is identified with the light of the setting sun.

If corroboration is needed for this reading, it is available, however ambiguously, in the reference to what appears to be a blind poet (see Joyce's own eye problems) in the next line. Such a figure must be yet another sublimation of the dreamer's identity.

The final exclamation, which is spaced gesturally to suggest its impact as an utterance, seems to be Joyce's own, undisguised dream-response to Lucia's announcement. It does not seem unreasonable to say that the allusion to two (if not four) of Joyce's literary self-projections, conjoined as they are to an undisguised evocation of Lucia, has brought the dreamer into painfully close proximity to his daughter and to a naked expression of his own controlled lust. This reading is reenforced by the next note, written in an identical hand and hence taken immediately after Joyce had recorded his dream: "A was rather lecherous/ B [was rather] lustful." It would appear that the writer had already set about rationalizing what he knew to be normal but felt to be dangerous dream impulses, turning them into literary/social matter.

Finally, it is worth noting that, not only does Lucia's name mean light, but Joyce, who was at this time being treated for glaucoma, needed reassurance and relief from the anxiety of impending blindness. Another note from this notebook makes the connection even more vividly by linking the abilities of Dr.

Borsch, Joyce's specialist, with those of the 16 year old, whose identity is screened by the sigla for Issy: "[Lucia/Issy was] wiser than Borsch [with regard to] face lotion."[13] Incest-related sexuality, ambiguous sexual impulses (see Wilde), profound guilt and fear, and endangered sight are joined in this dream even more forcefully than they have been in the earlier ones.

What I am suggesting is that at least two of these early dreams, all of which seem to have been important to Joyce, contributed to the development of the crime of HCE and perhaps to the liberation of the author from some of his own demons. Unlike Stephen Dedalus, who attempted in the last chapter of *Portrait* to separate himself from those who would act upon him, the mature Joyce seems to have tried to face down his urges and reenact his conflicts. In doing so, he was of course continuing the project of "Circe," if not of *Ulysses* in general. It is significant of course that the dreams he recorded, powerful, nightmarish, sexually charged as they are, all feature a Joycean persona, and that, like HCE, Joyce dreams of himself as seen and as acted upon rather than as acting. I suggest that his choice to make use of this oneiric material, however indirectly, was one of the most serious decisions made during his creative life. Through it he achieved some of the emotional intensity to drive the mighty engine that became *Finnegans Wake* through 18 difficult years and the stimulus for what became an intensely personal portrait of the nocturnal male psyche haunted by actions and urges and submerged in a sea of vibrant language.

Notes

1. *The James Joyce Archive* (Buffalo Notebook VI. B. 14) ed. David Hayman, (New York: Garland Publishing, 1978), 9.

2. *Scribbledehobble*, ed. Thomas Connolly (Evanston: Northwestern University Press, 1961). *James Joyce Archive* (Buffalo Notebook VI.A) ed. Danis Rose.

3. James Joyce, *Finnegans Wake*, 8th printing with the author's corrections incorporated in the text (New York: Viking Press, 1958), 185.34-186.6.

4. Jacques Lacan in *Joyce & Paris*, Vol. 1, eds. J. Aubert and M. Jolas (Paris: Publications de l' Université de Lille, III/CNRS), 13-17.

5. *The James Joyce Archive* (Buffalo Notebook VI.B.6), 560.

6. David Hayman, *A First-Draft Version of Finnegans Wake* (Austin: University of Texas Press, 1963), 63.

7. *The James Joyce Archive* (Buffalo Notebook VI.B.3), 153.

8. *The James Joyce Archive* (Buffalo Notebook VI.B.10), 46.

9. Such circling is unusual, but we do find a parallel instance on page 98 of this notebook. In the first instance the circle is roughly drawn, composed in fact of five or six lines enclosing rather insecurely a long sequence. In the second, the circle was apparently drawn in a single motion before Joyce began filling in what may have been another dream. It contains, however, only the suggestive words "serve her horse."

10. See Richard Ellmann, *James Joyce* (New York: Oxford University Press, 1959), 552-53 and *passim*; and David Hayman, *Shadow of His Mind: The Papers of Lucia Joyce*, in *Joyce at Texas* (Austin: The Humanities Research Center of the University of Texas, 1983), 65-79. See also "I Think Her Pretty: Reflections of the Familiar in Joyce's Notebook VI.B.5" in *James Joyce Studies*, No. I, 1990.

11. *The James Joyce Archive* (Buffalo Notebook VI.B.11), 31.

12. *The James Joyce Archive* (Buffalo Notebook VI.B.5), 107.

13. *The James Joyce Archive* (Buffalo Notebook IV.B.5), 14. This note is followed by another in the same hand: "obscenity insult of beauty/vulgarity ignore [beauty]." Even more relevant and startling is the close proximity of these notes to the draft of Joyce's oneiric poem "A Prayer."

An Introduction to *Finnegans Wake***

Colin MacCabe

Context

In 1922, on his fortieth birthday, James Joyce's *Ulysses* was published. The fruit of seven years' work, Joyce had started the book as an unknown English teacher in Trieste and had completed it an acknowledged major author in Paris. Ezra Pound's efforts on his behalf had ensured that both *A Portrait of the Artist as a Young Man*, Joyce's first novel, and the early drafts of *Ulysses* had been enthusiastically received in London literary circles. The public acclaim that Joyce now enjoyed was accompanied by financial security because Harriet Shaw Weaver, who had published *A Portrait*, made him a regular allowance. It was in these favorable circumstances that Joyce began to write a book which was to take him 17 years to complete and which, once published, was to be almost universally castigated as the product of charlatanism or insanity (or both). This is the book that we know as *Finnegans Wake*. Although a huge number of scholarly studies have since been written, explicating the text with reference sometimes to Joyce's life, sometimes to the books he read, sometimes to the languages he spoke, and very frequently with reference to all three and more, *Finnegans Wake*, nevertheless, remains inaccessible to most readers.

In *Finnegans Wake* Joyce attempted to write a book which would take all history and knowledge for its subject matter and the workings of the dreaming mind for its form. If one takes a page at random from *Finnegans Wake*, one may find reference to subjects as disparate as chemistry, Irish mythology, philosophy, American history, details from Joyce's life, all woven together in a language which constantly creates new words by fusing and shortening old ones or by borrowing from the many European languages that Joyce knew. The result of this deformation of language is that every word carries more than one meaning and each sentence opens out onto an infinity of interpretations. Joyce explained his method to a friend when he said: "In writing of the night, I really could not, I felt I could not, use words in their ordinary connections. Used that way they do not express how things are in the night, in the different stages—conscious, then semi-conscious, then unconscious."[1] The difficulty of the language is compounded by difficulty of divining what story this extraordinary language is recounting. Figures change name and transform themselves into their opposites, appear and disappear without any obvious rationality. Joyce's claim for his method was that it enabled the articulation of areas of experience which were barred from conventional language and plot. He told Miss Weaver:

**   This essay originally appeared in the British Council Series *Notes for Literature* and later appeared as "An Introduction to *Finnegans Wake*" in Colin MacCabe, ed. *James Joyce: New Perspectives* (Bloomington: Indiana University Press, 1982), 29-41. Permission for use granted by the Indiana University Press.

"One great part of every human existence is passed in a state which cannot be rendered sensible by the use of wideawake language, cutanddry grammar and goahead plot."[2]

Many critics have complained that Joyce's last book marks a major change from his earlier work and that his interest in language had become a self-indulgent aberration. But such criticism ignores the fact that from his earliest work, Joyce was obsessed with language, with its structure and its effects. Above all his writing focusses on the methods by which identity is produced in language. The opening passage of *A Portrait* demonstrates this production:

> Once upon a time and a very good time it was there was a moocow coming down along the road and this moo-cow that was coming down along the road met a nicens little boy named baby tuckoo. . . .
> His father told him that story: his father looked at him through a glass: he had a hairy face.
> He was baby tuckoo. The moocow came down the road where Betty Byrne lived: she sold lemon platt.
> *O, the wild rose blossoms*
> *On the little green place.*
> He sang that song. That was his song.
> *O, the green wothe botheth*
> When you wet the bed, first it is warm then it gets cold. His mother put on the oilsheet. That had the queer smell.
> His mother had a nicer smell than his father. She played on the piano the sailor's hornpipe for him to dance. He danced:
> *Tralala lala*
> *Tralala tralaladdy*
> *Tralala lala*
> *Tralala lala.*(P 7)

In this passage we move from the paternal narrator who tells us a story and fixes an identity (the listening child realises that he is baby tuckoo and that he can locate himself in a definite spatio-temporal identity) to the mother's voice in which stories are dissolved into the sounds, smells and sensations of the body. It is the deformation of language in "O, the green wothe botheth" that signals the transition to a world where the material of language (the sound of *Tralala*) has dominance over meaning. The identity of the story gets lost in the confused and disparate experiences of the body. While the father fixes with his eye, the mother displaces into the world of the ear. On the one hand we find the self and the father, the authority of meaning and society and, on the other hand, we find the body and the mother, the subversion of sound and desire. This movement from identity to infancy is one that we repeat each night as we enter the timeless world of dreams where words become things and we reverse the process each morning as we wake to the temporal continuity of meaning. Language changes its nature in the passage between these two realms. A normal syntax and morphology (cutanddry grammar) is appropriate to the normality of stories (goahead plot) but as soon as we begin to pay attention to the material constituents of words in either the spoken or written form then we find ourselves slipping into the world of desire. And this eruption of the material of language is not confined to the sleeping life or dreams. Jokes and verbal slips are the most obvious example in our waking life when another order of language interrupts the normal flow of communication. When Joyce claimed that in

Finnegans Wake he was investigating a "great part of every human existence" which escaped normal linguistic relations, he was not simply claiming to represent accurately a sleeping mind but rather to be investigating a vital dimension of our being which, although more evident in dreams, insists in our waking life as well. His earlier works and their experiments with narrative and language made the writing of *Finnegans Wake* possible but both his methods and his topics remain remarkably constant throughout his adult life as we can see in the extract that we looked at from *A Portrait*.

The importance of the opposition between the invisible language of the story and the material language of desire is evident throughout *Finnegans Wake* but it is towards the end as Anna Livia, both mother and river, flows to her death that it is stated in one of its simplest forms. As Anna thinks back over her past life, she remembers how much her husband (the ubiquitous figure who is indicated by the letters HCE) wanted a daughter, hoping for a female in the family who would believe his stories, who would give to him the respect that he feels is his due. But the father is inevitably disappointed for the mother teaches her daughter that beneath the stories and the identities lies the world of letters and desire. While the father tells the son stories, the mother teaches the daughter the alphabet: "If you spun your yarns to him on the swishbarque waves I was spelling my yearns to her over cottage cake" (*FW* 620). The father's yarns (stories) are displaced by the mother's yearns (desires); telling gives way to spelling. It is this struggle between meaning and sound, between story and language, between male and female that *Finnegans Wake* enacts, introducing the reader to a world in which his or her own language can suddenly reveal new desires beneath old meanings as the material of language forms and reforms.

If the language attempts to investigate the processes by which we are constructed in the world of sense and syntax, the stories that we piece together from the mosaic of the *Wake* constantly return us to the place of that construction: the family. As the text throws out references to the world's religions and philosophies, to geography, and to astronomy, we come back again and again to the most banal and local of all problems. What is the nature of the obscure sexual offence that the father, HCE, is charged with? And is he guilty? Only the mother Anna Livia Plurabelle, ALP, seems to know the definitive answers to these questions. The mother has written or will write (tenses become interchangeable in the timeless world of the *Wake*) a letter which will explain all but the letter is difficult to identify and decipher. It was dictated to one of her sons, Shem, a writer of ill repute, who is likely to have altered the contents, and may have been delivered by her other son, Shaun, a nauseating worldly success. The two brothers are engaged in a constant conflict, often occasioned by sexual rivalry. In some obscure way their sister, Issy, might hold the solution to the problems of her father and brothers but she refuses to say anything at all serious as she is quite content to gaze endlessly at herself in the mirror.

If language, the family and sexuality provide three of the emphases of Joyce's last work, there is a fourth which is as important: death. Indeed the title of the book, *Finnegans Wake*, makes clear this concern. The immediate reference is to a song of almost identical title (only an apostrophe differentiates them): *Finnegan's Wake*. This tells the story of an Irish bricklayer who went to work one morning with a terrible hangover and, as a result, fell off his ladder. His friends presume that he is dead and take him home to "wake" him, that is to spend the night before the funeral drinking beside the dead body. During the wake a fight breaks out and a bottle of whiskey breaks by Tim's head. No sooner has some whiskey trickled into his mouth than he revives and joins in the fun of his own funeral (which thus becomes a "*funferal*" [*FW 120*]). The ambiguity of the "wake" of Joyce's title, which refers both to part of the funeral process (Finnegan's wake) and to the general awakening of all the Finnegans (Finnegans wake without an apostrophe), indicates the inseparability of life and death in the world of language. To come to life, to recognise one's separate existence, is also to allow the possibility of its termination, its end. *Finnegans Wake* not only puns on two means of "wake" but the first word contains both an end ("fin" is French for "end") and a new beginning ("egan" tells us that everything will start "again"). And this process will be the negation (negans) of the ordinary processes of language, an attention to the trace ("wake" in its third sense) left by the passage of language. The clarity of communication will be disturbed by the material trace of the letter that any communication leaves in its wake.

Death and sexuality, the construction of language within the family drama, Joyce's text is no self-indulgent whim but an engagement with the very matter of our being. In his attempt to break away from the "evidences" of conventional narrative with its fixed causality and temporality, two Italian thinkers, Giordano Bruno and Giambattista Vico, were of profound importance in the writing of *Finnegans Wake*. In understanding the importance of these figures it is not enough to sketch the positive features of their thought, one must also understand what Joyce is avoiding by his use of these theorists, what presuppositions he is denying.

Giordano Bruno was a philosopher of the Italian Renaissance. After becoming a Dominican friar he flirted with the varieties of Protestant reformism as well as interesting himself in hermetic philosophy. His unorthodox beliefs and his final death at the stake as a heretic in 1600 had interested Joyce from an early age. Bruno's principle of the "coincidence of contraries" denied the existence of absolute identities in the universe. Bruno argued that oppositions collapsed into unities at their extremes, thus extreme heat and extreme cold were held to be indistinguishable, and all identities were, therefore, provisional. Bruno joined this belief to a belief in an infinite universe composed of an infinity of worlds. There is an obvious level at which such theories offer some explanations of the constant transformation of characters into their opposites in *Finnegans Wake* and the infinite worlds opened up by the "dream within a dream" structure of the text. But to understand Joyce as simply providing an artistic gloss to the theories of an obscure philosopher is to minimise crucially the importance of the *Wake*. Bruno is important insofar as he provides a philosophical trellis on which the philosophical and linguistic presuppositions of identity can be unpicked. At one level of consciousness we claim an identity and stability both for ourselves and our objects of perception. But such identities can only be produced by a process of differentiation in which other identities are rejected. This rejection, however, presupposes that other identities are possible. The paradoxical feature of identity is that its conditions of existence allow the possibility of its very contradiction. It is this play of identity that Joyce investigates in the *Wake* where language no longer has to presuppose noncontradiction and everybody becomes everybody else in an infinite series of substitutions and juxtapositions which never attain some imaginary finality but constantly break, reform and start again.

Giambattista Vico is, arguably, even more important to the structure and content of *Finnegans Wake*. His name occurs (in suitably distorted form) in the opening sentence of the book as does a reference to his cyclical theory of history. A Neapolitan philosopher of the eighteenth century, Vico was one of the first to propose a general theory of historical change. He held that history was a cyclical process in which civilisation proceeded from a theocratic to an aristocratic to a democratic age and that, at the end of the democratic age, civilisation passed through a short period of destruction, the *ricorso*, which recommenced the cycle.

The very plan of *Finnegans Wake*, with its three long books and a short concluding one, bears witness to Vico's importance. It is not only Vico's historical theories which figure in the *Wake*, there is also much play with his account of the birth of language and civilisation. According to Vico, primitive man, surprised in the sexual act by a clap of thunder, is stricken with fear and guilt at what he imagines is the angered voice of God. He retires into a cave to conceal his activities and it is this act which inaugurates civilisation. Language arises when man attempts to reproduce the sound of thunder with his own vocal organs. Once again, however, it would be wrong to understand Joyce's use of Vico as the artistic illustration of philosophical theses. What Vico's theory offers is both an initial articulation of language, sexuality and society and, more importantly, a theory to oppose to dominant historicist accounts of history. Historicism understands the historical process to be subordinate to a dominant principle, which can only be understood in terms of the "end" to which it is progressing. When Stephen Dedalus and Mr Deasy discuss history in the second chapter of *Ulysses*, Mr Deasy claims that "All history moves towards one great goal, the manifestation of God" (*U* 40). This historicism imposes on the individual a meaning in which he is already defined. Stephen refuses such a meaning and identity when he claims that God is simply a noise in the street, the undifferentiated sound from which we fabricate meaning. It is by plunging into this sound that we can unmake the meanings imposed on us and awake from the nightmare of history into the dream of language. By insisting on the infinite repeatability of any moment, by refusing a progression to history, one can refuse the ready-made identities offered to us in order to investigate the reality of the processes that construct us. By denying an end to history, we can participate in the infinite varieties of the present. Bruno and Vico are used in *Finnegans Wake* to aid the deconstruction of identity into difference and to replace progress with repetition. But if Joyce used these thinkers it was largely to displace the dominant conceptions of the everyday novel of identity and temporality and not because they hold some intrinsic truth.

The text

To attempt a summary of the events of *Finnegans Wake* is both necessary and misleading. Necessary in that there are strands of narrative that we can follow through the text, misleading in that such narratives are always dispersed into other narratives. In an essay of this length it is only possible to look at one of the seventeen chapters of the *Wake*, and I have chosen chapter 7 of Book 1, the portrait of Shem the Penman, as one of the more immediately accessible sections of the text. The six chapters that lead up to it have taken us through both a synopsis of all the themes of the book (chapter 1) and then through a series of accounts of HCE's obscure and unmentionable crime and his trial (chapters 2-4). The letter which is so crucial to an understanding of all the issues at stake is discussed in chapter 5. Chapter 6 is composed of a set of questions and answers about the characters discussed in the letter and ends with a question about Shem. The whole of chapter 7 (the one we shall consider in a little more detail) is devoted to Shem the writer and at the end of this chapter he gives way to his mother, Anna Livia, whose life and activities are discussed in chapter 8. Book 2 transfers the scene from the whole city of Dublin to a particular public house in Chapelizod, one of Dublin's suburbs. In chapter 1 the children play outside the pub and in chapter 2 they have been put to bed in one of the rooms above the bar where they conduct their nightlessons, lessons which intermingle academic subjects with the discovery of sexuality. Chapter 3 takes place in the bar over which the children are sleeping. Customers and publican (HCE) gossip the evening away and when they have all left the innkeeper falls asleep on the floor in a drunken stupor and dreams about the story of Tristram and Iseult, this dream composing the major topic of chapter 4. Book 3 finds the innkeeper asleep in bed and chapters 1-3 deal with Shaun in his various manifestations as man of the world. At the end of chapter 3 Shaun dissolves into the voices of other characters and in chapter 4 the father and mother, woken by the cries of one of the children, make rather unsatisfactory love as dawn breaks. Book 4 sees the coming of dawn and the start of a new cycle. The mother Anna Livia is now old and looks back over her past life before she dissolves into the sea of death which starts the cycle again.

The portrait of Shem (*FW* 169-95) is unflattering in the extreme. He is accused of endless crimes and perversions. The officious tone of the opening sentences suggests that it is the rival brother, Shaun, speaking. Shaun, a pillar of society and an exemplar of moral rectitude, accuses Shem of refusing to be a proper member of society. To this end Shaun employs every kind of racist and anti-semitic slur. Shem is accused of being a sham and a forger, never able to be himself, to assume a definite identity, but constantly imitating others in his writing. His immense pride goes together with an absolute refusal to join in the patriotic struggle which would offer him the chance of achieving true manhood. Instead he prefers to occupy himself with the affairs of women. Shaun describes the particularly obscene process by which Shem's books are composed (we will look in detail at this description) and how Shem was arrested because of his books. After we have read the details of the arrest, we find ourselves at a trial where Shaun, in the person of Justius, tries Shem, in the person of Mercius. Mercius is accused of irreligion, of corrupting women, of squandering money and, most importantly, of being mad. It would seem that Mercius (Shem) is going to be unable to answer the last charge (the quintessential accusation aimed at those who refuse to conform), but, at the last moment, Anna Livia speaks through his mouth and evades Justius' (Shaun's) accusations. The process by which the mother speaks through the son reduplicates the whole effort of writing *Finnegans Wake*, in which the mother is finally given a voice. Shaun's demand that Shem identify himself, the policeman's request for identification, is avoided by a throwing into doubt of sexual identity. The apparatus by which the police of identity control the progress of history can be undercut by the assertion of an interminable, never complete, bi-sexuality.

If this imperfect summary indicates some of the drift of the chapter on Shem, we can now look, in a little more detail, at the description of Shem's method of writing. The lines in question occur after an explanation, in Latin, of the alchemical operations by which the body's waste matter is transformed into ink with the aid of a perverted religious prayer:

> Then, pious Eneas, conformant to the fulminant firman which enjoins on the tremylose terrian that, when the call comes, he shall produce nichthemerically from his unheavenly body a no uncertain quantity of obscene matter not protected by copriright in the United Stars of Ourania or bedeed and bedood and bedang and bedung to him, with this double dye, brought to blood heat, gallic acid on iron ore, through the bowels of his misery, flashly, faithly, nastily, appropriately, this Esuan Menschavik and the first till last alshemist wrote over every square inch of the only foolscap available, his own body, till by its corrosive sublimation one continuous present tense integument slowly unfolded all marryvoising moodmoulded cyclewheeling history (thereby, he said, reflecting from his own individual person life unlivable, transaccidentated through the slow fires of consciousness into a dividual chaos, perilous, potent common to allflesh, human only, mortal) but with each word that would not pass away the squidself which he had squirtscreened from the crystalline world waned chagreenold and doriangrayer in its dudhud. (*FW* 185-86)

We can get an initial perspective on how this sentence functions by examining earlier versions which occur in Joyce's notebooks.[3] The first, very short, draft of chapter 7 contains some preliminary suggestions, in Latin, of the equation between writing and excretion which the final text insists on but there is no hint of the English passage we are considering. In the next draft, however, we can read: "With the dye he wrote minutely, appropriately over every part of the only foolscap available, his own body, till integument slowly unfolded universal history & that self which he hid from the world grew darker & darker in outlook." Joyce then started to revise the sentence (all additions are italicised): "With the *double* dye he wrote minutely, appropriately over every part of the only foolscap available, his own body, till *one* integument slowly unfolded universal history *the reflection from his individual person of life unlivable transaccidentated in the slow fire of consciousness into a dividual chaos, perilous, potent, common to all flesh, mortal only,* & that self which he hid from the world grew darker & darker in *its* outlook."

In the first version of the sentence we are given an account of how the writer produces his work. The sentence is not syntactically difficult or lexically complex with the exception of the word "integument" which means a "covering" or "skin" and which refers here to the parchment, the material, on which the text is written. The text itself is, of course, *Finnegans Wake* (a universal and atemporal history) but it is also earlier manuscripts. There is no question of understanding writing as an aesthetic production of a disembodied and creative mind; to write is to engage in a transaction between body and language, word and flesh. It is not surprising that this activity may seem to resemble the small infant's play with all the parts and productions of his body for throughout *Finnegans Wake* adult behavior is never far distant from children's play and phantasy. But if the writer is transforming his body into the text we are reading, his self, hidden from the world, is becoming more and more pessimistic. The first editions emphasise that Joyce is working with a "double dye" (both ink and excrement) which he is transforming into the "one integument" that we are reading. The major addition to the text ("the reflections" to "mortal only") is one of the clearest statements of the process that produces *Finnegans Wake*. The text starts from the "unlivable" life of the "individual" and "transaccidents" it into a "dividual chaos." The invented word "transaccidentated" refers to the Catholic Mass and to the doctrine of *transubstantiation* which holds that the consecrated bread has been transformed into the body of Christ. The Church explains this process with reference to the Aristotelian distinction between the essential nature of a thing (its substance) and the inessential features (its accidents). After the consecration in the Mass, the bread is merely an "accident" while the "substance" is Christ's body. Joyce's writing also involves a transformation of the body but there is no question of an appeal to any ultimate "substance." Shem's whole life is a series of accidents, both in the modern sense of "unfortunate and arbitrary events" and in the philosophical sense that Shem is all inessential features ("accidents") without any essential identity ("substance"). Through concentrating on the "accidental," the writing unmakes the "individual" to investigate the "dividual chaos" that constitutes the "unlivable life." The presuppositions of identity are displaced to reveal the divisions from which we are all fabricated into unity.

In the text's final version we find that Joyce has added a proper name ("Eneas"), a demonstrative phrase ("this Esuan Menschavik") and a definite description ("the first till last alshemist") to expand the pronoun "he" at the beginning of the sentence. The first proper name is modified by a clause governed by a present participle modelled on the Latin ("conformant . . ."). This clause in turn contains a relative clause ("which enjoins . . .") which contains within it a further subordinate clause ("that . . . he shall . . . or bedeed . . .") which is itself modified by an adverbial clause of time ("when the call comes"). The effect of this syntactic complexity is that one has a tendency to read each clause or phrase in a variety of relations with surrounding groups of words. Without seriously transgressing the rules of English syntax at any stage, Joyce so confuses the reader that although each grammatical step will be followed, the phrases and words begin to function outside any grammatical relationship, taking on a multitude of meanings.[4] At the same time Joyce repeats, with variations, the main theme of the sentence as well as introducing topics from elsewhere in the book. Vico's thunder God makes an appearance in "fulminant firman" (through the Latin *fulmen*, a thunderbolt). His command equates the "call of nature" which reminds one of the necessity of excretion with the writer's "call" or vocation. A further term is added to this equation with the introduction of a set of chemical references which link writing to digestion. The first meaning one might attach to "tremylose" would be *tremulous*, fearful, but the -ose suffix is a biochemical suffix indicating a sugar. Similarly "nichthemerically" suggests some bio-chemical process although the "nicht" refers both to the nocturnal (night) and the negative (through the German *nicht*, not) features of the writing of *Finnegans Wake*. The reference to copyright and the United States of America refer to Joyce's own law suits in that country where *Ulysses* was both condemned as obscene and published without Joyce's permission. It thus provides more details of Shem's life but the presence of "anus" in "Ourania" and "copro" (Greek for dung) in "copriright" insist on the presence of the body in all Shem's activities.

The opening phrase of the final version ("Then, pious Eneas") illustrates a common device of the *Wake* in quoting famous phrases from European literature in a context which robs them of their sense. The phrase is used frequently in Virgil's epic, the *Aeneid*, where it functions in the narrative as an indication that one part of the action is finished and another is about to begin. Within the *Wake* such a phrase merely emphasises that we are reading a narrative which has no ability to distinguish between ends and beginnings as everything is written in an atemporal present. The other description conferred on Shem ("this Esuan Menschavik") confirms the charge that Shem is a loser in the game of life as it identifies him with Esau (who lost his birthright to Isaac) and the Mensheviks (who lost to the Bolsheviks in the Russian Revolution).

If we now turn to the end of the sentence and look at the transformation from the first draft to the final version then we find once again that the simple meaning has been multiplied through a series of lexical coinages and literary references. The original version claims that there is a correspondence between the degeneration of the artist's self and the production of the book from the material of his body. The final version states that the words that he is producing will not disappear and that the self which he had tried to hide behind the skirts of women and squirts of ink ("squirtscreened") is becoming sadder and older as it is affected by the book. In the coinage "doriangrayer," there is a reference to Oscar Wilde's *The Picture of Dorian Gray*, a story of a beautiful young man whose picture ages although he, himself, remains young. In its confusion of art and life, of body and representation, Wilde's story is also Joyce's. What *Finnegans Wake* suggests is that it is the story of us all and that if we wish to read this story of ourselves then we must enter into an experience of language more radical than any offered by the literary tradition.

This reading of a sentence from *Finnegans Wake* is not in any way exhaustive. All I have indicated is some of the processes by which *Finnegans Wake* involves the reader in a complicated network of signification which is never completed. *Finnegans Wake* does not ask for an interpretation that will identify it but for another set of elements to continue its work.

Notes

1. Max Eastman, *The Literary Mind* (New York: Scribner's, 1931), 101, quoted in Richard Ellmann, *James Joyce* (London: Oxford University Press, 1959), 559.

2. Ellmann, 597.

3. David Hayman, *A First-Draft Version of Finnegans Wake* (Austin: University of Texas Press, 1963), 112, 118-19.

4. For a more detailed consideration of the linguistic procedures adopted by Joyce see Colin MacCabe, "Joyce and Chomsky: The Body and Language," *James Joyce Broadsheet*, Vol. 1., No. 2, June 1980.

SHEM THE TEXTMAN

Hugh Kenner

As early as the titlepage we're in mild perplexity. "Finnegans Wake"—what does that tell us? Perhaps just that the typesetter has been careless, for should the word not be "Finnegan's"? But the author's name, "James Joyce," suggests otherwise, for from that author we've learned to expect odd things. The very first sentence of his *A Portrait of the Artist as a Young Man* arrays words of one or two syllables in a syntax of utter naivete, and three of those "words" we will never have seen before: "moocow" and "nicens" and "Tuckoo." (A "word," by the way, is something we've learned to perceive between spaces fore and aft. Thus "moocow" is one word, not two.)

So back to that titlepage. "Finnegan's Wake," with the apostrophe, is the title of a song about a wake, for a certain Tim Finnegan imperfectly deceased, perhaps merely besotted, and certainly resurrected by whiskey. (We may learn one day that it is not an Irish song; no, an American song about a stage-Irishman, a being who in his American incarnation was understood to be normally drunk. It was in America they coined the name paddy-wagon for the Saturday night drunk-tank express.)

Or is "Wake" perhaps a verb, and are we being told that whole constellations of Finnegans are coming awake? If so, then at least the orthography is accurate, though it does seem odd to be reminded too of that song.

One more possibility: may "Wake" exemplify that recourse of the dialect novelist, phonetic misspelling? For "wake" is what you hear when a Dublin voice says "weak," and can something be made of that? Well, perhaps.

What we have here, in ideal isolation, is the very condition of literacy: a confrontation with silent marks on paper, in utter absence of contexts save such as we ourselves may furnish, sometimes in desperation. Partly, these marks prompt our eyes to recognize familiar sequences (like "Once upon a time," which we've seen too often to reflect how odd is "upon"). Partly they suggest sounds we might make, in imitation of sounds we may imagine ourselves hearing. I've adduced phonetic misspelling to recall ways these promptings may interact, non-standard spelling connoting non-standard speech, to connote in turn intricacies of region and "class." (Look at *Huckleberry Finn*. Also, listen to it: though you'll be responsible yourself for whatever sounds you listen to. There's no guiding voice but your own, responsive to those guiding marks.) It's easy to make the whole subject seem to defy analysis, with such non-analytic naturalness have we all learned to be denizens of Text.

En route to becoming deconstruction's buzzword, the word "Text" has been sundered from its own history, part of which we should start by recalling. It's a word highly pertinent to the great Irish theme of orality, the story-teller's endless improvisations, since one thing no story-teller will ever produce is a text.

For a word that hovers back of "text" is "textile," woven stuff, with its cognate "texture," a quality you test with your fingers, not pertinent to anything made from a mouthful of air. Another antecedent is the name the Greeks had for a carpenter; he was a *tekton*, and appraisal of his skills gave occasion for the word *tekhne*: as we now say, "technique." So the family tree of "text" includes loom-and-shuttle Latin words like "textile" and "tissue," saw-and-hammer Greek words like "technician," and their kinship though surely real has not been fully traced.   Between them though they turn a text, however arrived at, into something made by hand, like a blanket or a boat. It follows that there can be no spoken text. It's only a text when we can get our hands on it. *Verba volant, litterae manent*, goes the proverb; words vanish as they're uttered, letters stay.

Eric Havelock and Marshall McLuhan are not the only writers who have tried to help us imagine what a shock that all was, when writing was invented and speech broke loose from what is within us—breath—to get outered by scribes. The word outside ourselves, not vanishing but staying: that is what "text" connotes. It even connotes, for that matter, the word itself, an entity created by the *space*, the last alphabetic character to be invented. Before the coming of Text, the only discrete elements employed by speakers were *names*, which reflect the separateness of physical things. Apart from names, spoken languages have no words: only a flow of modulated sound. As Ernst Mayr put it bluntly in *Animal Species and Evolution*, "The transfer of the food-uptake function from the snout to the hands further facilitated the specialization of the mouth as an organ of speech."[1] Mouths are speech-factories, notably Irish mouths; and all that they've uttered all these centuries is gone, all gone, all.

But the lettered words a text is made of exist in space the way threads and boards do. Unlike Homer himself, who could call no utterance back, the weaver of a text can reconsider words, scratch them out, rearrange them. We even speak of "cutting" a manuscript, something writers will sometimes do with actual scissors, though more likely with a blue pencil.

The words can be selected from lists (Joyce's frequent practice), and once firmly in place will even lie still to be counted. Thus 11, as every reader knows, is a number that dominates *Ulysses*. Little Rudy died 11 years ago, aged 11 days; that year Stephen Dedalus was 11, and he's now 22. The names of Marion Bloom and Hugh E. Boylan have 11 letters each; their tryst commences in the book's 11th episode. Bloom owns 22 books (the 23rd in the catalogue belongs to a library). "Oxen of the Sun" takes 11 paragraphs getting Bloom into the hospital; the coda, on the street and in Burke's pub, is 11 paragraphs too. In between, 40 paragraphs tally with the 40 weeks of gestation. The first sentence of *Ulysses* has exactly 22 words; the third has exactly 11. And Anna Livia's final utterance—hardly to be called a sentence—"A way a lone a last a loved a long the"—yes, that's 11 words also.

None of these facts is new; I rehearse them to illustrate one thing textuality means: the sheer detachment that permits such counting. And is it accidental, by the way, that in "Circe" the elements "black" and "white" occur in nearly perfect equilibrium, 51 whites, 49 blacks?   Or that "Circe"'s next most common color, with 35 mentions, is British red, with next in order the 29 manifestations of Irish green? I don't know if the color-census signifies or not, but it's one kind of question Joyce does lead you to ask. You'd not think to undertake a like scrutiny of any chapter by Dickens.

But the instincts of Dickens were those of a story-teller, a manufacturer by mouth, albeit one who resorted to pen and paper and printing-press as a ready way to get his stories disseminated. Though all those tens of thousands of readers will have been gratifying, still it was a penance never to be near them while they tasted their pleasure. So Dickens drew his deepest satisfaction from the spoken performances (read, to be sure, from his text) by which he drew laughter and tears from countless paying hearers on countless nights. As to why people paid to hear Dickens read what they had themselves already read, one part of the answer is surely that both he and they thought of the text as somehow coming *between* them. A machine-age expedient, a text, though it couldn't be dispensed with, could still never evade the radical unsatisfactoriness of anything Ersatz. Also, whether you're reading aloud or silently, the voice you hear as you pick your way through a text can only be your own: not the voice of the author, whence authenticity stems. Dickens and his public were agreed about that, agreed therefore that whenever possible it was the voice of Dickens that should be audible, even at the cost of booking theatres and buying tickets. And just such an agreement is one that James Joyce abrogated. The voice you hear as you scan James Joyce's texts remains your own, but in no way is it a stand-in for the voice of James. Auctorial authenticity has been cancelled. Not in this room, and certainly not in a theater, are we to imagine the author speaking to us. He is elsewhere, paring his fingernails, while we cope on our own with his text.

And here we encounter an especially acute contradiction, one that lies at the very root of Joyce's art. To get at it we must invoke his Irishness. Joyce, it goes without saying, is the most Irish of Irish writers; but in Ireland, generally speaking, nothing does go without saying, they're all such great *sayers.* I've written elsewhere about their distrust of print; they associate the production of printable matter with vices practiced in solitude behind a closed door upstairs, the producer suspect of calculating effects, even of scratching out sentences to start them over, unnatural behavior indeed were it taking place in a pub. Yet it is to be a writer that Leopold Bloom aspires— to be, even, a writer as respected as Philip Beaufoy —and his one effort to *tell* a story that we know of would benefit by writerly recalls and cancellations. He's recounting the disgrace of Reuben J. Dodd Jr. First he plunges, like Homer, *in medias res* ("There was a girl in the case," a phrase you're far more likely to read than to hear). Soon he's not being understood and has to adjust the reference of a pronoun (not old Reuben in danger of drowning, no, "the son himself"); whereupon Martin Cunningham takes over and finishes the story properly, and Bloom is reduced to saying ("eagerly"): "Isn't it awfully good?" As it is, if you know how to tell it.

Viewed in that light, it's a strange aura indeed that attends the first page of *Dubliners.* "There was no hope for him this time: it was the third stroke." That's demonstrably a *written* sentence, since a speaker would have said "*that* time"; and when the writer does get around to transcribing *spoken* sentences, what they're remarkable for is how little they say. Speakers hesitate, leave out words, leave gaps; three dots laid by the pen upon the page constitute the most eloquent parts of the transcriptions. "No, I wouldn't say he was exactly . . . but there was something queer . . . I'll tell you my opinion . . ." (though he never does). What's happening here is that Old Cotter is doing something essentially writerly: he's gauging the effect of each word, the way it may fall on the ears of an impressionable boy. Or that's one possibility; another is that he hasn't an idea in his head. Either way, the net result is he can find hardly any speakable words at all.

"The Sisters" is in many ways not only the first but the pivotal Joyce text. By the time he had done with revising the *Irish Homestead* version he'd published at 21, he had in hand much of his mature technique, to set the spoken and the written into ceaseless interaction. What came to fascinate him about his garrulous people was all the things they couldn't find ways of saying, or bring themselves to say, so his texts from end to end are peppered with tacit ellipses.

Then Fritz Senn has remarked on what at first glance seems un-Irish, the sheer quantity of reading and writing that goes on in *Ulysses*. Though in "Telemachus" no one reads or writes, it displays much quotation of printed texts, from the Roman Missal to the work-in-progress of W.B. Yeats. Thereafter literacy is omnipresent. In "Nestor" boys read (and one, who's supposed to be reciting, reads illegally); Mr Deasy writes, even typewrites. In "Proteus" Stephen reads signatures of all things, and inscribes a quatrain. In "Calypso" Bloom reads postcard and letter and the Agendath Netaim leaflet and *Tit-Bits*, and imagines himself writing, for publication, a story based on "some proverb." (It is Bloom, not Stephen, who is the most text-centered human the fiction of James Joyce has ever yet shown us.) Molly has been reading *Ruby*, and offstage she reads the cards. That's a detail Bloom remembers in "Lotus Eaters," where he also reads Martha's letter, part of the point of which is his disinclination to ever be in Martha's presence: these titillations go better on paper. In "Hades" he's reading gravestone inscriptions. "Aeolus" is wholly occupied with marks being put on paper or interpreted. "Lestrygonians" has Bloom reading about evangelist Dowie, then throwing the document into the Liffey. "Scylla and Charybdis" is all about Stephen's reading of what Shakespeare wrote. Mid-afternoon will revolve around finding Molly a book. In "Sirens," amid all the singing, behold Bloom writing, and the point is made that writing entails deceit. I can't think of another novel that keeps its people so busy reading and writing. In non-literate "Penelope," even, "write" and its inflections get 23 mentions, "read" 10, "letter" 15 (though one time to be sure the "letter" in question is "French," i.e., a condom), and we hear of Molly mailing envelopes stuffed with scraps of paper but addressed to herself, just so there'll be, if not words, at any rate mail. In courtship's great time Bloom would write her two letters a day. Now a mere delivered envelope serves as methadone. For the written word is addictive: its pushers urge schoolchildren, even, to acquire "the reading habit," a habit by the way that's been the ruin of Gerty MacDowell. Give us this day our daily fix.

At the time of which Joyce was writing, the strange phrase "reading matter" had already been invented, to denote what had become the single most fervently mass-produced item in any industrial society: print, print, print. That underlay the economic push, in the 1880s, toward mechanized typesetting: anything to get print out faster, never mind what print, and by all means less labor-intensively. It was only authorship that couldn't be mechanized. Philip Beaufoy: true, you might think a machine could supplant *him*: but that never proved really feasible.

People craved print because scanning it uses up time and they had time to kill, which is Molly's problem. (No, sex is not her problem; boredom is her problem.) Though reading for her isn't facile, she's read *Ruby, the Pride of the*

Ring clear to the end. That is no mean feat, I can assure you.[2] And Blazes Boylan's steno, Miss Dunne, fills boring hours at the office with *The Woman in White* ("too much mystery business in it"). And Bloom consumes time at the stool, time otherwise vacant, with Philip Beaufoy's "Matcham's Masterstroke"; it even provokes Aristotelian *katharsis*. Indeed, as long ago as about 1845, W.H. Smith in England had discerned that the place to sell cheap books was in railway stations, where throngs confronted the prospect, and commuters the daily prospect, of a vacant hour or two, just sitting. The genteel press duly railed at "The Railway Novel," an order of paper trash like Pampers, mass-produced for contingencies.

And by about 1900 James Augustine Joyce in Dublin began to wonder how on earth any reader made sense of anything at all. What strange new order of skill was now deployed? "Glancing round hastily to see that he was unobserved, the intrepid fellow mounted the steps, and after wrestling with the window fastenings with his knife, gained admission to the house." That sentence comes from *Tit-Bits* for 1 May 1897, where it's ascribed to the authentic Philip Beaufoy, paid a guinea a column, and the closer you look the more it disintegrates. "Gained admission" is queer enough; in Dublin as in London, native speakers of English never think of *gaining admission*. They just *get in*. But "wrestling," done "with his knife," is queerer still. For what Text is woven of is no longer language: it's a sequence of shared typographic conventions, akin to the convention, later challenged by Joyce, that cats say what Bloom pronounces as "miaow."

And the most mysterious aspect of the readerly skill is the reader's sure knowledge of what sense, just here and there, is *not* to be entertained, not even to be considered. There's nothing we're quicker at than *discarding* meanings. How early Joyce commenced playing with this phenomenon is well known; *Dubliners* has accreted but three paragraphs when word of Old Cotter "talking of faints and worms" suddenly divides all readers into two classes: the unsuspecting, who accept the phrase for its graveyard ring, and the knowledgeable, who assimilate it to a phrase that follows it, "stories about the distillery," aware as they are that "faint" and "worm" are distiller's jargon, hence that it's appropriate to discard the mortuary meanings. Here the unsuspecting reader will not so much as guess that the other possibility exists. Then there's "the black mass" in "Eveline," which pertains not to a rite but to the obdurate bulk of a ship at dusk; or the company the word "grace" is made to keep in "Grace," a cluster that includes "calling" and "gaiters," two more words that might summon ecclesiastical contexts were the present context not mere respectability.

And a way to describe the text of *Finnegans Wake* is that it leaves us forever uncertain what possibilities we can safely discard. "[F]allen lucifers" (*FW* 183.16), are those Miltonic devils? Given the litter that's being inventoried, it's more likely they're burnt matches, and the phrase has little point unless we are somehow aware of our need to decide. So readers of the *Wake* find themselves oddly engaged at what one never does while reading anything else, making actual lists of just such possibilities as skill at reading has long since taught us to ignore. It's a process not devoid of peril; Clive Hart in particular has been rightly eloquent about the dangers of over-interpretation. Still, criteria are not easy to formulate, confronted as we are with perpetual uncertainty about the number of people who may be speaking at once, or the language(s) being spoken. In a polyglot city, even a polyglot citizen may be a moment making sure in which of several tongues he's being offered the gift of discourse. ("Gift": was that German for poison or English for a benison?) We may want to surmise that many such experiences in Trieste and Zurich may have been what drew Joyce to the project of a whole book that keeps us on the qui vive because any known tongue may be audible somewhere or other.

Moreover, how we page-turners so much as pronounce a string of letters can depend very much on which language is governing. We know a French book is in French just by glancing at a page, and can generally tell that much whether we understand a word of French or not. But in the latter case we'll not know how to pronounce what we're looking at: in such a strait can the allegedly "phonetic" alphabet leave us. Still, not knowing French but needing the sense of a French phrase, can we not expect help from a dictionary? Often; but that strategy too has its perils. It takes Brendan O Hehir to help us unriddle a sequence of eight words that look as Gaelic as dammit but aren't any of them to be found in an Irish dictionary: "mhuith peisth mhuise as fearra bheura muirre hriosmas" (*FW* 91.4-5). What we have to do is sound the words out by Irish conventions, whereupon (assuming we've the skill to do that) we find ourselves making noises ("Wit pest wishi as fare vére mwiri hrismos") that resemble "With best wishes for a very merry Christmas": Irish look, English sound.[3]

It's evident that by the time he got to *Finnegans Wake* Joyce's unit of attention had narrowed to the single letter. He had fully absorbed the great lesson of his seven years with *Ulysses*, that what he was engaged in day after day was not "telling stories," no, but formulating minute instructions for printers, whose habit of attention goes letter-by-letter likewise. Type, in the days before the Linotype, existed in the form of little leaden objects, a letter apiece, for compositors' fingers to handle. (A text, remember, is something made by hand.) The first thing an apprentice compositor learned was how by attending to a guiding notch he could always avoid getting letters upside down (no way you can get speech upside down). After that it was all a matter of learning where to reach for the right ones, then setting them in the right order. (And note the word "set": it means putting something in place, a spatial but not an acoustic concept.)

Now it happened that, fully four decades into the era of mechanized typesetting, *Ulysses* was set by hand in Dijon, every letter of it. For as typesetting got mechanized to a craft a man performed sitting at a keyboard, the handset book became equated with Art, one definition of Art being any formal skill that's no longer of practical use.[4] Following the lead of William Morris's Kelmscott Press, much obsolete equipment saw a new life in all the fancy presses that could charge a high price indeed for the limited press-runs of their hand-set wares. The Cuala Press in Ireland was one such outfit, and Maurice Darantiere's Dijon operation was another. Nothing could have served Joyce better than did his interaction with Darantiere, to force his attention toward the power of the single letter: even, as happens once or twice in *Finnegans Wake*, the single letter inserted (at the author's behest) upside down.

So (p. 4) "waalworth" (two a's) turns the Woolworth Building (two o's) into something erected in America where, as *Tit-Bits* readers by the million well understood, people say "waal"; while as for "this man of hod, cement and edifices" (*FW* 4.26-27), three initial letters suffice to turn an Irish-American bricklayer into the polyvalent polysemous HCE.

A closer connection exists between these two examples than the mere fact that I fetched the pair of them from the same paragraph. For if the HCE initials are part of the *Wake*'s special code, "waal" is part of a special code too, special in that it ignores much of the human race but is shared by every denizen of English-language demotic textuality. The list of such codes, if we had one, might prove surprisingly long. They are as wholly arbitrary—as wholly disconnected from extra-textual reality—as are the *Wake*'s HCE and ALP. For you'll listen long and hard in America before you'll hear "waal." It's typographic encoding merely. Another example is the apostrophe in place of an initial "h," as when "'e" and "'er" say (1) Non-standard English; (2) "Cockney." Moreover, story-book Cockney means nothing very specific except non-standard English as spoken by natives of England. Listen to authentic Cockney speech, transcribe it phonetically the way Bernard Shaw did to guide the actors of *Major Barbara*, and what arrives on your page will look barbarous indeed, Cockney speech being most identifiable in its vowels. English having but five official written vowels, Shaw was forced to contrive diphthongs and elisions ("Aw'm gowin to give er a doin that'll teach er to cat awy from me"). Undriven by his practical purpose, fiction writers had recourse to that simple arbitrary code, the dropped "h," in which their readers concurred.

I use "code" in a sense quite different from that of Roland Barthes, whose famous interactive codes are very general, just five in number, and only to be discerned by abstract analysis. Mine are highly particular, indefinitely numerous, and visible right on the surface of the page. Thus doors in English text go "bang" (but in German, "bums"), dogs on an English page say "bow-wow" (but in China, "Wang wang"), Anglo-Irish cats say "miaow," American ones "meow" (but the cat in *Ulysses* says things far more intricate). Conan Doyle in *A Study in Scarlet*, by a single recourse to the verb "reckon," conveyed the American origin of a man who drove a cab in London. True, after forty years of a reasonably attentive exposure to the speech of Connecticut, of California, of Virginia, of Maryland, I cannot recall ever hearing anyone say "I reckon." But that is not the point. We are not dealing with anything that's there to be heard; we are in a domain of purely textual codes, alphabetic arrangements, and they occupy exactly the same plane of existence as the palpably arbitrary codes of the *Wake*. They tell the reader which stereotype is being evoked. For all the dense interweaving of its alphabetic codes, most of them public though a number of them peculiar to itself, *Finnegans Wake* is a book of stereotypes, and we'd get nowhere with it at all if it wasn't.

A neat instance is the "us" on which the very first sentence turns: "riverrun . . . brings us back to Howth Castle and Environs." That's the "us" of tourbooks, which abound in such locutions as "to our left we see. . .". Though behind it lingers the fiction of a loquacious guide shepherding his party, the Baedeker "us" is a purely typographic convention, since a book implies but one reader at a time. Many passages of *Finnegans Wake* are cued by this Baedeker first-person plural, and at least once (*FW* 62.26) the "us" makes an arch comment on itself: "We seem to us (the real Us!). . .".

And as for the dropped capital on the first word, "riverrun," that's a direct way to encode the fact that this book has somehow managed to start in mid-sentence. As everyone knows, for the real start of this sentence we must look to the last page: "A way a lone a last a loved a long the," some slippage of pagination having interfered with the book's attempt to start where the alphabet itself starts, "A." The alphabet too is a continual presence. "[I]t's as semper as oxhousehumper" (*FW* 107.34) will tell us "It's as simple as ABC," seeing that ox, house, camel—Aleph, Ghimel, Daleth—are the pictograms alleged to underlie the opening of the Hebrew litany of letters. And if "simple" has mutated to "semper," (Latin for "always"), well, whoever has read that far into *Finnegans Wake* has agreed that what all Western printed books are made of is, when you come down to it, some set or other of alphabetic units; *always* ABC or something related.

And we're back to the thing that fascinated Joyce very early, the intricate web of agreements, sometimes signaled by a modification of but one letter, that readers and writers, whether of *Tit-Bits* or of the *Aeneid*, had somehow come to share, and that accounted for people's ability to read at all. To disregard those agreements, or modify them, was one way for a writer to get regarded as "difficult."

The short story, as we have already remarked, in Joyce's young days was by no means "Art." It was the most widely practiced of sub-literary genres, the entire alphabetized world's time-killer of choice. Being sub-literary, it kept its repertory of devices right up in the foreground, where the least experienced of readers could not miss them. And it was James Joyce's point of entry into literature, the commencement of his career of wholesale modification. Among the first agreements he called into question was the one about closure: the agreement that an "ending" will be produced. What exactly has been happening in "The Sisters" the narrator himself seems not to know, or to remember not having known, and as for an ending, the story doesn't so much as have a last word: rather, it offers a last ellipsis, " . . . " .

By the time he had gotten to *Ulysses* he was nullifying standing arrangements wholesale. A novel ought to open by establishing the narrating voice, the pseudo-person we are to trust clear to the end whatever else may break up. *Ulysses* doesn't. It ought to tell us where it's opening and when; not so *Ulysses*, where two generations of readers have depended on commentaries for elementary data, as about the place (Martello Tower, Sandycove), and the year (1904). It ought to have the decency to let, for instance, any ordinary cat make an ordinary meow; not so the utterly ordinary—indeed nameless—*Ulysses* cat, with its four-word vocabulary, each word unpronounceable except by a cat. And part of the game *Ulysses* plays with its ideal reader is the presumption that such modifications of contract are empirically based; as for instance that since no real cat says "meow," we'll benefit by an improved transcription. But no sooner is that idea in place than the book is forsaking empiricism, partly because empiricism was after all the convention old-fashioned novelists had always pretended they were observing, and is not observance of a convention itself a convention?

Return, then, to the *Wake*, thinking now of Shem the Penman as Jim the Textman. What he's up to is what he was up to from the first, an intricate play with that old never-specified contract between any reader of "fiction" and any writer of it. It had become, he's reminding us now, an agreement that established whole stereotypical worlds by simply modifying the spelling of words, even by a single letter. Homer had not that resource at his disposal, since neither could he spell nor had he even any letters to think of spelling with. But having at our resource the technology of Gutenberg, we can accomplish absolutely anything with spelling. *Finnegans Wake* is mankind's isolated tour de force of misspelling: that's certainly one claim we can safely make for it. I've remarked elsewhere in connection with the Gabler *Ulysses* that Joyce's texts have this special quality when they grow corrupt, that the direction in which they degenerate is not away from the normal but toward it.[5] That is something we may see illustrated just as often as the very title of his last book gets cited with an inserted apostrophe, a theme we may end by pondering: the way, in imitation of his circling book, it served us for point of entry.

Notes

1. Ernst Mayr, *Animal Species and Evolution* (Cambridge, Mass.: The Belknap Press of Harvard University Press, 1963), 635.

2. The Yale Library possesses a copy of the unreadable book Joyce has her reading; it is Amy Reade's *Ruby: A Novel Founded on the Life of a Circus Girl*. But *Ruby, the Pride of the Ring* is a more Joycean title, for mightn't you guess, in the absence of context, that the phrase pertained to jewelry?

3. Brendan O Hehir, *A Gaelic Lexicon for Finnegans Wake and Glossary for Joyce's Other Works* (Berkeley and Los Angeles: University of California Press, 1967), 62.

4. Similarly, "Art" slowly took over the Short Story even as radio and video were usurping its truly profitable usefulness as time-killer. We lose a whole dimension of *Dubliners* in forgetting that its author was working with the most commercial of forms.

5. Hugh Kenner, "Reflections on the Gabler Era," *James Joyce Quarterly* 26 (Fall 1988): 11-20.

FW 606.13–607.16
[Lines not equal]

606.13   Bisships, bevel to rock's rite! Sarver buoy, extinguish! Nuotabene.
The rare view from the three Benns under the bald heaven is on
.15   the other end, askan your blixom on dimmen and blastun, something
to right hume about. They were erected in a purvious century, as a
hen fine coops and, if you know your Bristol and have trudged the
trolly ways and elventurns of that old cobbold city, you will
sortofficially scribble a mental Peny-Knox-Gore. Whether they were
.20   franklings by name also has not been fully probed. Their design is a
whosold word and the charming details of light in dark are freshed
from the feminiairity which breathes content. *O ferax cupla!* Ah,
fairypair! The first exploder to make his ablations in these parks was
indeed that lucky mortal which the monster trial showed on its first day
.25   out. What will not arky paper, anticidingly inked with penmark, push,
per sample prof, kuvertly falted, when style, stink and stigmataphoron
are of one sum in the same person? He comes out of the soil very
well after all just where Old Toffler is to come shuffling along-soons
Panniquanne starts showing of her peequuliar talonts. Awaywrong
wandler surking to a rightrare rute for his plain utterrock sukes,
.30   appelled to by her fancy claddaghs. You plied that pokar, gamesy,
swell as aye did, while there were flickars to the flores. He may be
humpy, nay, he may be dumpy but there is always something racey
about, say, a sailor on a horse. As soon as we sale him geen we gates
a sprise! He brings up tofatufa and that is how we get to Missas
607.01   in Massas. The old Marino tale. We veriters verity notefew demmed
lustres priorly magistrite maxi-mollient in ludubility learned. Facst.
Teak off that wise head! Great sinner, good sonner, is in effect
.05   the motto of the Mac-Cowell family. The gloved fist (skrimmhandsker)
was intraduced into their socerdatal tree before the fourth of the
twelfth and it is even a little odd all four horolodgeries still gonging
restage Jakob van der Bethel, smolking behing his pipe, with Essav of
Messagepostumia, lentling out his borrowed chafingdish, before
cymbaloosing the apostles at every hours of changeover. The first
.10   and last rittlrattle of the anniverse; when is a nam nought a nam
whenas it is a. Watch! Heroes' Highway where our fleshers leave their
bonings and every bob and joan to fill the bumper fair. It is their
segnall for old Champelysied to seek the shades of his retirement
.15   and for young Chappielassies to tear a round and tease their partners
lovesoftfun at Finnegan's Wake.

The Femasculine Obsubject: A Lacanian Reading of *FW* 606-607

Sheldon Brivic

I. Gender as Signification, or Taking a Stand

Masculine and feminine are modes of language in *Finnegans Wake* as they are in the theories of Jacques Lacan. After showing how the genders are divided linguistically, I will describe how the subject or self is formed by their interaction. Masculine and feminine language functions contribute to every personality, but the opposite sex is usually projected onto someone or something else in order to separate the subject from an object. This process can be illustrated vividly by close reading of a passage from the *Wake* that assembles the family complex of the book, showing how masculine and feminine arise as aspects of a single mind that sees itself in other things.

Building on Freud, Lacan argues that the infant has a closeness to the mother in which feelings flow freely until the father imposes phallic authority that separates the child from direct pleasure and obliges him to use language as a substitute for it.[1] We recall that in the first chapter of *A Portrait of the Artist*, Stephen Dedalus was separated from his mother and struggling to understand words. As the authority that enforces language, the phallus stands for a firm center that controls the unclear shifting of meaning, which Lacan associates with the feminine.

These two sides, "woman formed mobile or man made static" (*FW* 309.21-22), are represented in the *Wake* by ALP and HCE. She is a river who has no definite form and keeps going on, while he is a tower who tries to stand firm and take a definite position. As Colin MacCabe points out, both genders are described as involved in the act of writing, which expresses "the vaulting feminine libido," but is also " sternly controlled" by a "male fist" (*FW* 123.8-10).[2]

As Joyce's images suggest here, the masculine function can no more exist apart from the feminine than muscles could contract without expanding in the act of writing. It was a basic observation of Freud's that everyone includes both genders, as the dreamer of the *Wake* seems to include both HCE and ALP. Ellie Ragland-Sullivan suggests that the two lobes of the brain, in their distinct functions, correspond to the two genders.[3]

Society, however, is organized to define certain people as masculine and others as feminine. Lacan, emphasizing that the word *phallus* (as opposed to penis) refers to a symbol rather than an organ, insists that masculine and feminine are social constructs and linguistic codes with no necessary relation to the biological body. The phallus is seen by Lacan as built on emptiness because it is an idea generated in the child by the fear of castration. In the second chapter of *Portrait*, Stephen's interest in E__. C__. first appears in a scene that immediately follows one in which he is mistaken for "Josephine" (68), so that his sexuality seems to spring from castration anxiety. For Lacan, the penis is only a sign used to validate something bigger, the power of significance claimed by men.[4]

The elevation of the phallic over the feminine is parallel to the effort to

45

fix the meanings of words clearly and to deny the shifting uncertainty behind them, which is linked to the womanly. When words are clear it seems as if we can see reality through them, but Lacan emphasizes that the meaning of a sign can only refer to other signs, so that signification keeps sliding away from what it aims at and attaching itself to alternatives. At any point in the *Wake*, one finds that a variety of meanings are true at once; and the reader, who can only be conscious of one at a time, feels the sliding of other choices (or joyces). This sliding seems to be what Lacan means by *la jouissance*, a word that may be translated as 'joyance' or 'orgasm.' Lacan says that Joyce's main purpose is to express *jouissance*, the free movement of the meanings of words. Writing in a style like that of the *Wake*, Lacan plays on the term *jouissance* so as to equate it with Joyce's name.[5]

If the *Wake* is made up of sliding away, a *Wake* critic should not hope for a bull's eye, and Margot Norris has revealed that the center of the *Wake* is empty in *The Decentered Universe of Finnegans Wake*.[6] Yet everyone who interprets the *Wake* has to install some center, some principle around which to arrange things. The attempt to read the *Wake* coherently is like the erection of a phallus in the face of a flow. By finding a center, this tempting attempt will leave out many alternatives; and, like the phallus, its pride will not last long. The interpretation I make below is perhaps the most detailed treatment of the forty-six lines I examine, but it leaves out most of what is there, and I realize that other views can be taken. The *Wake* teaches us that our stands are, like HCE's phallic tower, bound to fall. This does not mean, however, that we should not interpret. Christine van Boheemen points out that reality cannot be represented without using the phallic focus.[7] Even when Norris posits an empty center in the text, she is using this emptiness as a Lacanian phallus, a stand that exerts significance to draw details around itself.

One valuable feature of Lacan's theory of genders is that if masculine and feminine are linguistic categories used by all people, then men or women can be as masculine or feminine as they want at any time—if they can escape artificial social restrictions. Patrick McGee shows in *Paperspace* that the sexual excitement people feel in *Ulysses* usually is situated in an uncertain area between masculine and feminine, especially in the cases of Leopold and Molly Bloom.[8] Joyce's main women all exert strong phallic powers, as Gretta Conroy, Bertha, and Molly do by having (or thinking of) their own men in opposition to their mates, and as ALP does by deciding to leave HCE. Each shows the will to fix on her own identity apart from the role given her by society. On the other hand, all of the men whom Joyce respects have substantial feminine components. On the linguistic level, each of these figures has to use both masculine and feminine modes if (s)he is to generate discourse that has both the firmness to be coherent and the vitality to be expressive.

II. Subobjectifying

More than any other figures in literature, the characters in the *Wake* exist as signs, as is evident from the letters and sigla that represent them. And these signs keeps shifting, for names rarely take the same form twice. Whether they be trees, words, or people as gestures, signs always function as objects because they are defined as sharable with others. Lacan argues, however, that the self can only be manifested in signs. Therefore the self can never exist independently, but only as a circuit between its impression of itself and the environment of signs that makes up that impression.

To show how the subject exists as an interaction with objects, and masculine as an interaction with feminine, I will analyze a passage of the *Wake* that describes the formation of the self through reflection by the environment.[9] Richard Beckman, who recommended this passage to me, described it as a microcosm of the *Wake*.[10] The earliest form of the two paragraphs I consider here (606.13-607.23) was a separate manuscript added to the *Wake* in 1938 (*JJA* 63:64-66), so they form a single late compositional unit. This passage appears in Book IV between the story of St. Kevin and the debate between the Archdruid Balkelly and St. Patrick. Directly before the main paragraph I examine (606.13-607.16), Kevin sinks into his pool in meditation. Directly after it, HCE is seen in bed with ALP, following which dawn begins to appear (607.24). It seems, then, that this paragraph moves from oblivion toward waking, and this movement evidently involves the formation of self consciousness, which is represented through the landscape. Assuming the dreamer is continuous, he passes from Kevin's emptiness to HCE's fullness.

The puzzling opening of this paragraph seems to follow from the last word of the previous one, "Yee" (606.12), which (as "yed") was added in 1938 as the final sentence of a paragraph about Kevin substantially written in 1923.[11] "Yee" may express Kevin's shock from the water he is entering, and this shock may lead to the image of swerving ships that opens the new paragraph: "Bisships, bevel to rock's rite! Sarver buoy, extinguish! Nuotabene" (606.13-14). Perhaps Kevin loses his identity when the buoy (or candle) goes out, for he is like a church server boy. But he seems still to influence "Nuotabene," which is Italian for ('he swims well,') as McHugh says,[12] as well as an injunction to observe the following landscape. It may be because the dreamer found Kevin's meditation unbearably dull (another level of "Yee") that a new identity is taken on here, so that the water imagery suggests birth.

The whole cycle of life is represented in our paragraph, and birth is followed by the development of the self. In Lacan, the self begins by being reflected from others. Moreover, according to Lacan's theory of the gaze, one can only see something by imagining that it is looking at one; for perception has to be motivated by desire, and desire seeks a response.[13] The lines of the *Wake* that follow emphasize that the landscape returns the viewer's perception: "The rare view from the three Benns under the bald heaven is on the other end, askan your blixom on dimmen and blastun, something to right hume about" (606.14-16).

Ben is Gaelic for 'peak,' and the rear view of the mountains on the other end of the subject's sight is shown actively soliciting (asking) his glance (German *Blick*) by means of a pattern of dark and light (dim and blaze, which is cognate with *blast*). This is not only something to write home about, but it will be news to Hume because the vitality of the outside world refutes his skepticism.

The mountains become constructions with the opening of the next

sentence: "They were erected in a purvious century, as a hen fine   coops . . ."
"Erected," "hen," and "coops" introduce HCE with the usual order of his letters
reversed, perhaps because he is seen from the other end. McHugh points out
that Howth has three peaks, so the mountain, which turns into a city in this
sentence, seems to be the father; but the image of the father tends to obstruct
the image of the mother. In the past, when things were more permeable (or
pervious), these structures were built to contain a hen. The word *fine* is derived
from *finire*, the Latin verb for 'end' or 'terminate.' As the hen is a figure of
woman in the *Wake*, it may be that the outlines of the landscape and of
civilization were constructed by patriarchal convention to con-fine the feminine
flow of language.

In any case, the landscape turns out to be imbued with womanhood. This
pattern recurs throughout the book: HCE projects the image of ALP to create
the physical attraction of the world and to bring his mind into the "reality" of
involvement. The man needs the feminine flow to motivate him, but he cannot
contain it because it breaks down his sense of identity and reason, so he projects
it on woman as the Other, and then blames her for inconstancy. The pattern is
developed as the observer of this paragraph finds the cityscape increasingly
attractive:

> Their design is a whosold word and the charming details of light in
> dark are freshed from the feminiairity which breathes content. *O
> ferax cupla*! (606.21-23)

There is synesthesia here in that the breathing feminine air that freshes the
details of light is a smell that creates a picture. This indicates strong sensuality,
which is confirmed by "*ferax cupla*," which, as McHugh indicates, combines the
Latin for 'fruitful' with the Irish for 'pair.' Feeling is expressed by the shifting
of language, and (other things being equal) the bigger the shift, the stronger the
feeling. The relation to the object has grown lustful, and the fact that the
design imaged is a "whosold" word suggests a woman everyone talks about, or
one who sold herself.

The Fall (*felix culpa*) appears here because the subject has separated
himself from his feelings and derogated them to the level of object. This may
be a necessary step in the formation of civilized man as opposed to woman, but
it alienates him from part of himself. The voyeuristic aspect of HCE's crime in
the park involves his distancing himself from the object that expresses him, but
through this crime he gains his public identity. The subject now finds himself
in Eden after original sin, and he is now HCE: "The first exploder to make his
ablations in these parks was indeed that lucky mortal which the monster trial
showed on its first day out" (606.23-25).

Werner Heisenberg states that you cannot observe a phenomenon without
changing what you observe.[14] The first explorer is an exploder because when
he sees things, he destroys what they were. As a version of Adam, he has been
a mortal on trial since history began. His crime was making ablations, a play on
ablutions and *oblations*. Ablation means surgical removal, and this fits with
what I have said about his cutting himself off from the feminine. He has,
however, also taken his identity *from* the landscape, and the Latin ablative case
means "from."

A passage from the "Gramma's Grammar" section of the lesson chapter (II.2) refers to the to-and-fro nature of relationships: "Take the dative with his oblative for, even if obsolete, it is always of interest, so spake gramma . . ." (268.22-24). On the surface, it says, "Take what your date offers, for even if he is old, he has money." "Oblative" refers not only to the date's offering, but to his round belly (compare "this oblate orange," *U* 15.4427). Since the dative is the Latin case for 'to,' as ablative is, for 'from,' and *inter-est* means 'between is,' a secondary meaning is "Take the to and from, for even if he is inanimate, there is still interaction." This recognizes that the truth lies *between* in any relationship rather than in either party.

Returning to our exploder, we find that the statement that he goes back to the first trial leads to a questioning of his identity, which is now attached to a document:

What will not arky paper, anticidingly inked with penmark, push,
per sample prof, kuvertly falted, when style, stink and
stigmataphoron are of one sum in the same person? (606.25-28)

Paper is "arky" because it lasts through the disasters of history, and this text is written "anticidingly" because it expresses several opposing forces at once. HCE now uses the phallus of interpretation, and "per sample prof" means that if the right professor is found, the text can be made to "push" anything. It can also be "kuvertly falted," secretly folded or faulted by hidden prejudice, so that parts of the text are hidden and recombined. HCE has now become involved in an elaborate effort to prove that he is unified, to deny his dependence on otherness. Yet "one sum in the same person" equates the Latin 'I am' with sumthing added up, and he continues to be created by the feminine.

III. Our Her-o

O being the standard Lacanian abbreviation for *object*, we can call HCE our her-o. He actually becomes an object at this point (in two stages), but only when ALP displays herself:

He comes out of the soil very well after all just where
Old Toffler is to come shuffling alongsoons
Panniquanne starts showing of her peequuliar talonts.
Awaywrong wandler surking to a rightrare rute for
his plain utterrock sukes, appelled to by her fancy
claddaghs. (606.28-32)

It seems that Old Toffler is the form of the initial "He" that is completed by the display of the Pan-Ann or 'All-Ann,' for the shuffler is apparently the one who searches for a route in the following sentence. The nameless narrator of "Cyclops" makes an offensive remark about a lewd picture: "Get a queer old tailend of corned beef off that one, what?" (*U* 12.1176); and the "talonts" ALP shows to supplement HCE's identity are primarily obscene. The P/Q split, a shift from *P* sounds to *K* sounds in Celtic and other Indo-European languages, is frequently referred to in the *Wake*.[15] Here it becomes an image of the feminine shifting of language as attractive. What appeals to HCE is ALP's uncertainty: one cannot tell whether she is coming or going, and her genitals are both in front ("pee") and in back (*le cul*). This arrangement follows St. Augustine's famous line "*Inter urinas et faeces nascimur.*"[16]

ALP's uncertainty gives HCE phallic certainty, so her fancy clothes (Swedish *kläder*), or Claddagh skirts (see McHugh) not only appeal to him, but give him a definite name or appellation. She allows his stones (British slang for 'testicles') to speak ("utterrock"), and he now appears as the phallus, keeping the fire going by poking; "You plied that pokar, gamesy, swell as aye did, while there were flickars to the flores" (606.32-34). *Flicka* is Swedish for 'girl,' as McHugh notes, so he played (or danced) a polka while there were girls on the floor. But he also plied the phallus of signification while the lights (flickers) on the flowers drew him. On one level, these were flowers of speech, for Lacan's idea that everything occurs in words is the rule for anyone who lives in writing.[17] After all "gamesy" is one of the frequent references to the fact that Joyce is behind HCE and all of the other signifiers in the *Wake*.

Yet the phallic signifier is a linguistic construct that cannot be filled by anyone; and having gained a sense of fulfillment by seducing or masturbating over every available woman (two more meanings of the last sentence cited) and debasing the object through which he exists, HCE is now beginning to decline, as indicated by the past of "while there were flickars." His inability to fit his definition is emphasized here:

> He may be humpy, nay, he may be dumpy but there
> is always something racy about, say, a sailor on a
> horse. As soon as we sale him geen we gates a sprise!
> (606.34-36)

Another reference to the Fall appears by way of Humpty Dumpty as HCE fails to fit into the expected shape because he is humpy and dumpy. As a sailor on horseback, he is out of place, but his incongruity, the surprise with which he greets you "we gates" (German *wie geht's*? ['how are you?'] as McHugh notes) is what makes him vital (racy). He comes alive whenever he goes beyond the fixed meanings in which he could be enclosed. That may be why, having become a third person on line 24, he now gains an audience in the first person plural.

The movement beyond definition that makes HCE attractive is now portrayed as an eruption: "He brings up tofatufa and that is how we get to Missas in Massas" (606.36-607.1). Joyce may have known of tofu, Japanese bean curd, which was eaten in the West by the turn of the century.[18] He certainly refers to *tufa*, an English word of Italian origin for porous stone, often volcanic (*OED*), and its repetition suggests redundancy. The excess that streams from our her-o reveals his feminine aspect, the miss (or going amiss) in the master. This sentence also says that he projects another by which he creates himself: by bringing up thou, he creates me. "Tofatufa" and "Missas in Massas" go together to form the last version of a major motif in the *Wake* for which Clive Hart lists fifty-six occurrences under the name of the first form in which it appears, "mishe mishe to tauftauf" (3.9-10).[19] Critics have not developed the idea that me and thou form a circuit that constitutes the subject.

"*Mishe*," as McHugh points out, is Gaelic for 'I,' and Joyce may have been influenced by Martin Buber's *I and Thou* (1923). Buber says that "I-

Thou" forms a single primary word. He argues that *I* cannot exist except in combination and that when *Thou* is spoken, *I* has to be said along with it.[20] Joyce emphasizes the objective form *me* rather than *I* to indicate that the self only exists by return from the other.

If HCE at this point has generated the fullness of the other, the personality of the environment, to develop himself, this may relate to "The old Marino tale" (607.1), for Coleridge's "Ancient Mariner" learns by telling his story to accept his bond to nature. HCE, however, may show the weakness of a subjection to religion in "Missas in Masses." He is moving toward a middleaged accommodation like that of the "womanly man" Leopold Bloom (*U* 15.1799), for whom, as Bella Cohen points out, ". . . the missus is master" (15.2759). One reason for this is that the masculine cannot live without expressing itself through the feminine.

HCE is thoroughly surrounded after this by the social connections he now needs to support his position as patriarch. He is vouched for in legal terms (607.1-3) and his family motto, history, and heraldry are presented to affirm his status (607.4-10). The Four Old Men sit in judgment over him and his sons appear in ceremonial form as Jakob (Shem) and Essav (Shaun, as indicated by "Messagepostumia"). HCE is striving for a propriety that will protect him from his irrational side, and the more he encloses himself with external specifications and extensions, the less he can live by interacting with otherness.

His position is summed up near the end of the paragraph through another familiar motif; "The first and last rittlerattle of the anniverse; when is a nam nought a nam whenas it is a. Watch!" (607.10-12). Patrick A. McCarthy points out that HCE is reduced to a mere name here.[21] As "nam," he is a man in reverse because he is seen from the other end. Lacan argues that if identity is based on how others see one, it is inherently reversed and distorted.[22] In *Ulysses*, when Bloom is in Nighttown, his guilt is evoked and he imagines the voice of society criticizing him in the form of "the watch" (15.676-1223). Kimberly Devlin points out that Joyce shows that shame is always caused by a sense of being watched.[23] HCE is a "Watch" because he consists of what others see. And because a major component of what sees and generates him is feminine, he is between the genders; so he lives in an "anniverse" ruled by ALP, and he takes the neuter pronoun *it*.

The assemblage of social obligations around HCE constricts him by enveloping him in so many definitions. Yet the potential that is being cut down in him is also being dispersed among his dependents. The whole construct that is wearing HCE out is seen as a big clock run by the Four Old Men, and as Michael O'Shea suggested at a reading session, the two sons are carved figures that ring the hour:

> . . . all four horolodgereies still gonging restage Jakob
> van der Bethel, smolking behing his pipe, with Essav
> of Messagepostumia, lentling out his borrowed
> chafingdish, before cymbaloosing the apostles at every
> hours of changeover. (607.7-10)

A cymbal is struck for the hour here; but since McHugh says that *cymbal* is derived from the Greek for 'cup,' something is also being let out of a cup.

Apostle is based on the Greek for 'one who is sent forth,' and HCE's spirit is being loosed among his apostles in a process of changeover that takes place at every hour.

HCE now faces old age, which may be a heroic highway in the sense of a place where everyone confronts death:

> Heroes' Highway where our fleshers leave their bonings and every bob and joan to fill the bumper fair. It is their segnall for old Champelysied to seek the shades of his retirement and for young Chappielassies to tear a round and tease their partners lovesoftfun at Finnegan's Wake. (607.12-16)

"Fill the Bumper Fair!" (as McHugh notes) is a song written by Thomas Moore to a tune called "Bob and Joan." A book could be written about the hundreds of references to Moore's *Irish Melodies* in the *Wake*. The present poem, an advertisement for alcoholism, says that when Prometheus stole fire from the gods, he needed a place to put it, so he put it in Bacchus's cup, where it mixed with wine, and this is why drinking gives such spirit. In our passage, the spirit passes from the old vessel to the new.

The appearance of Shem and Shaun suggested a particularly strong version of two figures who cannot exist except by interaction with each other; and the present passage adds another version of reciprocity, this time inverse, for it repeats the idea that the decline of HCE is the growth of the young people around him. Compare Stephen's statement in "Scylla and Charybdis": ". . . his growth is his father's decline . . ."(*U* 9.856). If HCE declines by linking himself to too many identities, we may say that as "Old Champelysied," the palsied old champ has the sophistication of a boulevardier; but he is also a ghost, for *Champs Elysées* means 'fields of Elysium.'

The apostrophe in "Finnegan's" makes the end of the paragraph refer primarily to the wake rather than to the book. If the young rejoice while HCE fades, it seems that 'love's oft fun' at the wake because the decline of the parent is stimulating to the children. On the other hand, love is seen here as soft fun in which one teaches by teasing. These images show the mixing of active and passive, subject and object, indicating how men and women both give and take to create each other by exchanging feeling. The successor of Old Champelysied will be like him, "young Chappielassies," figures each of whom combines subject and object, masculine and feminine, in a single signifier.

In the next paragraph, which originally completed the compositional unit of 1938, HCE apparently half wakes to find himself so entangled with his wife that he cannot tell which is which:

> That my dig pressed in your dag si . . . . Mees is thees knees. Thi is mi. We have caught oneselves, Sveasmeas, in somes incontigruity coumplegs of heoponhurrish marrage from whose I most sublumbunate. (607.17-21)

John Bishop has amply demonstrated in *Joyce's Book of the Dark* that the dreaming of the *Wake* seems to be influenced by the "external" events of the physical reactions of the sleeper,[24] so the dream passage we have been examining may have been influenced by the feelings of HCE's body touching ALP's. Bishop does add, however, that we cannot be certain of any of the supposedly external events that impinge on the dreamer.

Whether or not ALP is actually there, the situation illustrates a psychological truth of marriage; one is often kidding oneself if one tries to distinguish whether a given feeling, thought, or action comes from one mate or another. In such situations it is clear that the source of the impulse is really a field of interplay between the two. Joyce presents marriage as a 'marring' of distinctions between 'he' and 'her' in such elements as the reversal of "is" in the first sentence quoted and the positing in the third of "oneselves."

Lacan represents an indeterminate third party at every dialogue by the term *the Other*.[25] The Other can never be known or seen, but it feels like an external, personal agency or consciousness. Its presence here is indicated by the pronoun "whose": "heoponhurrish marrage from whose I most sublumbunate." Since *lumbar* means 'of the loins' and *nates* means 'buttocks,' this has the physical meaning of taking one part of the body out from under another. But its main meaning is that he must sublimate out of 'its' entanglement, the entanglement of an indefinite third party.

HCE must pretend that he is he and she is she to avoid realizing that the truth of his being lies between them. After this the dawn appears that will end the book, and presumably return to the external world of clear definitions in which man and woman are opposed. The vision of the *Wake*, however, is a vision in which personality is located in the field between individuals, a field in which subject is object and masculine is feminine.

Notes

1. Ellie Ragland-Sullivan, *Jacques Lacan and the Philosophy of Psychoanalysis* (Urbana: University of Illinois Press, 1986), 55-57. This is the most comprehensive summary of Lacan's theories available.

2. Colin MacCabe, *James Joyce and the Revolution of the Word* (London: Macmillan, 1979), 146.

3. Ragland-Sullivan, *Philosophy*, 291. Ragland-Sullivan points out that the differentiation of the lobes of the brain takes place at the age of five, when sex differences have been learned. She argues that differences between male and female brains may be caused by social conditioning rather than by biology.

4. "The Meaning of the Phallus," in *Jacques Lacan and the école freudienne, Feminine Sexuality*, eds. Juliet Mitchell and Jacqueline Rose (New York: Norton, 1982), 74-85. The Introductions to this book by Mitchell and Rose are the clearest introduction to Lacan's thought available.

5. Jacques Aubert, ed., *Joyce avec Lacan* (Paris: Navarin, 1987), 27, 36. Four of Lacan's writings on Joyce are in this collection. Eight more appeared soon after they were composed (1975-1976) in the undated periodical *Ornicar?*, numbers 6-11.

6. Margot Norris, *The Decentered Universe of Finnegans Wake: A Structuralist Analysis* (Baltimore: Johns Hopkins University Press, 1976).

7. Christine van Boheemen, *The Novel as Family Romance: Language, Gender, and Authority from Fielding to Joyce* (Ithaca: Cornell University Press, 1987), 38-42.

8. Patrick McGee, *Paperspace: Style as Ideology in Joyce's Ulysses* (Lincoln: University of Nebraska Press, 1988), 117, 128. McGee joins Norris, MacCabe, and van Boheemen as one of the best Lacanian critics of Joyce working in English.

9. The best available analysis of this passage seems to me to be William York Tindall, *A Reader's Guide to Finnegans Wake* (London: Thames and Hudson, 1969), 315-316. Another good treatment of it is Danis Rose and John O'Hanlon, *Understanding Finnegans Wake: A Guide to the Narrative of James Joyce's Masterpiece* (New York: Garland, 1982), 299-300.

10. I participated in an Ensemble Interpretation of this passage with the Philadelphia *Wake* Circle at the Milwaukee Joyce Conference on 13 June 1987. I am grateful to Dick Beckman, our leader, and to the other members of the group: Martha Davis, Morton Levitt, Timothy Martin, and Michael O'Shea.

11. Joyce wrote "Yed" on a typescript "probably early" in 1938, the time listed for our two paragraphs (*JJA* 63:41,63). "Yed" is typed in two later typescripts, but becomes "Yee" in a galley proof of November 1938 (63:93,113,301). Among the *OED* meanings for the Anglo-Saxon *yed* are 'tell, sing, and dispute.' Compare *FW* 605.4.

12. Roland McHugh, *Annotations to Finnegans Wake* (Baltimore: Johns Hopkins University Press, 1980), 606. Because McHugh, who takes many points from earlier scholars, uses the same page numbers as the *Wake*, I will not have to use notes for my further references to him. There are many fine points on the present *Wake* passage in McHugh, and in Tindall and others, that I do not mention because they are not relevant to my interpretation.

13. The idea of the self originating in reflection appears in "The mirror stage as formative . . ." (1949), in *Écrits: A Selection*, trans. Alan Sheridan (New York: Norton, 1977), 1-7. The theory of the gaze is in *The Four Fundamental Concepts of Psycho-Analysis*, ed. Jacques-Alain Miller, trans. Alan Sheridan (New York: Norton, 1978), 72-83.

14. Werner Heisenberg, "Non-Objective Science and Uncertainty," in *The Modern Tradition: Backgrounds of Modern Literature*, ed. Richard Ellmann and Charles Feidelson, Jr. (New York: Oxford University Press, 1965), 444-450.

15. The P/K Split is explained in Brendan O Hehir, *A Gaelic Lexicon for Finnegans Wake and Glossary for Joyce's Other Works* (Berkeley: University of California Press, 1967), 403-405.

16. 'We are born between piss and shit,' cited in Norman O. Brown, *Life Against Death: The Psychoanalytical Meaning of History* (Middletown, Conn.: Wesleyan University Press, 1959), 187-188.

17. Lacan hears a voice saying, "Everything is language: language when my heart beats faster . . ." in "The Freudian thing . . ." (1955), in *Écrits*, 124. He means that a sensation can only be perceived by comparing it to other sensations, and this puts it into language.

18. L. Patrick Coyle, *The World Encyclopedia of Food* (New York: Facts on File, 1982), 642.

19. Clive Hart, *Structure and Motif in Finnegans Wake* (London: Faber and Faber, 1962), 222-223.

20. Will Herberg, ed., *The Writings of Martin Buber* (New York: Meridian Books, 1956), 43-44. According to Michael O'Siadhail, *Learning Irish* (Reprint, New Haven: Yale University Press, 1988), 12, 40, *mise* is the first person disjunctive pronoun, a form that is either the object or implies contrast. Thanks for advice on the Gaelic to Mary Ellen Cohane.

21. Patrick A. McCarthy, *The Riddles of Finnegans Wake* (Cranbury, N.J.: Associated University Presses, 1980), 101-102.

22. This idea is explained well in Juliet Mitchell, *Psychoanalysis and Feminism* (New York: Vintage, 1974), 39-40.

23. Kim Devlin, "'See ourselves as others see us': Joyce's Look at the Eye of the Other," *PMLA* 104 (1989): 883. I have also learned from her "Self and Other in *Finnegans Wake*," *JJQ* 10 (Fall 1983): 31-50.

24. John Bishop, *Joyce's Book of the Dark: Finnegans Wake* (Madison: University of Wisconsin Press, 1986), 278-286. Bishop observes also that HCE cannot exist independently of his consort, so that the hero of the *Wake* is "dyadic" (367).

25. "The subversion of the subject and the dialectic of desire . . . ," in *Écrits*, 305.

Quinet in the *Wake*:
The Proof or the Pudding?

Bernard Benstock

Several theories have been proposed regarding the narrative structure of *Finnegans Wake*, and each has had its advocates: that it is a continuous narrative, *or* that there is a narrative line that is constantly being interrupted, *or* that multiple narratives are embedded into each other, *or* that there is a thematic structure containing narrative analogues, *or* that a series of points of reference operate within oscillating perspectives, *or* that a narrative coexists with various near-narratives and constant commentaries—none of these theories need be discarded and all may function in conjunction with each other. With no organizing schema available, these approaches may provide structuring possibilities.

There has on occasion been the suggestion that some basic concept underlies the shifting narrative(s) of *Finnegans Wake*, and a certain amount of attention has been paid to a sentence from Edgar Quinet's *Introduction à la philosophie de l'histoire de l'humanité* that has an almost unique existence in Joyce's *Finnegans Wake*: it is quoted in its entirety and in the original language (*FW* 281.4-13) as a paragraph unto itself. Except for three slight discrepancies, probably due to Joyce's habit of quoting from memory, the sentence stands undistorted in the middle of the Night Lessons chapter. Its privileged condition as one of the few self-contained references gives it the stature of the highly focused set-pieces, yet its placement within the lessons context, like the placements of its variants in other contexts in the *Wake*, raises important questions regarding its overall position in Joyce's scheme of things. Does it provide a philosophic grid for the narrative ventures of the text, or is it there because, as Joyce indicated, he appreciated the balance and rhythms of the sentence? Does it provide a context for the events in the particular episodes, or does it derive its potency from the context that contains it? Like the materials from the Dublin Annals, the Quinet sentence has only a handful of echoes in the text and is therefore all the more suitable for an attempt at thorough analysis.

What actually constitutes a context? In this case a foreshadowing of the full French sentence exists some ten pages earlier, and numerous glimpses into the gist of the sentence are spotted along the way. These "indicators" are:

puny wars (*FW* 270.30-31)
The O'Brien, The O'Connor, The Mac Loughlin and the Mac Namara (*FW* 270.31-271.2)
duo of druidesses...and the tryonforit (*FW* 271.4-5)
From the butts of Heber and Heremon...brood our pansies (*FW* 271.19-20)
As they warred (*FW* 271.22-23)
Dark ages clasp the daisy roots (*FW* 272.9)
Hengegst and Horsesauce, take your heads out of that taletub! (*FW* 272.17-18)
threehandshighs...twofootlarge (*FW* 272.22-23)
span of peace (*FW* 273.4-5)

we keep is peace (*FW* 276.26-27)
With a pansy (*FW* 278.5)
Since alls war that end war (*FW* 279.5-6)
using her flower (*FW* 280.24-25)
a field of faery blithe as this flowing wild (*FW* 281.3)

These may seem disparate and disconnected elements, especially when applied to the Quinet sentence, but at this juncture almost halfway through the *Wake* various echoes have already conspired to establish something of a context even before we read the sentence itself:

> *Aujourd'hui comme aux temps de Pline et de Columelle la jacinthe se plaît dans les Gaules, la pervenche en Illyrie, la marguerite sur les ruines de Numance et pendant qu'autour d'elles les villes ont changé de maîtres et de noms, que plusieurs sont entrées dans le néant, que les civilisations se sont choquées et brisées, leur paisibles générations ont traversé les âges et sont arrivées jusqu'à nous, fraîches et riantes comme aux jours des batailles. (FW 281.4-13)*

Issy's footnotes to the sentence acknowledge the French locale with references to the Gallic chief that fought the Romans and to the Arch of Triumph, and calls for a translation from the obviously foreign language. Shaun's marginal note, "THE PART PLAYED BY BELLETRISTICKS IN THE BELLUM-PAX-BELLUM. MUTUOMORPHOMUTATION" (*FW* 281.R) calls attention to the appreciation of the beauty of the sentence, the War-and-Peace context, and the system of change—significantly in Latin. Shem's marginal note spots "Twos Don Johns" in Pliny and Columella and "Threes Totty Askins" in hyacinth, periwinkle and daisy, the two girls and three soldiers with their sexes reversed. These three commentators on the text reflect an awareness of several aspects of the governing context, as does the paragraph of "commentary" that follows the Quinet sentence.

Unlike the frequent instances at which "sober" commentary follows "imaginative" narrative (the preceding paragraph is a case in point: Issy's attempt at letterwriting leads into the observations that become the introduction to Quinet), the fanciful and rather wild comments that evolve from the Quinet sentence begin with exclamations regarding the three flowers: "Margaritomancy! Hyacinthinous pervinciveness! Flowers" (*FW* 281.14-15). Despite floral innocence, and Quinet's "long view" of history, a suggestion of divination has intruded, a hint of Stephen Dedalus's concern about the course of Roman history had Caesar listened to the Soothsayer. And Roman history for Stephen had been suggested by knives, the stabbing of Caesar by his betrayers, so Shakespeare's *Julius Caesar*, as well as his *Othello* (betrayal, knifing, jealousy), quickly produce the literary context ("But Bruto and Cassio are ware only of trifid tongues"; "What if she love Sieger less though she leave Ruhm moan?"—*FW* 281.15-16, 22-23). The triumph of peace in Quinet's observation fails to materialize in the world of "brothers' broil." There is an implication of a natural belligerency that belies the promises of peace, a masculine compulsion overturning the feminine "heptarched span of peace" (*FW* 273.4-5). World conquest implied in "That's how our oxyggent has gotten ahold of half their world" (*FW* 281.24-25) seems hardly the conquest of battlefields by wild flowers; nor can we mistake the instinct for battle in "A flink dab for a freck dive and a stern poise for a swift pounce was frankly at the manual arith sure enough which was the bekase he knowed from his cradle, no bird better, why his fingures were giving him whatfor to fife with" (*FW* 282.7-12), although the martial arts could be offset if the fife were to replace the fight. The cynical reaction to Quinet apparent in the commentary is relaxed when combat turns into sports, and Issy can add her comment: "Gamester Damester in the road to Rouen he grows more like his deed every die" (*FW* 283.F2).

Quinet's belletristic gambit (*Aujourd'hui comme aux jours de Pline et de Columelle*—Joyce replaced *jours* with *temps*) provides the text with something that the author was constantly in search of, a traditional narrative beginning; and a narrative beginnings parallel historical beginnings. A false opening that anticipates the Quinet sentence exists ten pages earlier and, introducing Heber and Heremon, the legendary founders of the Irish people, it stresses warfare in contradistinction to Quinet's stress on *paisibles générations*:

> From the butts of Heber and Heremon, *nolens volens*,
> brood our pansies, brune in brume. There's a split in
> the infinitive from to have to have been to will be. As
> they warred in their big innings ease now we never
> shall know. (*FW* 271.19-24)

This intrusion of an Irished Quinet belongs to Issy: while the boys are doing their mathematics lessons ("jemmijohns will cudgel about some a rhythmatick or other over Browne and Nolan's divisional tables"—*FW* 268.7-9), Issy is learning "gramma's grammar" (*FW* 268.17), apparently from the Latin. She is aware in the diametric oppositions of her two brother (Shem notes "M. 50-50," while Shaun adds "POLAR PRINCIPLES"—*FW* 269.L, 271.R), so that she comments, "You may spin on youthlit's bike and multiplease your Mike and Nike with your kickshoes on the algebrars but, volve the virgil page and view, the O of woman is long" (*FW* 270.22-26). (Issy is divining the future by select pages of Virgil, a method commented upon by Shaun at the reference to "Margaritomancy": "SORTES VIRGINIANAE"—*FW* 281.R.) As Kev and Dolph move toward the geometry figure that will result in their broil, Issy has read her Irish history and Roman history and anticipates their *split in the infinitive*. Co-founders of a civilization they are also its dividers, akin to the Horsa and Hengest of Britain, reduced to embroiled school-boys: "Here, Hengegst and Horsesauce, take your heads out of that taletub!" (*FW* 272.17-18).

Issy's feminine perspective takes her somewhat afield, although her roots are specifically in Ireland and close to home. Ireland's four fields in particular provide the battleground: Shem lists them as "*Ulstria, Monastir, Leninstar and Connecticut*" (*FW* 270-271.L), while Issy names the clans that provide the four corners of the field, "The O'Brien, The O'Connor, The Mac Loughlin and The Mac Namara" (*FW* 270.31-271.2)—which here serve as the Four Master Annalists of Ireland, who have their own contextual relationship to the Quinet sentence. She is reading Livy's History of the Punic Wars ("Hireling's puny wars"—*FW* 270.30-31), so that Roman history once again adds to the context, but it is particularly Julius Caesar and his particular version of the Three Soldiers that she fastens on: "Sire Jeallyous Seizer, that gamely torskmester, with his duo of druidesses in ready money rompers and the tryonforit of Oxthievious, Lapidous and Malthouse Anthemy" (*FW* 271.3-6). Intimations of the scene in Phoenix Park, involving Earwicker, the two girls and the three soldier, are certainly present in this conjuring up of the field of combat (the letter she writes as prologue to the Quinet sentence is sent from "Auburn chenlemagne," and Shem's marginal note refers to "*la jambe de marche*" —*FW* 280.27-28, L), the sin in the park. That the "park" in question is the Garden of Eden locates Issy's version of the "butts of Heber and Heremon," as she adds:

> Eat early earthapples. Coax Cobra to chatters. Hail,
> Heva, we hear! This is the glider that gladdened the
> girl that list to the wind that lifted the leaves that
> folded the fruit that hung on the tree that grew in the
> garden Gough gave. (*FW* 271.24-29)

A statue of Sir Hugh Gough, British general in India, stands in the heart of Phoenix Park.

The positioning of the Quinet quotation at mid-point in the *Wake* does not make it the first allusion to the concept (assuming that we still read *Finnegans Wake* in sequential progression): a full adumbration appears early in the first chapter and a last echo late in the closing chapter (*FW* 14.35-15.11; 615.2-11). The process of transmutation is a familiar one: whatever the form of the "original," various changes are wrought upon it, pulling in factors from the immediate context and weaving parodic variations, so that at other instances a mere fragment from the original (or from a variant) synecdochally awakens a recollection of the whole. The most significant change wrought by Joyce is to expand the trinitarian floral structure to a tetratarian one, from a trifoil to a quadrifoil, citing as "authority" the Four Master Annalists of Ireland. The opening Quinetian allusion follows from the four citations from the Annals, and the four alternatives regarding the changes in time since the absconding of the copyist with his scroll. Unable to read the transcription of history, we read the remains of history, the Irish landscape (in preference to the world of history, the Irish landscape (in preference to the world of antiquity posited by Edgar Quinet). The Annalists are named as historical sources (Quinet is not), although the text credited is a Latin one that translates into an image of the color of the cover of the original *Ulysses*. In this case the "Irish" version of the sentence does not stand alone as a paragraph but is the second sentence of a paragraph that begins with both contextual transition and a Quinet-like sentence of its own, a "false" opening that contains potent elements of the "true" rewriting:

> Now after all that farfatch'd and peragrine or dingnant
> or clere lift we our ears, eyes of the darkness, from the
> tome of *Liber Lividus* and, (toh!), how paisibly
> eirenical, all dimmering dunes and gloamering glades,
> selfstretches afore us our fredeland's plain! Lean neath
> stone pine the pastor lies with his crook; young pricket
> by pricket's sister nibbleth on returned viridities;
> amaid her rocking grasses the herb trinity shams
> lowliness; skyup is of evergrey. Thus, too, for
> donkey's years. (*FW* 14.28-35)

Just as the four clan chieftains had been invoked by Issy as a prelude to the "butts of Heber and Heremon," so the Four Master Annalists in the conflation of "farfatch'd and peragrine or dingnant or clere" are present in this prelude; peace in abundance reigns in "paisably eirenical . . . fredeland"; the pastoral scene is luxuriant, although it is essentially the shamrock's three leaves that serve as the three Quinetian flowers of antiquity. All is now set and strongly foreshadowed for the world of Edgar Quinet:

> Since the bouts of Hebear and Hairyman the
> cornflowers have been staying at Ballymun, the
> duskrose has choosed out Goatstown's hedges, twolips
> have pressed togatheerthem by sweet Rush, townland
> of twinedlights, the whitethorn and the redthorn have
> fairygeyed the mayvalleys of Knockmaroon, and,
> though for rings round them, during a chiliad of
> perihelygangs, the Formoreans have brittled the tooath
> of the Danes and the Oxman has been pestered by the
> Firebugs and the Joynts have thrown up jerrybuilding
> to the Kevanses and Little on the Green is childsfather
> to the City (Year! Year! And laughtears!), these
> paxsealing buttonholes have quadrilled across the
> centuries and whiff now whafft to us, fresh and made-
> of-all-smiles as, on the eve of Killallwho. (*FW* 14.35-
> 15.11)

Translated to the four provinces of Ireland, Quinet's world is much reduced,
even trivialized, but his triad of flowers and battlefields augmented to the
Joycean four, while an implication of a fifth (the domain of the High King of
Ireland at the center of the quincunx) is expanded from the whitethorn to a
redthorn as well, a battle of thorns to complement the War of the Roses. The
waves of invaders that have created the history of Ireland as a series of wars
between defenders and invaders persist *despite* the constant growth of flowers,
and return to idyllic nature; while Quinet's *jours des batailles* are assumed to
reside in the past, the "eve of Killallwho" projects into an Armageddon of the
future.

Such an ominous projection is soon tempered, however, by the
progenitive "war of the sexes." Wave after wave have come and gone,
particularly the Danes and the Norse who founded Dublin, so while the "blond
has sought of the brune" (*FW* 15.16), their "fighting is also their "seeking," the
attraction of opposites ("the duncledames have countered with the hellish
fellows" (*FW* 15.17-18), as males and females enounter one another, and
interaction takes place between the flora and fauna: "all bold floras of the field
to their shyfaun lovers" (*FW* 15.20-21).

The "bouts of Hebear and Hairyman" at this juncture are bracketted by
the sighting of the "Dyoublong" landscape and the confronting of the first
inhabitant, the Jute. Written history, whether the "facts" of history as presented
by the Annalists or the philosophy of history as recorded by Edgar Quinet, are
soon lost: the copyist has departed with his copy, and has probably been
murdered by the "scribicide" (*FW* 14.21). Without a governing text, one reads
the landscape, as Quinet suggests, although a great deal depends on *how* one
reads the landscape—and where.

At its most Irish the Quinet situation concerns Heber and Heremon, a
beginning, yet the mere presence of those progenitors of the Irish populace is
not necessarily grist for the Quinetian mill. When Matt the Evangelist takes the
floor to narrate the amorous events on the Tristram-Iseult love vessel ("the
clipperbuilt and the five fourmasters"—*FW* 394.17), this Annalist seems intent
on applying Quinet to the business at hand, especially as his invocation conjures
up "that time of the dynast days of old konning Soteric Sulkinbored and

Bargomuster Bart" (*FW* 393.7-8)—both Joyce's *temps* and Quinet's *jours*—but except for a nod toward "mother of periwinkle buttons" (*FW* 393.19-20) and the predictable "Huber and Harman" (*FW* 394.29), nothing much comes of it. Heber and Heremon fare somewhat better in the last chapter, although again only as a "teaser" for the final development of Applied Quinet. In the narrative exposition on Saint Kevin, the Irish bog is shown capable of producing flowers ("The bog which puckerooed the posy"—*FW* 604.3), introducing the dramatis personae of those Irish progenitors and a solid suggestion of a floral landscape. The short sentence proves disappointing, however: "The vinebranch of Heremonheber on Bregia's plane where Teffia lies is leaved invert and fructed proper but the cublic hatches endnot open yet for hourly rincers' mess" (*FW* 604.3-6), apparently because the pub is not yet open for business, as the reiteration attests: "Malthus is yet lukked in close" (*FW* 604.7). Quinet will soon have another opportunity, this time in full proportions, although only as the last half of a much longer sentence that first calls upon Giambattista Vico and the Four Old Men: "Our wholemole millwheeling vicociclometer, a tetradomational gazebocroticon (the 'Mamma Lujah' known to every schoolboy scandaller, be he Matty, Marky, Lukey or John-a-Donk)" (*FW* 614.27-30).

Just as the first use of Quinet served as a stepping stone to the interview between Mutt and Jute, so the last one follows the colloquy of Muta and Juva, and just as the intrusive statement in the original French followed Issy's version of the letter, so does the closing echo user in Anna Livia's writing of the final letter, with an acknowledgment of "heroticisms, catastrophes and eccentricities transmitted by the ancient legacy of the past, type by tope, letter from litter, word at ward":

> since the days of Plooney and Columcellas when Giacinta, Pervenche and Margaret swayed over the all-too-ghoulish and illyrical and in our mutter nation, all, anastomosically assimilated and preteridentified paraidiotically, in fact, the sameold gamebold adomic structure of our Finnius the old One, as highly charged with electrons as hophazards can effective it, may be there for you, Cockalooraloomenos, when cup, platter and pot come piping hot, as sure as herself pits hen to paper and there's scribings scrawled on eggs.
> (*FW* 614.35-615.10)

Masculine "heroticisms, catastrophes and eccentricities" notwithstanding (even heroism here is highly suspect), Edgar Quinet's pronouncement suffers a sex change and has been feminized as well as domesticated. Although Quinet's Pliny-Columella pair are present, his flowers have been corporealized as three women, and his battle areas mocked and negativized. The world which might have been assumed patriachically determined, a fatherland, has been mutated in a "mutter nation," and the hero himself, "our Finnius," reduced to a "Cockalooralooraloomenos," a husband eager for his breakfast, prepared by a wife who is writing history.

Anna Livia's immediate reaction, once she has effected her salutation to the "Reverend . . . majesty," is to acknowledge the gist of the Quinet concept, although somewhat dismissively. "Well," she writes, "we have frankly enjoyed more than anything these secret workings of natures" (*FW* 615.12-14). Her concerns are elsewhere, and she quickly comes to the point: the fields she

remembers are prelapsarian, and rather than wait for flowers to grow again
when the battles are over, she retains her pristine innocence, unlike the guilty
male who "woke up in a sweat besidus" (*FW* 615.22-23). As far as she is
concerned, preventative measures must be taken to keep the "Peace!" that she
proclaims (*FW* 616.12), and to do so she warns against the dangerous serpent:
"Sneakers in the grass, keep off!" and "Wriggling reptiles, take notice!" (*FW*
615.28-29; 616.16). Her park is signposted in advance, although the park she
returns to in her thoughts is "backed in paladays last" (*FW* 615.25). Like Issy
she is aware of the potential menace and catalogues the personages who
comprise the Fall: an "Eirinishmhan, called Ervigsen," "three Sulvans of Dulkey
and what a sellpriceget the two Peris of Monacheena," as well as the "cad with
the pope's wife, Lily Kinsella, who became the wife of Mr Sneakers for her
good name" (*FW* 616.3, 10-12; 618.3-5). All the potentials are still operative for
the initiation (or the repetition) of Quinet's *jours des batailles*.

The privileging of Pliny and Columella in this instance returns the
situation closer to the Quinet source, and only one other case of such privileging
is extant in the *Wake*, although the two Roman historians are more deeply
embedded within the construct. At the close of the comic turn of Butt and
Taff, the two antagonists merge into "*now one and the same person*" (*FW* 354.8)
who offers the concluding commentary. The scene has temporarily shifted away
from Ireland to an Edenic setting somewhat determined by the Crimean War
battlefield, into which Irish elements filter back. Perhaps it is more accurate to
say that Quinet *invades* an already existing context, that of the Tale of Jarl van
Hoother and the Prankquean, as well as an overlay of the Genesis narrative,
"*umbraged by the shadow of Old Erssia's*" (*FW* 354.9-10). (The long stage
direction that introduces the "BUTT and TAFF" peroration adumbrates the Old
Earth, Old Eire, and Old Russia.) The Quinetian sentence breaks up within the
confines of the Joycean paragraph:

> When old the wormd was a gadden and Anthea first
> unfoiled her limbs wanderloot was the way the wood
> wagged where opter and apter were samuraised
> twimbs. They had their mutthering ivies and their
> murdhering idies and their mouldhering iries in that
> muskat grove but there'll be bright plinnyflowers in
> Calomella's cool bowers when the magpyre's babble
> towers scorching and screeching from the ravenindove.
> If thees lobed the sex of his head and mees ate the seep
> of his traublers he's dancing figgies to the spittle side
> and shoving outs the soord. And he'll be buying buys
> and go gulling gells with his flossim and jessim of
> carm, silk and honey while myandthys playing lancifer
> lucifug and what's duff as a bettle for usses makes coy
> cosyn corollanes' moues weeter to wee. So till butagain
> budly shoots thon rising germinal let bodley chow the
> fatt of his anger and badley bide the toil of his tubb.
> (*FW* 354.22-36)

The constant process of creating narrative openings and closings, usually
folded into each other so that a superfetation of narrations result in
multidimensional storytelling, characterizes Wakean contextuality. In this
instance the once-upon-a-timeness has been bypassed for the secondary gambit:
When old the wormd was gadden echoes "when Adam was delvin" (*FW* 21.6) of

the Prankquean tale, in which the male protagonist is replaced by the setting itself, and a Grecian "madameen," the Aphroditic Anthea, unfolds herself as progenitor (*mutthering ivies*), engendering the antagonistic Cain and Abel of the Crimean battlefield (*opter and apter*). The causes of their wars are relatively simplistic, Mother, Fate, Hatred (the opposite of love), *mutthering ivies, murdhering idies, mouldhering iries*, but the triad is also a progression, from motherhood to murder to mouldering, with flowers reclaiming the fields of combat. That they are not specifically Quinet's familiar floral arrangement of periwinkle, hyacinth, and daisy attests to the phasing out of one context and its replacement by others, yet synecdochally Quinet's Roman historians are transformed into flowers instead; *plinnyflowers in Calomella's cool bowers* are merely one facet of the *muskat grove*, among which can be found ivy and irises as well. (Pline and Columelle have on other occasions their own existences in the *Wake*, quite independent of Quinet, as when "Pliny the Younger writes to Pliny the Elder his calamolumen of contumellas" [*FW* 255.18-19] and when "plinary indulgence makes collemullas of us all" [*FW* 319.7-9].)

If the "adventures" of Grace O'Malley and the Earl of Howth had been a pre-existing text for the Tale of the Prankquean and the Jarl, then that Tale may serve as pretext for this Crimean-Edenic passage, with the wandering Anthea as protagonist, until her story is preempted by the *twimbs*, Hilary and Tristopher, interlocked in combat so they are not only interchangeable but two parts of a whole. The Lucifer combatant is a two-part *lancifer lucifug* played in the Mime by his Other, so that both opponents (*myandthys*) play each other's role. The rival sons of Adam and Eve soon give way to the tri-united sons of Noah, as one narrative succeeds another, and the field of battle becomes the flooded field (the Battle of Waterloo), and the three sons are co-existent with the two bird-girls (*ravenindove*), Three Soldiers and Two Maidens in Phoenix Park. Closure is effected by "separating" the antagonists, making tea (*weeter to wee*), and assuming a temporary peace until the story begins again. *Till* and *let* become the operative words for resolution (*till butagain budly shoots . . . let bodley chow . . . and badley bide*). Certain words serve as gambits, *It was, Once, When, Since*, words that *interrupt* an existing action or commentary, a sort of overall Wakean progression, to begin a framed narrative, an intrusive tale within the developing narrative. Quinet had perfectly "rounded out" his sentence, from *aux jours de Pline et de Columelle* to *comme aux jours des batailles*, while the Joycean variants invented for *Finnegans Wake* are replete with false openings and inconclusive endings, with set-pieces that seem rounded out with beginnings and endings but are in constant apposition to the contextual permutations.

In the Mime context the Quinet sentence, with Romulus and Remus for the only time the dominant pair, has very little excuse for being, probably even less than when the original intruded into the Night Lessons, where at least as a piece of belletristics it served a pedagogical purpose. The cavorting Issy accounts for the dance tunes, and her appetite for sweets gastronomically allows Thyme to stand in for *les temps* and flavor an indigestible stew. The focus is limited to Dublin and environs, where the only significant warfare is an election between Liberals and Conservatives. At a few instances the allusions weave their way close to Quinet, as when "the races have come and gone" parallels *leurs paisibles générations ont traversé les âges*, except that the "races" in question may have modulated (as in *Ulysses*) from generational races to horse races ("some progress has been made on stilts"), so that "lithe and limberfree" may mock *fraîches et riantes*, rather than echo. Domesticity provides the conclusive setting, pa and ma at tea, very much in the spirit of the closing of the Anna Livia version, and perhaps Edgar Quinet is best represented by the dance popular in his own age, the cancan. The Joycean "improvement" is again represented by "whatnot willbe isnor was" (past, present, and future—indefinite), heard elsewhere as "to have to have been to will be" (*FW* 271.22).

This Joycean improvement or variation on Quinet serves as the fulcrum for the only other fairly complete reverberation of the sonorous sentence, and the weakest one of the five. "So hath been, love: tis tis: and will be" (*FW* 116.36) opens the paragraph that precedes the quasi-Quinet sentence in the Letter chapter, a paragraph that begins with several triads evolving from the past-present-future configuration, but soon forming quadrivials along Vichian lines: "a good clap, a fore marriage, a bad wake, tell hell's well" (*FW* 117.5-6) is complete enough, yet is followed by a quartet that leaves its ricorso indeterminate: "such is manowife's lot of lose and win again, like he's gruen quhiskers on who's chin again, she plucketed them out but they grown in again. So what are you going to do about it? O dear!" (*FW* 117.6-9).

The "sentence' as such is the only one of the lot that actually acknowledges its source in Edgar Quinet, but not without the usual camouflage, in this case teaming him up with Michelet, Vico and Bruno, to form the four-cornered historical context previously consisting of the Four Master Annalists of Ireland, the heads of the four major tribes, the Four Old Codgers (four posts of the bed, four sails on the ship): "From quiqui quinet to michemiche chelet and a jambebatiste to a brulobrulo!" (*FW* 117.11-12). Fulsome as it is, the Quinet mock-sentence is weighted at both ends of the paragraph with introductory and concluding commentaries, attesting perhaps to its nebulousness in relation to the tight specifics of its prototype. The two Roman historians have disappeared, replaced neither by the founding pair of "Romans" nor of the Irish race, but a couple of theatrical dancers:

> Since nozzy Nanette tripped palmyways with Highho Harry there's a spurtfire turf a'kind o'kindling where oft as the souffsouff blows her peaties up and a claypot wet for thee, my Sitys, and talkatalka tell Tibbs has eve: and whathough (revilous life proving aye the death of ronaldses when winpower wine has bucked the kick on poor won man) billiousness has been billiousness during milliums of millenions and our mixed racings have been giving two hoots or three jeers for the grape, vine and brew and Pieter's in Nieuw Amsteldam and Paoli's where the poules go and rum smelt his end for him and he dined off sooth american (it would give one the frier even were one a normal Kettlelicker) this oldworld epistola of their weatherings and their marryings and their buryings and their natural selections has combled tumbled down to us fersch and made-at-all-hours like an ould cup on tay. (*FW* 117.16-30)

All that is left of Quinet's battlefield is a reference to the death of Roland, while the eternal presence of an old cup of tea is reaffirmed as a kind of domestic and pacific truth. The homely Irish (Old World) scene of tea-drinking by a turf fire, and the talk that accompanies it, conjures up scenes of America (the New World), with rum as the contemporary drink. The historic achievement of fermentation provides a continuum (the "billiousness" of "millenions") to parallel the cycles of war and peace, and now has resulted in the "warfare" of American Prohibition, from Amsterdam to Pieter Stuyvesant's Nieuw Amsterdam to the New York of Broadway's *No, No, Nanette*! As the historian reads the past in the landscape, the Irish peasant reads the future (emigration to America, the American Dream) in the turf fire, and newspapers record the present of rum-running and Broadway musicals. Folded into the analysis of the all-important missive this New World variant of Quinet's Old World view takes on broader, if also comic and trivial, proportions. The "oldworld epistola" is a letter from the new continent, where gangland pistols create new *jours des batailles*.

Finnegans Wake reads both the runes and the ruins, and does so with a certain degree of suspicion, attempting to separate the authorative from the authoratarian, while constantly questioning the authority. The printed text operative in the new Ireland, "our wee free state" (*FW* 117.34), is "our Irish daily independence" (*FW* 118.2-3), and we are (dubiously) instructed that "we must vaunt no idle dubiosity as to its genuine authorship and holusbolus authoritativeness" (*FW* 118.3-4). History as a completed process is assumed by this particular authority, "the affair is a thing once for all done and there you are somewhere and finished in a certain time" (*FW* 118.7-8), the "somewhere" undercutting the certainty. "Anyhow, somehow and somewhere . . . somebody" (*FW* 118.11-12) continues the new ambiguity, so that when the single somebody turns up as a Roman duo, "Coccolanius or Gallotaurus" (*FW* 118.13), Quinet's Pliny and Columella return to the scene: they "wrote it, wrote it all, wrote it all down, and there you are, full stop" (*FW* 118.13-14), while the insistence on certainty disintegrates into scepticism once again: "O, undoubtedly yes, and very potably so, but one who deeper thinks will always bear in the baccbuccus of his mind that this downright there you are and there it is is only all in his eye" (*FW* 118.14-17)—"all my eye" implying persiflage and "his eye" subjective vision.

Despite its tenuous relationship to Quinet's original, the nozzy Nanette-Highho Harry version has the distinction of persistent reverberations through the succeeding paragraphs, remaining contextually viable, as distinct from the intrusion of the self-contained French original in the Lessons chapter. The "continually more orless intermisunderstanding minds of the anticollaborators" (*FW* 118.24-26) impugns Pliny and Columella (if not Quinet), while "the calamite's columitas" (*FW* 119.11) isolates one of the pair for scrutiny of a sort. Echoes are apparent as attempts are made to read "the hidmost coignings of the earth . . . for wars luck . . . by the light of philophosy" (*FW* 118.36-119.4-5), but it all remains "a miseffectual whyacinthinous riot of blots and blurs," etc. (*FW* 118.28-30), "an Irish plot in the Champ de Mors, not?" (*FW* 119.32).

Whatever proof there is in the pudding may rest not in the authority of the document but in the elegance of the statement, not in the conclusions of the author but in the subsuming contemporaneity of the new rewriting. At the end of the first watch of Shaun a conclusive sendoff is framed in a sentence that carries over the belletristics of Quinet without its pontifications. The Four Evangelists are invoked formulaically in "the elders luking and marking the jornies, chalkin up drizzle in drizzle out on the four bare mats" (*FW* 428.3-4), while the four elements are thrown in for good measure: "the mosse . . . foggy dews . . . the fireplug . . . the barleywind" (*FW* 428.10-13). The farewell sentence reads:

> 'Tis well we know you were loth to leave us, winding
> your hobbledehorn, right royal post, but, aruah sure,
> pulse of our slumber, dreambookpage, by the grace of
> Votre Dame, when the natural morning of your
> nocturne blankmerges into the national morning of
> golden sunup and Don Leary gets his own back from
> old grog Georges Quartos as that goodship the
> Jonnyjoys takes the wind from waterloogged Erin's
> king, you will shiff across the Moylendsea and round
> up in you own escapology some canonisator's day or
> other, sack on back, alack! digging snow, (not so?) like
> the good man you are, with your picture pockets
> turned knockside out in the rake of the rain for fresh
> remittances and from that till this in any case, timus
> tenant, may the tussocks grow quickly under your
> trampthickets and the daisies trip lightly over your
> battercops. (*FW* 428.14-27)

Like many of the chapter endings in the *Wake* this one veers strongly toward the sentimental, an Irish wish of well-being for the departing emigrant. Only the waterlogged allusion to Waterloo retains anything of the field of combat (it is his name that Dun Leary gets back from King George IV, Kingstown reverting to Dun Laoghaire during the Free State), and no reader could be expected to glean any resemblance of the Quinet sentence until the closing daisies trip lightly by. Joyce is having a go at doing a "sentence" all on his own, making it as melodiously and nostalgically Irish as Quinet's had been sentoriously and concisely Gallic. Quinet had framed his floral images of peace between reminders of battles; Joyce hides his only battlefield in the middle of images of sleep and sunrise, sea voyages and fields of flowers, turning Quinet inside out and privileging the pacifistic.

As the kaleidoscope turns the image becomes less and less like itself, and yet particles persist in new arrangements. In the Night Lessons, halfway between the tentative "From the butts of Heber and Heremon" and the authorized "*Aujourd'hui comme aux temps de Pline et Columelle*," the Wakean insistence on the interrelationship of Past, Present, and Future ushers in a short, clinically concise sentence with intimations of the Quinet construction, unlike the elaborate and exaggerated versions developed throughout. Its prologue sets the stage for it:

> For as Anna was at the beginning lives yet and will
> return after great deap sleap rerising and a white night
> high with a cows of Drommhiem as shower as there's
> a wet enclouded in Westwicklow or a little black rose
> a truant in a thorntree. We drames our dreams tell
> Bappy returns. And Sein annews. (*FW* 277.12-18)

The self-renewing feminine principle contains the cycle from past to future in a universe that is temporarily without a father figure—even "as sure as there's a God in heaven" becomes "as shower as there's a wet enclouded in

Westwicklow." Resuscitation is at the mother's breast ("And Sein annews"), and the maternal version of *paisibles générations* supplants the paternal legal peace existing under threat, "with hoodie hearsemen carrawain we keep is peace who follow his law, Sunday King" (*FW* 276.26-277.1).

The Joycean definitive statement, in succinct phraseology and uncluttered precision rather than in any attempt to authorize a philosophy of the history of humanity, follows as a renewal from the maternal breast, somewhat shy and hesitant, modest but with a clear assertion, combining the city along with the countryside, aware of military legions as well as legends, and something of a conclusion since it is followed by the traditional closing of Polly Put the Kettle On ("So shuttle the pipers done"—*FW* 277.22-23):

> We will not say it shall not be, this passing of order
> and order's coming, but in the herbest country and in
> the country around Blath as in that city self of legionds
> they look for its being ever yet. (*FW* 277.18-22)

Finnegans Wake: All the World's a Stage**

Vincent J. Cheng

In James Joyce's vision, an artist is the god and creator of his own worlds—"After God, Shakespeare has created most" (*U* 212), as John Eglinton asserts (quoting Dumas *père*)—while God is but a very major artist, "the playwright who wrote the folio of this world" ("and wrote it badly," Stephen Dedalus adds; *U* 213). In *Finnegans Wake*, Joyce confirms and restates this notion, referring to Shakespeare as "Great Shapesphere" (295.4). To Joyce, artist and god were equivalent—the quintessential artist was the greatest bard of all, the lord of language at his Globe.[1]

Since artists-creators-gods are the playwrights who write the folios of their worlds, Joyce similarly conceived of the world in the *Wake* as staged drama. Like Shakespeare before him, Joyce viewed all the world as a stage, the "worldstage" (33.3) of the *Wake*. This is the notion I will refer to as the dramatic metaphor.

HCE, the archetypal father who "Haveth Childers Everywhere" (535.34-35) and who thus also creates and populates a world, is but another version of both poet and god—of "Great Shapesphere." Joyce himself, of course, is all of these things: like Stephen Dedalus' Shakespeare, he is "all in all" (*U* 212). As a god and an artist, a poet triumphs over confining reality by creating worlds through the imagination—and each of his works is an exploration into the possible "history" of such worlds.

HISTORY AND INFINITE POSSIBILITIES

Myths are cyclical in nature, and Joyce centered *Ulysses* on an ancient myth. Bloomsday is a modern reenactment of the Odyssey: Homer's *Odyssey*, however, is not reenacted precisely, nor linearly, but in more modern variations; in the typical terms of everyman Leopold Bloom, it is "history repeating itself with a difference" (*U* 655).

Bloom's comment could easily serve as a subtitle for *Finnegans Wake*, for Joyce carried the exploration of this general notion of cyclical history furthest—in *Finnegans Wake*—with the construct of a dream, the perfect vehicle for repeated motifs and variations, for everything happening at once, for all possibilities and all history in the course of a night's dream. He made *Finnegans Wake* into a Viconian river, "a commodius vicus of recirculation" (3.2).

**   Parts of this essay are freely adapted from Vincent J. Cheng, *Shakespeare and Joyce: A Study of Finnegans Wake* (University Park: Pennsylvania State University Press, 1984), chapters two and three. Permission for use granted by The Pennsylvania State University Press.

In contrast, for Stephen Dedalus, linear history ("a nightmare from which I am trying to awake"; *U* 34) is a destroyer, an ouster of possibilities. "Kingstown pier, Stephen said. Yes, a disappointed bridge" (*U* 25). "How, sir?" a student asks. A disappointed bridge, perhaps, simply because it *is* a pier—therefore severely limited in scope, the possibility of its being a bridge having been ousted by its clearly being a pier. Actual, factual history makes it so. Stephen Dedalus is himself remorseful because of the memory of his dead mother and the hurt he gave her. Her death is fact, and history makes it so; thus, his "agenbite of inwit" cannot be absolved—for she is dead, and nothing can change that absolute fact of history. This is why, to the aspiring artist, history is such a nightmare—because of its destructive qualities:

> Had Pyrrhus not fallen by a beldam's hand in Argos or
> Julius Caesar not been knifed to death? They are not
> to be thought away. Time has branded them and
> fettered they are lodged in the room of the infinite
> possibilities they have ousted. But can those have been
> possible seeing that they never were? Or was that only
> possible which came to pass? (*U* 25)

In these crucial lines, Stephen is referring to Aristotle's theory in the *Poetics* ("Aristotle's phrase" in *U* 25) that there is a room of infinite possibilities—if Caesar had not been knifed to death, he might have lived to a ripe old age, might have developed cancer, might even have come to America—but history limits, and chooses from that room one possibility, thus destroying all others. Linear history, then, is seen by Stephen as a usurper and a destroyer of creative potential, a restrictive force which limits other, perhaps more interesting, possibilities. Stephen goes on to quote Milton:

> *Weep no more, woful shepherd, weep no more*
> *For Lycidas, your sorrow, is not dead,*
> *Sunk though he be beneath the watery floor. . . .*
>
> It must be a movement then, an actuality of the
> possible as possible. (*U* 25)

To Stephen, the conflict lies between history and poetry: Lycidas's death is a historical fact; other possibilities are ousted by that certainty. The poet Milton, however, asserts that Lycidas is *not* dead; whereas factual history eliminates possibilities, poetry forges and creates new and other possibilities. Thus the poet, his poetry, and his imagination are placed in the role of revivifiers, re-creators, constructive counters to history's destructiveness: "It must be a movement then, an actuality of the possible as possible."

Through artistic creation, the artist can counter the death-dealing destructiveness of history and fact by bringing to life all the dead chances ousted and destroyed by linear history. It is a great and moving moment in *Finnegans Wake*, when Shem-Joyce, reviled and ridiculed by his brother Shaun, gets up to defend himself, lifting his only weapon—the life wand, the godlike phallic pen/knife of the artistic imagination: "He lifts the lifewand and the dumb speak" (195.5). The dead and the dumb can speak through the power of the creative, regenerative act; through the imagination are history and the past conquered. History, no longer just a nightmare, can be a dream vision, a resurrection of dead possibilities, a wake. Its destructive elements are exorcised through an exploration of myriad possibilities in the room of infinite ones.

Joyce's notions about the "room of the infinite possibilities" are carried out in the *Wake*, in which all history and literature are seen as uncertainty and gossip, the exploration of practically every possibility, and in which the study of the past is as uncertain as our knowledge of actual, factual truth. In a sense all of *Finnegans Wake* could be considered an attempt to answer the question, "What happened to HCE?" Finding the "truth"—if there is one—is a matter of digging (like Biddy the hen) through the countless possibilities, variations, and interpretations accumulated by the middenpile of time and cyclical history. Art and creation are, for the Joyce of the *Wake* as well as for Stephen Dedalus and Aristotle, a "movement, an actuality of the possible as possible," an exploration of potential actualities from the room of infinite possibilities. The problem is the same with the story of HCE: we try to choose one version. But which one? Unfortunately, "Zot is the Quiztune" (110.14), and Joyce, like Hamlet (also seeking the truth) and Aristotle before him, knew it:

> . . . me ken or no me ken Zot is the Quiztune. . . . we are in for a sequentiality of improbable possibles though possibly nobody after having grubbed up a lock of cwold cworn aboove his subject probably in Harrystotalies [Aristotle] or the vivle [the Bible] will go out of his way to applaud him on the onboiassed back of his remark for utterly impossible as are all these events they are probably as like those which may have taken place as any others which never took person at all are ever likely to be. (110.13-21)

In describing the *Wake*'s explorations as "a sequentiality of improbable possibles," Joyce appeals to the dean of the Department of possibilities and probabilities, Aristotle. Joyce explains in this passage that the book explores a history of resonant uncertainty and indeterminate sequentiality, a sequentiality of improbable possibles that are as possible as anything, or as much so as the sequentiality put out by linear "history": "for utterly impossible as are all these events they are probably as like those which may have taken place as any others which never took person at all are ever likely to be." What actually "happened" is ultimately determined by the beholder (in the forms of gossip, criticism, history books, and so on), and nothing is ever conclusive: every generation reinterprets history, just as each generation reinterprets Shakespeare. *Finnegans Wake* studies this effect by exploring all possibilities and all viewpoints which "are probably as like those which may have taken place."

Finnegans Wake's world history is thus one about gossip and uncertainty, about incommunicability and the impossibility of learning the truth, about the attempts of literature, scholarship, and history to state truth by fabricating varying accounts and interpretations of every incident. Repeatedly the *Wake* collects opinions and evidence from a host of characters. Each one espouses his or her own versions of the HCE tale; nothing can be proved, and they are all probably "meer marchant taylor's fablings" (61.28)—mere lies and fables about a sailor and a tailor. All this Irish gossip is erroneous misunderstanding, and,

Joyce tells us, HCE, "the Man . . . [was] subjected to the horrors of the premier terror of Errorland. (perorhaps!)"—perhaps, for even that is uncertain (62.23-25). We can only listen to (or read) the *Wake*'s compilation of all the gossipy possibilities and speculative misunderstandings of history and the Ballad of Persse O'Reilly. Thus, we are called to "List! List!" (*U* 188 and *Hamlet* I.v.22) to a review of human history: "*Hirp! Hirp! for their Missed Understandings! chirps the Ballat of Perce-Oreille*" (175.27-28). As such a compilation, the *Wake* is thus an exploration of the "Notpossible!" (175.5).

"Learned scholarch[s]" (31.21) also engage in such explorations. Scholarship and artistic creation, connected by the role of language (*litterae*, letters), are both concerned with finding, if possible, the right interpretation from the litterheap of infinite possibilities. Clearly aware of the similarity between reading the *Wake* and researching purple patches and problem passages of literature, Joyce, a twentieth-century foliowright, describes his own "problem passion play" (32.32) as "the purchypatch of hamlock" (31.23-24), the "patchpurple of the massacre" (111.2), "[t]heirs porpor patches!" (200.4), "paupers patch" (316.23), and so on. Joyce further emphasizes this similarity by his repeated references to holographs, folios, librettos, original manuscripts, and Shakespearean scholars and ghosters.

Finnegans Wake is Joyce's attempt to compile these error-possibilities of HCE's comedy of errors—in other words, all history. A problem play has purple passages which engender much critical speculation and scholarly research; in this sense, *Finnegans Wake* is, like the letter unearthed by Biddy the hen, an attempt to dig into the middenheap and find the "gossiple" truth. Resonant with the pun of *litterae*, the "letter from litter" (615.1) is broadly symbolic, representing both history and literature, especially *Finnegans Wake*. The letter contains all the contributions, from all generations, to the dirtmound of books, history and literature: "For that . . . is what papyr is meed of, made of, hides and hints and misses in prints" (20.10-11)—all the errors and missed understandings (and misprints) of the Ballad of Persse O'Reilly. Therefore, you hardly need to ask if every story in the bound book of history has a score of versions and possible interpretations: "So you need hardly spell me how every word will be bound over to carry three score and ten toptypsical readings throughout the book of Doublends Jined" (20.13-16). Here Joyce is commenting on the interminable fecundity of the past and of literature, both subject to endless interpretation, by using the *Wake* as a symbol of both world and word.

The problem play of *Finnegans Wake* is, like the letter unearthed by Biddy the hen, an attempt to dig the truth out of the middenheap of possibilities. As with history or literature, there are an infinite number of possible meanings for the letter's sequentiality of improbables, and scholarly study results in numerous schools of interpretation. Equated with Joyce's works, the letter is thus similar to great literature, and specifically to Shakespeare's *Hamlet*. In *Finnegans Wake*, Joyce concludes about this "dummpshow" (120.7-8—the dumb show on the middendump)—that it is a "prepronominal *funferal* [the *Wake* as a funeral and a fun-for-all], engraved and retouched and edgewiped and pudden-padded, very like a whale's egg farced with pemmican, as were it sentenced to be nuzzled over a full trillion times for ever and a night till his noddle sink or swim by that ideal reader suffering from an ideal insomnia" (120.9-14). In other words: this work, like Shakespeare's, has been retouched and worked over; and, like the plays or the *Wake*, it is meant to be puzzled over for a trillion nights by that ideal dreambook and insomniac reader. Finally, the passage describes the *Wake*'s Protean qualities as an exploration of infinite possibilities, which, like the cloud observed by Hamlet and Polonius, takes on many shapes, "very like a whale" (*Hamlet*, III.ii.367)—this line has been quoted before, by Stephen, in, appropriately, the "Proteus" episode (*U* 40), *Ulysses*'s exploration of infinite possibilities.

Like Shakespearean folios, then, or like littermounds, works of literature and of historical interpretation are comedies of errors, compilations of misunderstandings. The "purchypatch of hamlock" (*Hamlet*) is like the purple-patched *Wake*. In *Ulysses* and *Finnegans Wake*, Joyce's lifewand makes the dumb speak, exploring the infinite possibilities neglected by factual/linear history, those imaginative alternatives that allow a cloud to become a whale.

THE WORLD AS STAGE

As we have seen, *Finnegans Wake* explores "a sequentiality of improbable possibles" (110.15)—a history of resonant uncertainty, indeterminate sequentiality, and infinite possibilities: "for utterly impossible as are all these events they are probably as like those which may have taken place as any others which never took person at all are ever likely to be" (110.19-21). As early as 1962 Clive Hart had noted that "In *Finnegans Wake* [Joyce] was particularly concerned to reproduce relativity and the uncertainty principle. . . . There is in fact no absolute position whatever in *Finnegans Wake*. . . . [F]rom whichever standpoint we may examine the Joycean phenomena, all other possible frames of reference, no matter how irreconcilable or unpalatable, must be taken into account as valid alternatives."[2] In his recent study of *Joyce's Uncertainty Principle*, Phillip F. Herring has argued that "Incertitude may be the dominant theme of the *Wake*. . . ."[3]

After all, what the dream of all-history requires is a dream-like structure that allows for both specificity of detail and the endless flexibility of variable free-play—that is, both the concrete particulars of a specific possibility, and the simultaneous interchangeability of the particular for infinite possibilities. Characters and events must be infinitely flexible and variable. As Barbara DiBernard writes: "Correspondences juxtapose the individual and the universal, show the unity of life, and undercut any traditional notions of identity or reality. There are no characters or events in *Finnegans Wake* in the usual meanings of those terms";[4] Patrick McCarthy notes simply that "no character exists in his own right as a stable personality in the book [*Finnegans Wake*]."[5]

The infinite possibilities and cycles of Joyce's "Viconian" history, then, require infinitely flexible structures and forms in *Finnegans Wake*. Narrative form/structure in *Finnegans Wake* has been a primary focus of *Wake* scholarship in recent years, and there have been a number of major contributions to our understandings of the different structures by which the *Wake*'s narrative is held together: Clive Hart's motifs, Michael Begnal's narrative and dream voices, Roland McHugh's sigla, Patrick McCarthy's riddles, John Bishop's sleeper—among others—have helped to elucidate the structural mysteries of Joyce's final work.[6] I would propose still another structuring principle—the dramatic form of *Finnegans Wake*, the world as stage. This is a particularly illuminating structural principle given the nature of the *Wake*'s basis on history as infinite possibilities, history repeating itself with a difference. After all, the *Wake*'s fiction can hardly be considered a conventional narrative—and the usefulness of such necessary schemes and scaffolds as Adaline Glasheen's multitudinous charts titled "Who's Who When Everybody Is Somebody Else" suggests a shifting, kaleidoscopic set of references—like casts of characters in different plays.[7]

Margot Norris's important deconstructionist formulation argues that in the *Wake* "[t]he substitutability of parts for one another, the variability and uncertainty of the work's structural and thematic elements, represent a decentered universe, one that lacks the center that defines, gives meaning, designates, and holds the structure together—by holding it in immobility." It is the mobility/variability of setting and character that allows for the *Wake*'s infinite possibilities; as Norris goes on to argue, "It is freeplay that makes characters, times, places, and actions interchangeable in *Finnegans Wake*, that breaks down the all-important distinction between the self and the other, and that makes uncertainty a governing principle of the work."[8] In this sense, the dramatic stage provides both an appropriate analogy/metaphor and a precise form/vehicle for representing such infinitely varied reality: life/history are, in the *Wake*, presented as the infinitely varied repertory of plays produced nightly by a theater company, playing out the decentered variations of an archetypal all-play.

For, as Herring and many other commentators have long noted, in *Finnegans Wake* "Character is based on types that are identified in the *Wake* manuscripts and at *FW* 299 as sigla."[9] "In one sense," McCarthy writes, "*Finnegans Wake* has a cast of thousands: the latest edition of Adaline Glasheen's invaluable *Census of Finnegans Wake* requires more than three hundred, double-column pages to list and identify the characters, real and fictitious, who appear or are mentioned in the *Wake*."[10] But Glasheen's charts ("Who's Who When Everybody Is Somebody Else") are also based on only a handful of sigla, suggesting archetypal character types playing out an infinite variety of story-possibilities, like casts of stock characters playing different parts ("changing every part of the time") in a multitude of different plays. This is the nature of the both predictably repetitious and infinitely shifting nature of *Finnegans Wake*: "every person, place and thing in the chaosmos of Alle anyway connected with the gobblydumped turkery was moving and changing every part of the time" (118.21-23).

Thus, Joyce conceived of *Finnegans Wake* as essentially dramatic, a world-play acted out on the "worldstage" (33.3) by the archetypal family members of a dramatic company. This "dramatic metaphor"—that is, that all the world is a stage and all the figures of history merely players—underlies all the "action" in *Finnegans Wake*, Joyce's chronicle of Viconian history: an exploration into Aristotle's "room of the infinite possibilities," different variations of basic archetypal structures within the patterns of Viconian cycles. Joyce sets his dream of all-history in the context of the dramatic milieu: the dream as drama.

In *Finnegans Wake* these possibilities take on the forms of various plays, each re-creating a different view of the possibilities of history. There are consequently thousands of allusions to drama and to the stage in *Finnegans Wake*—from the works of Ibsen to W. G. Wills's Napoleonic drama *A Royal Divorce* to Dion Boucicault's *Arrah-na-Pogue*, from Synge to Gilbert and Sullivan. Cheryl Herr has convincingly argued the importance and familiarity of such plays in the life of Dublin, in which "the theater provided an experience available in some form to almost all of Dublin's citizens."[11] Elsewhere I have shown how Shakespearean plays are particularly central matrixes,[12] especially

Hamlet (in defining the family relations between father and son, and between mother and son) and *Macbeth* and *Julius Caesar* (in defining the relations between rival brothers and the sister they fight over). Most importantly, though, Joyce had come to think of an artist as a playwright and a creator-god, and of the artist's works as a stage peopled by his creations, "All the charictures in the drame" (302.31-32).

The metaphor of playwright as god is most insistent in the *Wake*, Joyce's chronicle of world history. The prime mover behind the force of destiny is a playwright, "the compositor of the farce of dustiny" (162.2-3);[13] this production of the play about Viconian history is presented by "the producer (Mr John Baptister Vickar)"—Joyce as the author of the *Wake* and God as the author of history, alias Giambattista Vico and John the Baptist (255.27). God-Shakespeare-Joyce-HCE is a "worldwright" (14.19) and a "puppetry producer" (219.7-8); like Prospero, he is a "pageantmaster" (237.13) and the "god of all machineries" (253.33). In the *Wake*, the most recurrent symbol for the creator-father-god-figure is, however, Michael Gunn, manager of Dublin's Gaiety Theatre, and father of Joyce's friend Selskar Gunn; repeatedly HCE is referred to as, or compared with, Michael Gunn, in the role of manager of his worldstage. In II.i, that most "dramatic" of *Wake* chapters, HCE is introduced as "HUMP (Mr Makeall Gone)"; as stage managers, Michael Gunn and God can both make all things come or go. At the end of the same chapter, after loud applause, the exiting HCE is described as "Gonn the gawds, Gunnar's gustspells" (257.34); Gunn as god is gone; the play, Gunn's and God's gospels, is over. In 481.19 Joyce describes HCE as a builder of cities, a populator and a patriarch: "We speak of Gun, the farther"—HCE as Gunn and God the Father. So also he is described in 434.8-10 as "the big gun," waiting "for Bessy Sudlow" (Michael Gunn's wife, and an actress in his troupe) to serve him his dinner. In keeping with the theme of Viconian *ricorso*, HCE will also become, in a felicitous coinage, "the cropse of our seedfather" (55.8)—the corpse will become the earth-laden seed and father of future crops and generations. Thus, finally, in the "worldwright" metaphor, HCE is a "gunnfodder" (242.10): at once cannonfodder; a phallic gun; Michael Gunn, a father and a creator, a grandfather, and the fodder for future Gunns, guns, and generations. Even after death, after Makeall Gone has made all gone, himself being but cannonfodder, even then will there be the "Hereweareagain Gaieties of the Afterpiece"—a joyous play (*pièce*) at the Gaiety in our afterlife. This will be supervised by this new Gaiety's manager, Michael Gunn, "the Royal Revolver of these real globoes" (455.25-26), the god and gun who makes this world turn, the stage manager of "these real globoes"—the Globe Theater and the global world. As "Makeall Gone," "Gun, the farther," "gunnfodder," and "the big gun," Joyce is a playwright-god whose real-life phallic gun is the creative pen of Shem the Penman.

Joyce, conceiving of the artist-creator as a playwright, necessarily came to think of his own creations as plays. In the "Shem" episode, for example, Joyce describes *Ulysses*—"his usylessly unreadable Blue Book of Eccles" (179.26-27)—as an S.R.O. hit and a Christmas pantomime at the Gaiety Theatre: "an entire operahouse (there was to be stamping room only in the prompter's box and everthemore his queque kept swelling) . . . in their gaiety pantheomime" (179.35-180.4). More importantly, Joyce thought of the *Wake* itself as a drama. If Stephen Dedalus saw history as a nightmare, in the *Wake* Joyce presents history as a dream, the universal story of "Allmen" (419.10)—at once the dream and drama of the world, dreamed and played nightly in countless versions and variations of the basic archetypal family drama about HCE, ALP, Shem, Shaun, and Issy. This dream unrolls the drama of universal history, a "dromo of todos" (598.2)—a dream and drama of everything (Spanish *todos*), of today and of everyday. In the book itself, the word "dream" rarely appears unaccompanied by a pun on the word "drama"; this equation between dream and drama is enforced throughout. "In the drema" (69.14) of the *Wake*, "We drames our dreams" (277.17) of universal history, peopled with the characters and caricatures of the past, "All the charictures in the drame" (302.31-32); in the *Wake*, dreams are history, and one might say, "Me drames . . . has come through!" (49.32-33)—my dreams have come true! In our own world of modern psychoanalysis, the drama of our dreams reveals our (and the world's) traumas; and so the *Wake* is (in the words of Shaun as "Professor Jones," alias Freudian/Shakespearean critic Ernest Jones) "a prepossessing drauma" (115.32; also *Traum*, German for dream). It may at times be depicted as *Hamlet*, "the drame of Drainophilias" (110.11)—a dream and drama of Ophelia's; or as Bottom's eerie dream in a midsummer night's drama, "*This eeridreme* . . . From Topphole to Bottom" (342.30-32); or as Stephen's nightmare of history, "a lane picture for us, in a dreariodreama" (79.27-28), a dreary Shakespearean drama at Drury Lane. However, behind the dream there is always the drama of cause and effect, of history-becoming-fact: "His dream monologue was over, of cause, but his drama parapolylogic had yet to be, affact" (474.4-5).

"[I]n this drury world of ours" (600.2), the Drury Lane counterpart to this dream-drama of the *Wake* is Shakespeare's "Miss Somer's nice dream" (502.29). Whatever it is that Miss Somer or HCE or Yawn or mankind (or whoever) dreams, it is equated in the *Wake* with Bottom's dream in *A Midsummer Night's Dream*. (There are many references to "bully Bottom" throughout the *Wake*.)[14] This is the central reason—as Father Boyle, Adaline Glasheen, and I have all discussed in variant ways[15]—that Bottom's dream in "Miss Somer's nice dream," along with the language of medieval and Elizabethan dream visions (methinks, meseems, etc.) is ubiquitous in *Finnegans Wake*: the Ass in *Finnegans Wake* remembers his dream of all-history on a "lukesummer night" (501.16); and since the *Wake* is both dream and drama, the Ass's dream vision thus finds a parallel in Bottom's dream from *A Midsummer Night's Dream*. The dream is at once a midsummer night's dream and all dreams, both "Miss Somer's nice dream" (502.29) and "Mad Winthrop's delugium stramens" (502.29-30). As such, it can be female ("Miss Somer") or male ("Mad Winthrop"), dream ("nice dream") or nightmare (delirium tremens), midsummer or midwinter ("Mad Winthrop"). It is all history.

The "prepossessing drauma," then, is both a traumatic dream sequence, the nightmare of history, and the archetypal family drama, *The Mime of Mick, Nick and the Maggies*. A poet-playwright—by analogy, HCE and all men—dreams the nightmare—"Me drames" (49.32)—of all time, the "drema" (69.14) of the world. The metaphor of the world as stage, the dramatic metaphor, is suggested recurrently in *Finnegans Wake* and most insistently on pages 30 to 33 and 219 to 221, the two passages in which Dublin's Gaiety Theatre is aptly transformed into the Globe.

James S. Atherton has observed that "one of Joyce's favourite images for the world, or the *Wake*, is as a stage—although the famous quotation is never made."[16] Of course, few direct quotations are made in *Finnegans Wake* without being refracted through puns and double meanings. Pages 30 to 33, however, contain a cluster of allusions to Shakespeare and to the stage, most conspicuous of which is the description of HCE as "our worldstage's practical jokepiece" (33.2-3). Clearly, this is a direct reference to Jaques' (the "jokepiece"?) famous lines, "All the world's a stage, / And all the men and women merely players" (*As You Like It* II.vii.139-140). As a drama on the worldstage, HCE's story is a nightly reenactment, to which the public is invited, of an archetypal story, a "druriodrama" (50.6) in this Drury Lane world of ours.

Here we first see HCE, like the "old gardener" Adam in his "prefall paradise," sitting about in his garden, "saving daylight under his redwoodtree" (30.13-15) as the king approaches. These lines again echo *As You Like It* and "Under the greenwood tree" (II.v.1), in a context which informs that the world has been a stage from the beginning of time, and that the Green World of the Forest of Arden, the world of dramatic romance, is none other than Eden and all gardens. The story which follows, the drama about human history, is a production to be "staged by Madame Sudlow" (32.10; Bessy Sudlow, actress and the wife of Michael Gunn) at the "king's treat house" (32.26; the Gaiety Theatre, a.k.a. King Street Theatre, was on King Street, Dublin) in a "command performance . . . of the problem passion play of the millentury" (32.30-32). Admission to this "pantalime" (32.11; Christmas pantomimes were a tradition at the Gaiety) is "two pitts paythronosed" (32.11-12; two bits for patrons paying through the nose) to sit in the "pit stalls and early amphitheatre" (33.9-10), or in the "Pit, prommer and parterre, standing room only" (33.12). The habitual theatergoers are all out tonight to see "our worldstage's practical jokepiece," HCE: "Habituels conspicuously emergent" (33.12-13). Like *Hamlet*, this piece is a "problem passion play"—and there are references in these pages to Ophelia ("Offaly" in 31.18), Hamlet, Polonius with his "metheg in your midness" (32.4-5), and the purple-patch of *Hamlet*—"the purchypatch of hamlock" (31.23-24).

In any event, the drama of history here is a play or pantomime presented on a worldstage, in its "homedroned and enliventh performance . . . of the millentury, running strong since creation" (32.31-33). As with *Hamlet* or with the plays of the "house of Atreox" (55.3), the pantomime is an archetypal family drama: it is the tragedy of HCE's fall and his falling-out with his wife ("*A Royal Divorce*" and "Napoleon the Nth" in 32.33 and 33.2) and his daughters ("*The Bo Girl*" and "*The Lily*" in 32.35). Brothers ("our red brother" in 31.25) and sisters ("his inseparable sisters, uncontrollable nighttalkers, Skertsiraizde with Donyahzade" in 32.7-8—Scheherazade and Dunyazade, skirt-raised sisters from the *Arabian Nights*) are also here, as is the Holy Family, the "triptychal religious family symbolising puritas of doctrina, business per usuals and the purchypatch of hamlock" (31.22-23).

The drama is a family affair. Joyce pursues this analogy in the *Wake* by frequently referring to the characters in the drama of the *Wake* as both family members and actors in a stage company. The drama on this worldstage is "real life"—or history—and the roles are played by a theatre company (whether the Gunns, Porters, Bonapartes, Hamlets, or Holy Family) whose cast members are the archetypal family itself: "Real life behind the floodlights as shown by the best exponents of a royal divorce" (260.F3). The cast members are, as we know by now, the members of HCE-Porter-Gunn's household, and their Gaiety Theatre globe-stage is none other than the publican's inn and residence in Chapelizod; thus, the word "house" is used throughout the *Wake* in three senses: domestic, tavernal, and theatrical (e.g., "the whole stock company of the old house of the Leaking Barrel" on 510.17-18). The cast is first introduced on page 13 of the *Wake*:

And here now they are. . . . A bulbenboss surmounted
upon an alderman . . . . A shoe on a puir old wobban
. . . . An auburn mayde, o'brine a'bride, to be desarted
. . . . A penn no weightier nor a polepost. And so.
And all. (13.23-28)

The family members are an "older man" with a hump ("bulbenboss") and a
stutter (Balbus), or Humphrey-HCE; his wife, ALP, a poor old woman; his
daughter, Issy, an auburn maiden; and his twin sons, the Pen and the Post, Shem
and Shaun. There are five so far in the cast, and yet that is not all.[17] At other
times this household troupe inflates to a "howthold of nummer seven" (242.5),
having two additional, nonfamily members in the household: a male servant
(Sickerson, Sanderson, etc.) and a female servant (Kate). At the start of chapter
1 of Book II, the performance of *The Mime of Mick, Nick and the Maggies* is
prefaced by the proper theatrical introductions of the cast; this reads:
"featuring: GLUGG (Mr Seumas McQuillad). . . . IZOD (Miss Butys Pott).
. . . CHUFF (Mr Sean O'Mailey). . . . ANN (Miss Corrie Corriendo). . . .
HUMP (Mr Makeall Gone). . . . SAUNDERSON. . . . KATE" (219.21-
221.12)—that is, Shem the Penquill, Issy the Beauty Spot, Shaun the Post, Anna
Livia (the running—*corriendo*—waters of the Liffey), HCE-Michael Gunn,
Saunderson, and Kate. These are the elements of our domestic drama, of "The
family umbroglia" (284.4).

In an acting troupe of only seven members, each actor or actress must be
able flexibly to assume a number of roles on call, depending on the particular
family imbroglio being performed that evening; thus, each member is symbolic
of a family "type," able to be recast into almost any old play or version of a
royal divorce. "Like the newcasters in their old plyable of *A Royenne Devours*"
(388.7), they must be ready pliably to take over history's old plays, each actor
performing the role assigned to him or her by the "worldwright" and puppetry
producer. This concept is important and fundamental. The notion of an
archetypal cast performing different plays, or interpretations of an archetypal
play, corresponds marvelously with Joyce's concept of history as a resonant
exploration of different possibilities. As the *Wake* is about history, the
different variations (and possibilities) of reality and history become the
different plays in the repertoire performed by the acting troupe and family, "the
whole stock company of the old house" (510.17), where each member is able to
act the part for his or her particular "type" in each new play. The *Wake* is full
of references to stock companies and acting troupes, with the same basic "types"
playing different roles under each character "type." What better model could
there be for Wakean history and Viconian *ricorso*? HCE can be the same basic
actor under the various historical guises of Adam, Tim Finnegan, Finn
MacCool, Shakespeare, and so forth; or the filial usurper (Cad, Hosty, Paul
Horan, etc.), "Under the name of Orani . . . may have been the utility man of
the troupe capable of sustaining long parts at short notice" (49.19-21). The
family is a house troupe, which performs "with nightly redistribution of parts
and players by the puppetry producer and daily dubbing of ghosters" (219.6-
8), an archetypal cast and stock company acting out the different plays and
infinitely various cycles of Viconian history.

Pages 323 and 324 provide an excellent illustration of how *Finnegans
Wake* is presented as a stage drama played by "the whole stock company of the
house":

> tummelumpsk . . . that bunch of palers . . . . Toni
> Lampi . . . . ghustorily spoeking, gen and gang, dane
> and dare, like the dud spuk of his first foetotype.
> . . . And ere he could catch or hook or line to suit their
> saussyskins, the lumpenpack. . . . Sot! . . . change all
> that whole set. Shut down and shet up. Our set, our
> set's allohn. (323.28-324.16)

Fritz Senn has pointed out that this passage (quoted here in part) refers to a particular stage performance of *Hamlet* in Dublin at the Crow Street Theatre. Referring to "the versatility of the Dublin stock companies" (and quoting from Samuel Fitzpatrick's *Dublin: A Historical and Topographical Account of the City* [1907], one of Joyce's source books for the *Wake*), Senn writes:

> "At Crow Street Digges ('Digges' in 313.26) was
> playing 'Hamlet' and ruptured a blood vessel. The
> play was immediately stopped and *She Stoops to
> Conquer* substituted for it. The manager's apologies
> having been accepted, the performers, who were all
> in the house, hastily dressed and went on. A
> gentleman in the pit had left the building immediately
> before the accident to Digges, for the purposes of
> buying oranges. He was delayed for some little time,
> and having left 'Hamlet' in conversation with the
> 'Ghost,' found on his return the stage occupied by
> 'Tony Lumpkin' and his companions at the Three Jolly
> Pigeons. He at first thought he had mistaken the
> theatre, but an explanation showed him the real state
> of affairs" (Fitzpatrick, 256-57). In *FW*, all actors play
> multiple parts, often simultaneously, and we [readers]
> all think, again and again, that we have mistaken the
> theatre. In particular, Joyce used the incident in the
> paragraph beginning 323.25, where *She Stoops* and
> *Hamlet* are among the things that go on at the same
> time.[18]

With much going on at once, the passage on pages 323 and 324 is a murky one at best; in context, it seems that HCE, in the role of the Norwegian Captain, has momentarily left the tavern for the outhouse (much as the spectator at Crow Street goes out to buy oranges), and returns to find the set (tavern = theater, of course) completely changed, as happened with *She Stoops to Conquer* and *Hamlet*. This historic worldstage seems to be constantly changing sets, exploring new and different variations and possibilities. The drinkers at the tavern have suddenly become "that bunch of palers" (a bunch of players); Tony Lumpkin appears as "tummelumpsk" and "Toni Lampi." The first play concerned Danish ghosts: both the ghost of King Hamlet, King of Denmark, ("ghustorily spoeking. . . . dane and dare") daring his son on (a father spooking and speaking, "like the dud spuk," to his firstborn, "his first foetotype"); and Ibsen's *Ghosts* (*Gengangere* in Dano-Norwegian; here, "gen and gang"). However, "ere he could catch or hook or line," the set has changed back to Tony Lumpkin and the Three Jolly Pigeons—back to the "lumpenpack" accompanied by the shout: "Sot! . . . change all that whole set. Shut down and shet up. Our set, our set's allohn"—our set's all one in the versatile drama of all-history. (The prop men, crying to shut down and set up, seem to be Sinn Feinners: ourselves, ourselves alone.) Change the set, but the show (and history) must go on, "like the newcasters in the old plyable" (388.7). The archetypal family drama is a tale renewed and reenacted nightly on the worldstage, a daily dubbing of *Hamlet* (and all family dramas) at the Globe.

If all the world's a stage, then all stages are the world. As a result of this "dramatic metaphor," we find the pages of *Finnegans Wake* repeatedly and ubiquitously peppered and textured with references to theaters and stage history (the Globe, Bankside, Blackfriars, Drury Lane, Phoenix Playhouse, Dublin's Crow Street and Smock Alley Theaters, and so on), with stage directions ("On. Sennet" [219.13]; "Exeunc throw a darras" [388.1]; "Lights, pageboy, lights!" [245.4]; "Act drop. Stand by! Blinders! Curtain up. Juice, please! Foots!" [501.7] and so on). With such parameters, the players in our world-history then are naturally the great stage-actors, and there are repeated references in the *Wake* to Richard Burbage, David Garrick, Spranger Barry, Henry Mossop, Thomas Sheridan, Peg Woffington, Ellen Terry, and many others. There is much more to say (than I can suggest here) about the ways dramas and stage history structure *Finnegans Wake*.[19] The more persistent references, of course, are to those actors most familiar to Joyce—the family troupe and stock company of Dublin's Gaiety Theatre on King Street, managed by Michael Gunn and Bessy Sudlow—who become the HCE and the ALP in the *Wake*'s "gaiety pantheomime" (180.4) performed nightly by the house troupe. And so *Finnegans Wake* abounds with references to Gunn, Sudlow, the Gaiety, and other members of their troupe, such as Valentine Vousden and E. W. Royce.

Finnegans Wake is most explicitly a play in II.i, on page 219 and following, where *The Mime of Mick, Nick and the Maggies* is presented. This mime, put on by Michael Gunn's troupe, is a model of the *Wake* dream-drama. It is a play given by the children before their parents—a family drama of temptation and frustration (in which Izod-Issy is frustrated in her sexual temptations of Glugg-Shem). The story reenacts some of the old themes of the story of the parents, and is thus a "daily dubbing." Like the *Wake* and like Joyce's Viconian history, this play comes in four acts, and is a microcosm of *Finnegans Wake* itself.

To Joyce, always punning, a "play" is also a game—and the plot of the children's mime is literally a game, the children at play. The game that the girls ("the Maggies," led by Izod) are playing, Joyce said, is one called "Angels and Devils or colours."[20] Shaun-Chuff is Mick, or Michael the Archangel; Shem-Glugg is Nick, common nickname for the Devil; and the Maggies—rainbow girls or flower girls—are the "colours." Their sport is a guessing game in which Shem-Glugg is the victim: Izod poses a riddle to him three separate times, and thrice he is baffled and disgraced; the Maggies meanwhile dance rings around Shaun-Chuff, for the answer to their riddle is "heliotrope,"[21] and the heliotropic Floras find their sunshine in Shaun. HCE then returns to commence the fourth act, in which he ends the children's hour of game and sends them upstairs to bed. At this point the play is over, the curtain falls, and the chapter ends.

The introduction/playbill to *The Mime* is particularly important, for it forms a key statement of the *Wake*'s dramatic metaphor, equating the action of Joyce's novel (here, *The Mime*) with a stage performance. II.i opens with a playbill announcing the performance of *The Mime* (pages 219-222):

> Every evening at lighting up o'clock sharp and
> until further notice in Feenichts Playhouse. (Bar and
> conveniences always open, Diddlem Club
> douncestears.) Entrancings: gads, a scrab; the quality,
> one large shilling. Newly billed for each wickeday
> perfumance. Somndoze massinees. By arraignment,
> childream's hours, expercatered. Jampots, rinsed
> porters, taken in token. With nightly redistribution of
> parts and players by the puppetry producer and daily
> dubbing of ghosters, with the benediction of the Holy
> Genesius Archimimus and under the distinguished
> patronage of their Elderships. . . . while the Caesar-
> in-Chief looks. On. Sennet. As played to the Adelphi
> by the Brothers Bratislavoff (Hyrcan and
> Haristobulus), after humpteen dumpteen revivals.
> Before all the King's Hoarsers with all the Queen's
> Mum. And wordloosed over seven seas crowdblast in
> cellelleneteutoslavzendlatinsoundscript. In four
> tubbloids. . . . *The Mime of Mick, Nick and the
> Maggies*, adopted from the Ballymooney Bloodriddon
> Murther by Bluechin Blackdillain (authorways 'Big
> Storey'), featuring:

> GLUGG (Mr Seumas McQuillad. . . .)

> THE FLORAS. . . .

> IZOD (Miss Butys Pott. . . .)

> CHUFF (Mr Sean O'Mailey. . . .)

> ANN (Miss Corrie Corriendo. . . .)

> HUMP (Mr Makeall Gone. . . .)

> THE CUSTOMERS. . . .

> SAUNDERSON. . . .

> KATE. . . .

> . . . the show must go on.

> Time: the pressant. (219.1-221.17)[22]

A partial explication for the playbill announcement reads thus:
Performed every evening at lighting up time and until further notice in the
Phoenix Playhouse. (Bar and conveniences always open, a club downstairs for
"diddling," or passing the time.) Entrance fee: for vagabonds, a crab-apple; for
the quality, one large shilling. Newly billed for each weekday performance.[23]
And Sunday matinees (for somnolent ones who doze through Sunday mass). By
arrangement, there can be special children's hours, expurgated, and expertly
catered, with jampots and rinsed porters taken in token. The play will be

performed by the whole stock company, with nightly redistribution of parts and players by the puppetry producer (Michael Gunn, stage manager) and daily dubbing of ghosters with the blessing of the Holy Genesius Arch-Mime himself (St. Genesius, patron saint of actors; Greek *archimimos*, chief actor) and under the patronage of their Elderships . . . while the Caesar-in-Chief (God) looks on. Trumpets, please; begin the play. As previously performed at the Adelphi Theatre by the Brothers Bratislavoff (*brat* is slavic for brother; Greek *adelphoi*, brothers) after humpteen revivals (and revivals-ricorsos of HCE = Humpty-Dumpty). Played before all the King's Horses (Chamberlain's Men) and the Queen's Men. Wiralessed and broadcast over the seven seas in Celtic-Hellenic-Teutonic-Slavic-Zend-Latin-Sanskrit soundscript. In four tableaux. . . . Called *The Mime of Mick, Nick and the Maggies*, adopted from a Senecan tragedy of blood (like *Hamlet*) by Bluechin Blackdillain (otherwise known as the author of "Big Story") featuring: Glugg (Shem the Penman); The Flower (heliotrope) Girls; Izod (Miss Beauty Spot); Chuff (Sean the Postman); Anna Livia (the running waters of the Liffey); Hump (Michael Gunn); The Customers; Saunderson, the manservant; Kate, the maid. . . . The show must go on. Time: the present, urgent (French, *pressant*) and pressing ever onwards.

The playbill continues with a list of props used in "the Pageant of Past History" (221.18-19)—masks, lighting, pipes, hats, bags, trees, rocks, venetian blinds, doorposts, gladstone bags, and so on. Credits are given for a musical score ("Accidental music providentially arranged by L'Archet and Laccorde" [222.1-2]—John F. Larchet was the Abbey Theatre's orchestra leader), and singers are mentioned (including "Joan MockComic" [222.7]—John McCormack). Next, "the whole thugogmagog . . . to be wound up for an after-enactment by a Magnificent Transformation Scene showing the Radium Wedding of Neid and Moorning and the Dawn of Peace, Pure, Perfect and Perpetual, Waking the Weary of the World" (222.14-20)—the whole thingamajig is then to be wound up for an after-enactment in a Magnificent Transformation Scene showing the Radiant Wedding of Night and Morning, the Dawn of Peace, the Wake, and Ricorso. (Here, too, is found yet another play, Congreve's *Way of the World*; and, as in the Gaiety pantomimes, there is a "transformation scene."[24]) These lines provide an apt description of Book IV of the *Wake*, and, thus, the four acts of *The Mime* appear to be a microscosm of the *Wake* itself.

Once again we have learned that the *Wake* family drama is being staged at the Gaiety, with "Makeall Gone" taking the lead role of Hump (HCE). "Every evening at lighting up o'clock sharp and until further notice in Feenichts Playhouse. . . . Newly billed for each wickeday perfumance": the nightly performance reminds us that HCE's story is an archetypal "drema," dreamt, performed, and reenacted during all times; and, like a reborn phoenix ("Feenichts"), Gunn-Hump rises each morning in order to replay a tragic fall in the evening's performance. The stage thus becomes a precise, concrete, and practical application of Joycean-Viconian *ricorso*. The various dramas in the *Wake* become the parameters of the dream-stories of cyclical history played out in its infinite possibilities. *The Mime* is thus a "nightly redistribution of parts and players by the puppetry producer and daily dubbing of ghosters." Our lives are, in this way, literally "played out" every night—in dream and drama.

Notes

1. Page and line references are to *Finnegans Wake* (New York: Viking, 1939, 1959). Page references to *Ulysses* (New York: Random House, 1961) are preceded by a *U*.

2. Clive Hart, *Structure and Motif in Finnegans Wake* (Evanston: Northwestern University Press, 1962), 65-66.

3. Phillip F. Herring, *Joyce's Uncertainty Principle* (Princeton: Princeton University Press, 1987), 182.

4. Barbara DiBernard, "Technique in *Finnegans Wake*," in eds. Zack Bowen and James F. Carens, *A Companion to Joyce Studies* (Westport, Conn.: Greenwood Press, 1984), 681.

5. Patrick A. McCarthy, "The Structures and Meanings of *Finnegans Wake*," in eds. Zack Bowen and James F. Carens, *A Companion to Joyce Studies* (Westport, Conn.: Greenwood Press, 1984), 564.

6. Clive Hart, *Structure and Motif in Finnegans Wake*; Bernard Benstock, *Joyce-Again's Wake* (Seattle: University of Washington Press, 1965); Michael Begnal and Grace Eckley, *Narrator and Character in Finnegans Wake* (Cranbury, NJ: Associated University Presses, 1975); Roland McHugh, *The Sigla of Finnegans Wake* (Austin: University of Texas Press, 1976); Patrick A. McCarthy, *The Riddles of Finnegans Wake* (Cranbury, NJ: Associated University Presses, 1980); and John Bishop, *Joyce's Book of the Dark: Finnegans Wake* (Madison: University of Wisconsin Press, 1986).

7. See Adaline Glasheen, *Third Census of Finnegans Wake* (Berkeley: University of California Press, 1977), lxxii ff.

8. Margot Norris, *The Decentered Universe of Finnegans Wake* (Baltimore: Johns Hopkins University Press, 1974), 120-121, 123.

9. Herring, 189.

10. McCarthy, "The Structures and Meanings of *Finnegans Wake*," 564.

11. Cheryl Herr, *Joyce's Anatomy of Culture* (Urbana: University of Illinois Press, 1986), 98.

12. See Vincent J. Cheng, *Shakespeare and Joyce: A Study of Finnegans Wake* (University Park: Penn State University Press, 1984), especially chapters 3 to 6.

13. Operas are one of the forms of drama in the *Wake*. A recurrent theme in this drama of Viconian history is the force of destiny, or Verdi's *La Forza Del Destino*.

14. See Cheng, *Shakespeare and Joyce*, 214-216.

15. Robert Boyle, S.J. *James Joyce's Pauline Vision: A Catholic Exposition* (Carbondale: Southern Illinois University Press, 1978), x; Glasheen, 36; Cheng, 35-38.

16. James S. Atherton, *The Books at the Wake* (Carbondale: Southern Illinois University Press, 1959), 149.

17. McCarthy, "The Structures and Meanings of *Finnegans Wake*," 564: "In one sense, *Finnegans Wake* has a cast of thousands. . . . In another sense, the book has only one character, *Everyman*; or two characters, who represent the male and female principles. Somewhere between these extremes, however, it is possible to discern five main characters, who may be regarded as the members of a single family: H.C. Earwicker, his wife Anna Livia, their twin sons Shem and Shaun, and a daughter, Issy or Iseult. Surrounding and associated with these figures are secondary characters who often represent aspects of the family members: the cleaning woman Kate; the manservant; four old men . . . ; seven girls who are associated with the colors of the rainbow; and a jury of twelve citizens . . . . "

18. Fritz Senn, "Notes on Dublin Theatres," *A Wake Newslitter*, Old Series 2, 6.

19. See Cheng, 43-53 and 230-233.

20. James Joyce, *The Letters of James Joyce*, Vol. I, ed. Stuart Gilbert (New York: Viking, 1957), 295.

21. See *Letters*, I, 406; William York Tindall, *A Reader's Guide to Finnegans Wake* (New York: Farrar, Straus, & Giroux, 1969), 153; and McHugh, *The Sigla of Finnegans Wake*, 55-61.

22. McHugh calls these pages "programme notes." He also notes the play's similarities to Christmas pantomimes at the Gaiety (see *Sigla*, 57-58). So do Margaret Solomon and Cheryl Herr: see Solomon, *Eternal Geomater; The Sexual Universe of Finnegans Wake* (Carbondale: Southern Illinois University Press, 1969), 21; and Herr, 120 ff.

23. See Herr's analysis of the religious implications of "wickeday" and "Holy Genesius Archimimus"; Herr, 124-125.

24. The *Freeman's Journal* of December 24 and 26, 1892, carried an ad for a Christmas pantomime at the Gaiety, including the climactic "THE GRAND TRANSFORMATION / Entitled / WINTER AND SUMMER." Robert M. Adams shows that page 678 of *Ulysses* is based on this ad; it describes a show "commissioned by Michael Gunn, lessee of the Gaiety Theatre, 46, 47, 48, 49 South King Street . . . the grand annual Christmas pantomime . . . (under the supervision of Mrs Michael Gunn, ballets by Jessie Noir, harlequinade by Thomas Otto) and sung by Nelly Bouverist principal girl." See Adams, *Surface and Symbol: The Consistency of James Joyce's Ulysses* (New York: Oxford University Press, 1962), 76-82; see also McHugh, *Sigla*, 58.

The Convertshems of the Tchoose:

Judaism and Jewishness in *Finnegans Wake*

John Gordon

When Edouard Drumont, professional antisemite, charged that Alfred Dreyfus "does business in the manner of the sons of Sem,"[1] he was citing tradition stretching back to Genesis 10, according to which Shem, eldest of Noah's sons, founded the Hebrew race.[2] Etymologically, to be antisemitic is to be anti-Shem.

That, surely, is why so many of the insults thrown at Shem by his antagonist Shaun come from the Jew-baiting repertoire. For example, the account given (149.11-168.12)[3] by Professor Jones, who associates Shem with four famous Jews, Spinoza, Einstein, Bergson, and Lucien Levi-Bruehl (the last the author of "*Why am I not born like a Gentileman*" published by "Feigenbaumblatt and Father, Judapest" [150.26-28]), who is strangely indignant about the word "talis" (Hebrew for "prayer-shawl") as misused by a "passim" or "pessims," (person or persons celebrating Passover and Pessach), and who characterizes Shem as a bad-smelling (163.9) unwashed (159.27) money-grubbing (149.21-22) arriviste (161.20), variously employed as pawnbroker (164.23) and robber (160.19), in all capacities tricky (154.2, 159.30, 165.6), who despite his earlocks (165.32) wants to be accepted as a "genteel" (161.4). Jones's fable is in the same vein: the Gripes, skulking from his "temple" (155.4), is a "sly" (154.2), greasy (156.17), double-talking seducer/seditionist (156.7-18).

The fable also repeats the innuendo about Shem's odor and assigns it a cause: like the Shem described in I.7 (e.g. 177.6-7, cf. 153.13-14), the Gripes soils himself when frightened. In fact much of the Mookse-Gripes exchange falls into focus once we recognize that the Gripes/Shem is a pair of fouled (male or female) pants (alternately handkerchief or handkerchiefs) opposite, in the person of the Mookse/Shaun, a blood-stained (butcher's or bishop's) apron (alternately sheet or shirt), the two separated by the stream where they have both been taken to be washed.[4] Thus in I.8 one washerwoman scents the "*eau de Colo*" "oder" of "greasy" pair of drawers (204.30-35) and remarks that they are "flush-caloured" (205.8-9), "flush" in the context suggesting toilet rather than glow, while the other recognizes the tell-tale bridal-night red stain on the "hostel [and, as Shaun-Mookse, hostile] sheets" she is washing (213.24-25).

This opposition of insignia, of brown-stained Jew versus his blood-stained tormenter, of the letter's brown tea stain opposite the X or X's identified with a bloody wound, is, I will argue, emblematic of the relationship of Shem to Shaun, Jew to Christian, in ways which bear on the shape of the *Wake*. Before that, however, it will be useful to review what kind of Jew Shem is. Most obviously, he is pure caricature—a music-hall stage sheeny to vie with Shaun's stage mick. (When, as he sometimes does, Shem doubles with Noah's third son Ham, founder of the black races, he becomes a type from a music-hall coon show.) In fact he is called a sheeny (173.27, 179.6, 626.25), also an ikey (424.3), a jewboy (463.17), a gombeen-man (344.6; cf. *Ulysses* 10.890), a yid (318.7), and, countlessly, some variant of "jew," "yude," "ju," "jewy," "yu," etc. As the fouled-pants routine illustrates, he is cowardly, with a shambling, insinuating

85

manner. He is also relentlessly associated with excrement,[5] hence with the brown stain on letter and pants, which makes him Shaun's "lowbrown," "old brown freer" (424.36, 588.13). He has the traditional exaggerated Jewish nose: his attacker in I.7 mocks his "shiny [shiny, shemmy, sheeny] shnout" (179.6); the same chapter's account gives him a hell of a nose (169.12); in the Wakean aviary he is associated with the large-beaked raven (contrasting with the petite-billed Shaunian dove); the "probscenium" at which he fantasizes enthusiastic females throwing favors (180.3) is a proboscis as well as a proscenium and phallic probe. (According to 403.13, he shares this feature with his father.) His greasiness (or, at 570.22, oiliness) accounts for the "suet" which falls from him at 86.2, for the oiliness of Napoleon-Lipoleum[6] at Waterloo, above all for the wet and slithery trail that HCE's Shemian attacker invariably leaves after him. The trades ascribed to him include tailor, "Ole Clo" pedlar (453.15), pawnbroker (192.11), "loanshark" (193.5), and pornographer (*passim*), all stereotypically Jewish. At one time or other he doubles with Fagen (150.27, 593.15), Shylock (165.32), Marlowe's Aaron (204.31—as in the play, he is poisoning the waters), and, especially, the antisemitic apostate Jew Nathan of Mosenthal's *Leah the Forsaken*.

As both Jones and the Shaunian narrator of I.7 repeatedly tell us, he is a naturally "low"[7] individual who keeps trying to get above himself and has to be put in his place—in other words, he is an upstart. In spite of the Yiddish into which he and the narrative accompanying him are prone to slip,[8] he is likely to affect a high-toned English accent, to lie about his background (180.34–181.5), to ape various fashions in order to look more like a gentile/gentleman (343.13–14) while trumpeting his degrees in the way no true gentleman ever would (179.21-24). Most reprehensibly, he leches after what Alexander Portnoy, employing the Yiddish he learned at his mother's knee, calls "shiksas" (cf. 342.7) and the *Wake*, quite wonderfully I think, dubs "goyls" (182.22). Worse, there are signs that the feeling may be reciprocated: ALP still remembers how, when about Issy's age, she was swept off her feet by her husband's "sheeny stare" (626.25), and Shaun's anxiety that his blonde blue-eyed sister may go the same way often seems justified. Thus throughout the book, and especially in III.2, Shaun plays the Victorian older brother, warning his sister against the blandishments of the cosmopolitan insinuator.

With his pretensions to establishment respectability and his taste for gentile women, Shem, like Leopold Bloom, aspires to assimilation—one reason he is always making overtures to Shaun. And as for Bloom, the price will be conversion to Christianity, a conversion which will probably be insincere and will always be suspect. The story of Shem's conversion—his initial resistance, his capitulation, his intermittent lapses—is one of the narrative strands which runs through the whole of the *Wake*. In Book I we are told indignantly that Shem would not submit to the church (154.30-32), that he "would not put fire to his cerebrum [experience the Pentecostal descent of faith]; he would not throw himself in Liffey [be baptized]; would not explaud himself with pneumantics [receive the Holy Spirit]; he refused to saffrocake himself with a sod [take communion]" (172.18-20), that in short he would not commit intellectual and spiritual suicide by becoming an Irish Catholic. But in the next book, beginning with II.1, the pressure increases and Shem, hoping to ingratiate himself with Issy, is weakening: the long paragraph at 240.5-242.24 includes his tormented testimony that he has left or will leave the temple and join the church: "No more singing all the dags in his sengaggeng" (240.9-10) [No more singing all day in the synagogue], and in the next two chapters the conversion is confirmed as a preliminary to his marriage into a "roomyo connelic" family (326.13-14): at 317.12, as what on the next page will be called a "yester yidd" (318.7), he orders a (non-kosher) oyster and (leavened) "doroughbread" (317.1), explaining that "my old religion's out of tiempor" (317.2-3). His antagonist "kerrse" doesn't believe him—the gist of his outburst at 320.1-17 is that once a "shinar" always a sheeny sinner, and the "resistance" (316.4) thrown up against Shem's incursion into the family is "aerian" [Aryan] (316.4)—and indeed at 367.2 we learn, after a spate of Hebrew (366.34-36), that as he got older Issy/ALP's husband "grew back into his grossery baseness" (367.2) [his gross baseness, his grocery business]. Throughout Book III HCE/Shaun's Shemian, Jewish past, always threatening to return, is remembered as a skeleton in the closet, to be repudiated: the David who danced before the ark and chased after women, the "Ole Clo" (453.15), the schoolgirls are urged to avoid, the Nathan-nation whose name and anthem are banned (588.16).

In all such outbursts, there is the unmistakable accent of someone protesting too much—as for Mosenthal's Nathan, Shaun's antisemitism comes across as the overreaction of someone with something to hide. The same is true of the HCE whose voice, on page 538, emerges from Shaun's, and who proceeds to tell us all about his "genteelician arms" (546.5)—though, alas, "genteelician" contains the Yiddish "T.L." (pronounced "tea el," abbreviation for "*tokheth lecken*," ass-licking[9]—well-known as the exercise required of parvenus seeking family crests (see *Ulysses* 9.924-927, 568.16-26), and the king from whom he received it is not only a sovereign and a Sullivan but a Solomon as well (546.2), and the word in the middle of its legend is, alas alas, not "*Cross*" but "*Crass*" and the "holocryptogam" it adds up to sounds a lot like "Tetragrammaton," and the—as always with HCE—incriminating commentary on this authenticating emblem which follows makes a point of nervously dismissing any speculations as to whether he, in the "elder disposition," derived from the "essenes"—ancient Jewish sect—and, like the people of Israel, was "carried of cloud [the pillar of cloud] from the land of locust [Egypt, of the plague of locusts]" (546.11-14).

In other words, the story of Shaun, and of the elder HCE, is the familiar one of what the Irish of Joyce's day called a shoneen and the Jews a *meshumed*, someone who for reasons presumed to be less than honorable has gone over to the creed and customs of the ruling faction, and who typically overdoes things, both in aping the manners of the new set and repudiating those of the old. If we try reading *Finnegans Wake* as the history of one *paterfamilias* and family, then its progress from Book I dominated by Shem (hectored from above by Shaun) to Book III dominated by Shaun (menaced from below by Shem) reflects the biography of an uneasy convert from Judaism to Christianity, from someone who in his youth was prevailed on by the carrot-and-stick of persecution and opportunism to renounce his ancestral faith and who in later years is guiltily haunted by voices from the former life. In making this change he has gone, as the racialist conventions of the day would have it,[10] from the earthy and avid sensibility of the Semite to the otherworldly, static sensibility of the Aryan.

As it happens, this transition corresponds to the growth, as *Finnegans Wake* represents it, from young-manhood to old-manhood: "For all of these have been thisworlders, time liquescing into state, pitiless age grows angelhood" (251.8-9). It also corresponds to the progress of the book from which *Finnegans Wake* draws most, the Bible. One big reason for Shaun's resentment of Shem, for the way he spurns Shem's overtures of reconciliation and suggestions of kinship, is that as a Christian, an adherent of the New Testament, he is unsettled by reminders that his creed might be seen as related to, even an outgrowth of, the Judaism of the Old Testament. To an extent, antisemitism in the *Wake* symptomizes the anxiety of influence. What really infuriated the antisemitic Citizen of *Ulysses* was being reminded that his god was a Jew, that he himself was a recent guest in the house established by Bloom's people; what really infuriates Shaun are intimations of continuity, even identity between Shem's low earthy-excremental Hebrew/Semite and his own high celestial-crusader Aryan/Christian. That is one reason why he repeatedly describes Shem—the "yester Yidd" whose "old religion's out of tiempor"—as woebegone (104.12), as old, aged, decrepit if not defunct (e.g., 153.13-19, 169.20-170.3, 422.14, 463.27), and affects to be surprised at his survival or return: the relationship must be one of replacement rather than displacement. It is also why, for instance, when at his most indignant, just before striking Shem, he should taunt him with "Weepon, weeponder, song of sorrowmon!" (344.5)—an epithet which not only casts Shem as a Jewish son of Solomon and seductive singer of erotic songs (like Solomon's), but reveals Shaun's anxious awareness that his god, the man of sorrows, was prophesied (Isaiah 53:3) in Shem's book, and that he was a Jew, a Shem.

Old Testament Shem dominating I, New Testament Shaun dominating III: I would be willing to bet that someone more versed in the Bible than I am could demonstrate a sequential point-by-point correlation between it and the *Wake*, similar to the sequence of correspondences between the *Odyssey* and *Ulysses*. Certainly I.1 is drenched in "Genesis"; certainly IV, with its blowing trumpet, floods of light, resurrecting bodies and souls, and so on, recalls "Revelations," and the four apostles arrive about when they should.

More to the point of the Shem-Shaun conflict in particular, however, is what seems to me another, similar pattern governing the *Wake* as a whole: that as, like the Shemian/Joycean "Jambs," it goes "Dawncing . . . round the colander" (513.9-12), it enacts, more or less chronologically, the major holy days of Judaism and Christianity and the events they commemorate. Specifically, Book I corresponds to Rosh Hashanah and Yom Kippur in September, Book II to the Christmas season in December, and Books III and IV to Lent, Holy Week, and Easter in Spring.

The last of these equations needs little support. Many commentators have identified Book IV with Easter, and we know from Joyce's letters that the first two chapters of Book III re-trace (in reverse) the stations of the cross. The four apostle/inquisitors of III.3 are pretty clearly crucifiers as well; at the same time the Shaun who flinches beneath their assault is also descending into hell, hitting bottom, I would suggest, at 500.1-501.5, from which point he begins the ascent that reaches its celestial culmination in IV. Meanwhile, the events of III are typically those of Lent and Holy Week: Shaun's thou-shalt-not sermons, followed by a dark spell of mourning and self-mortification, followed by the vigil of III.4, then Easter.

As for Book I, consider this summary of it. In the wake of his gigantic predecessor's fall, a new man arrives on the scene. He achieves eminence but soon becomes weighed down, both in his conscience and in the eyes of others, by the memory and rumors of some great, protean sin. In fact before long he is completely incapacitated—closed in a dark room, assailed by a rising chorus of reproach and self-reproach. There follows a prolonged exposure and scrutiny of the sin, carried out as trial and as exegesis of a document (which at one point is reviewed one letter at a time, eventually covering the whole alphabet), then as a systematic examination (in two senses), from which emerges one figure on whom the whole rigmarole is blamed. This figure is driven out, after which a cleansing river carries away afflictions and washes away stains. The book ends at sundown.

I have just described, admittedly in somewhat re-shuffled order, many of the salient rituals of the High Holy Days, encompassing Rosh Hashanah, Yom Kippur, and the intervening days of penitence. The new man is the new year commemorated at Rosh Hashanah. The evocation, review, and confession of sins corresponds to the days of penitence and the Confession of the Yom Kippur evening service, which Confession presents an alphabetical catalogue of sins. Shem is the scapegoat in whose expulsion from temple and town the Yom Kippur ritual originated. ALP's arrival in I.8 corresponds to *Taschlich*, the ceremonial visit to a river and casting of crumbs into it, washing away the sins which in the other ceremony are loaded on the scapegoat. ("JUSTIUS" to Shem: "You will need all the elements in the river to clean you . . . " [188.5-6].) The moribund HCE of the middle chapters, closed in his room, is observing the Day of Atonement, with its prohibition of all work or distractions. The book ends, like Yom Kippur, at dusk.

And possibly—I'm not as confident of this—the hundred-letter thunderwords of Book I may be, among the usual other things, the blowing, at intervals during the service, of the ram's horn shofar, the "Trist/ram" introduced at the outset. In any event, near the end of the next book's first chapter we are commanded to "Blare no more ramsblares" and to put out the "kindalled bushies," the burning bush of the Mosaic law, because "the holy language" is "Soons to come" (256.11-14). Book II is, I think, the site in which the *Wake*, like Shem, so to speak crosses over from Judaism to Christianity: "Please stop if you're a B.C. minding missy, please do. But should you prefer A.D. stepplease" (272.12-14). Which is to say it corresponds to Christmas and Christmastide, commemorating the arrival of a figure who, as the hinge of the epochal change, was both a Jew and the founder of Christianity.

One difficulty with this proposed reading is that, aside from the caroling of 236.10-18 and the "youlldied" Nightletter of 308.18-27, there isn't much about Book II that's particularly Christmasy. Or so it seems. I propose that the whole of Book II, and not just the first chapter, be read as relating the annual Christmas Pantomime at the Gaiety. The announced pantomime program of 219.1-222.20 accords with the whole of Book II, and particularly the actions of II.3, better than it does with the mime of II.1. It is in II.3 that we encounter the forecast "chuting [of] rudskin gunerally" (220.15), carried out by "The interjection (Buckley!) by the firement in the pit" (221.36-222.1), that the customers and Kate (featured in the program but barely detectable if at all in II.1) make prominent appearances, that the drinkers, in their "exodus" from the pub (222.5), enact what can with the license of Wakean wordplay be called a "chorale in canon" (a choral rendering of various songs accompanied by—for canon read "cannon"—"Guns").[11]

This seems to me the main sequence of events. I.1 is a round of games, interrupted for tea at about midpoint, played by children while waiting for the show to start. Because like all game-playing children (at least in Joyce), they are imitating their parents, acting out the fundamental patterns of human community throughout history, their "mime" adumbrates the main action to follow, which is to say it is, as it is called, an "argument" (222.21), a preliminary synopsis. At 257.8-10 they are called in as the lobby bell rings at (there are eight "nin"s) eight o'clock, the customary curtain time. As it still does in British theaters, the safety curtain drops (257.29-32), to the commotion and applause of the audience, happy that the show is beginning. At 259.10 everyone goes "Mummum." II.2 is a program of variety-show acts or "turns." The capital letter legends in the right margin are the placards, traditionally situated upstage right, pompously announcing the titles of the turns or the scenes of performances; at 286.3 and 286.18 Shaun is reminded to "turn over" the next in order to signal that the turn is over; licking a plate, he was evidently (as usual) busy eating, with the result that it has been almost four pages since the last right-margin announcement—as 222.15-16 predicted, there has been a gap during which the titles did not appear. The left-margin Shem is, as he is called at 435.20, the prompter (the program specifies "Promptings by Elanio Vitale" [221.22], Shem designated by the *elan vitale* of the Jewish "Bitchson" [149.20] with whom Shaun/Jones yokes him), whispering cues onto the stage: Joyce's British Museum notes link the first half or so of the left-margin notes to specific phrases in the main text (there are no such links for the right-margin notes), and usually the association is fairly plain: thus "*Allma Mathers*" and "*Old Gavelkind the Gamper*" on page 268 prompt, respectively, "gramma's" and "to your grappa." As for the footnotes, they are the sound of the family (the "Doodles" family of 299 F.4) in the audience reacting to the show. They are dominated by the chatty Issy, but as others have remarked different voices can sometimes be heard—271 F.4, for instance, is in the idiom of Shaun's sermon of III.2, and it is probably Shem who answers a reverential reference to the Church of England with an anti-English epithet (264 F.2). The long footnote on 279 occurs during an intermission, when Issy goes to the lady's room and, applying makeup, talks to her reflection in the mirror; the long monologue of 287.17-292.32 occurs when the father nods off in his seat. Perhaps for the benefit of the children in the audience, perhaps simply according to Barnumesque conventions of ersatz uplift, Shaun's announcements make most of the turns sound onerously educational. In fact, there is a good deal of knockabout farce and dialect cross-talk (282.5-286.2), giving us a set between an absurdly stodgy "*stodge Angleshman*" [284 L.1] [stage Englishman, by analogy with stage Irishman] and his barbaric stage-American counterpart, "*Finnfinnotus of Cincinnati*" (285 L.1) culminating, from 286.4 to 306.7, in a razzle-dazzle magic-and-hypnotism show.

The main event is the Gaiety "Christmas pantaloonade" later identified as "*Oropos Roxy and Pantharhea*" (513.21-22). The Oedipus component of the events needs no underscoring, and "*Pantharhea*," combining "panta rhei," the Heraclitean catchphrase for fluvial flux, with Rhea, Magna Mater, doubtless epitomizes the female being fought over. The show ends at about 11:00, as a rowdy group of customers, realizing that "The playgue will soon be over" (378.20), leaves their seats early to mulct a final round from the barman before heading home. A good deal of II.4 following is taken up with reviewing the performance and recalling others from the past; the chapter ends with echoes of "auld luke syne" (398.26) as the Christmas season comes to a close.

So, to repeat: Book I is dominated by Jewish, Old Testament ritual, Books III and IV by Christian, New Testament ritual. In between, Book II is dominated by the season commencing the transition from one to the other.

Often this transition is violent, especially in II.3, which features a prolonged assault on Shem-types over issues of religion or race. The more his persuasion seems in the ascendant, the more Shaun resembles those Christian inquisitions whose prescription for Judaism and other out-of-date creeds has been the stake and the faggot. In I.6, identifying Shem with Levi-Bruehl, Shaun (in the person of Professor Jones) ominously spells his name "Levi-Brullo," as if to suggest the French for Jew-burn (151.11); in II.2 the "COP," re-introducing "GUBERNANT," the burning of Jews, restores order and terror to the town (306 R.1); in Book III, in charge, Shaun promises both to burn Shem (426.1-4) and his books (439.34-35). In II.3, Taff/Shaun's animus against the Russian general in particular fuses with this program of converting and/or annihilating Butt/Shem by burning him at the stake. He supplies a match—a "*spurts flash*" [a flash of fire, spurting from the struck matchhead] at 342.34-35, a "*strafe from the firetrench*" (344.9) a little later; after adding fuel to the fire and showing consternation that his victim still survives, he finally observes (349.6-350.9) the transformation through fire into both corpse and good Christian (349.17-24; cf. *Ulysses* 15.1926-1939), though the unconverted remnant survives, "*miraculising*" as Daniel, Hebrew survivor of Nebuchadnezzar's fire (352.27-28, cf. 354.3).

II.2 is a little trickier. The Jew-Christian story is also registered here by dialogue and narrative, but the main issue is the layout itself, which simultaneously accommodates distinctively Christian and Jewish figural patterns. First (remembering especially the "Tunc" page of the Book of Kells) a crucifixion scene—good thief on right, bad thief on left, Mary, alternately Virgin and Magdalene, along with the occasional supernumerary, at the foot of the cross, HCE the suffering "upright one" (261.23) the vertical column in the center. Second, a page from the Torah, the distinguishing visual feature of which—and I have never come across any book quite like it, in its resemblance to the II.2 layout—is the columns of commentary literally surrounding the column of text in the middle of the page. (In this regard, it's worth noting that II.2 is the one chapter that can't be read as we are always being urged to read the *Wake*, out loud.)

That is, whereas II.3 is a conflict between old Jew and new Christian in which the latter wins a qualified victory, II.2, the crossroads and formal center of *Finnegans Wake*, is a stereoscopic fusion of the two, a moment in time when "goy and jew" (273.14) are suspended in solution, and the question of which is to prevail is literally the question of how the chapter's bivalent text is to be read, which pattern they and we will foreground to the exclusion of the other. So it is not accidentally that around the center of the center, the geometric figure of page 293, Shem/Dolph should lead Shaun/Kev through a reading (later writing) lesson with the hidden purpose of advancing his own creed, his own reading. Consider the figure's coordinates:

Four dots, two of them plotting a vertical line, the other two equidistant from the midpoint of that line, one on either side. What does that resemble? For the Catholic inhabitants of Latin America and the missionary-indoctrinated peoples of the South Pacific, the answer was obvious, which is why we call four indifferent stars arranged thus in the sub-equatorial skies the Southern Cross.

Not for Shem. He directs Shaun to connect the dots angularly, ignoring the vertical, and so to produce two triangles connected at the base. Then he urges that the result be read as the hexagonal Solomon's seal (297.3), a "Sexuagesima" (298.27), with its powers of magic and wisdom—in other words that six-sided star of overlapping triangles also called the Star of David, symbol (by Joyce's day) of Judaism.

Shaun's response is characteristic. He is captivated for awhile, then becomes confused, indignant, and, soon, violent,[12] reacting with two gestures both of which typify his role throughout the *Wake*. One, he strikes out against his tutor, leaving him with a "bloody face" (303.32). Two, he punches a hole in the paper (with a "blast through his pergamen" [303.22-23], putting a stop to what had become a handwriting lesson), leaving the "foliated gashes" (124.2) which, as X's, invariably end the *Wake*'s letter, and which are repeatedly identified as the mark of some sharp instrument poked through the manuscript.

In doing so, Shaun introduces into the text that red-on-white, blood-on-linen motif, the "paper wounds" (124.3) which, I have earlier suggested, are persistently identified with the Shaunian Christian in distinction to the brown tea stain of Shem's earthy, vilified, brown-stained Jew. Literally into the text, in fact—once he has struck his blow the two triangles become (probably doubling with the Bass Ale label) a "red mass" (304.7). In fact throughout the book this red-on-white mark is a sign to be read, often quite literally, as red print on white paper. And where does one encounter printing like that? In the Gospel passages of those Bibles—typically the volumes used in the mass—which print the words of Jesus in red, thus asserting for those words an absolute truth beyond the black-and-white of the Jewish Old Testament. And so in the *Wake*: the "X ray picture turned out in wealthy red in the sabbath sheets" (530.8-9). Whatever the actual origin of this typographic convention, in *Finnegans Wake* its significance is clear: Christ's words are red because written in blood, the blood flowing from the gashes inflicted on his body—a connection made explicitly when, in one variant of his jab-to-white-surface gesture, hoisting his "pederect to the allmysty cielung," Shaunian Mookse strikes "blueild" which flows and spatters out, (155.23-24), thus imitating the centurion whose hoisted lance (jabbed into the chest, therefore lung) gave the king of the Jews his fifth wound. That is why Shaun's blow against person and paper produces a "red mass"—it is Shaun's version of the incarnation and transubstantiation, of the act which makes his lord's blood manifest.

It is also, more literally, a blow against Shem, against a Jew (once again, that obnoxious fact, that Christ was a Jew) and against a manuscript. In fact to Shaun, and to the book as a whole, the two go together. One meaning of "Shem" which does not seem to have been noted yet is given under "golem" in the 1925 edition of *The Jewish Encyclopedia*:

> In the Middle Ages arose the belief in the possibility of infusing life into a clay or wooden figure of a human being, which figure was termed 'golem' . . . and could carry any message or obey mechanically any order of its master. It was supposed to be created by the aid of . . . a combination of letters forming a 'Shem' (any one of the names of God). The Shem was written on a piece of paper and inserted either in the mouth or in the forehead of the golem, thus bringing it into life and action.

> The best-known golem was that of Judah Low b. Bezaleel, or the "hohe Rabbi Low," of Prague . . . who used his golem as a servant on week-days, and extracted the Shem from the golem's mouth every Friday afternoon, so as to let it rest on Sabbath.[13]

I have earlier noted the "anxiety of influence" suffered by New Testament Shaun at the prospect of Old Testament Shem. Much of that anxiety focuses on writing—a skill which Shaun possesses rudimentarily or not at all. The Shem/Gripes that he encounters (153.9-19) is (as always, among other things) a book that he can't read, with flyleaf and colophon, waterlogged from having been cast on the waters at *Wake*'s end according to the conventions of the *envoi*, and the "pressing" to which he consigns him (155.18) is both winepress and printing press. Among Shaun's charges (188.8-189.27) is that Shem could have been a popular singer but chose perversely to scribble instead, that for instance he "mangled Moore's melodies," flattened them out, as with mangle/steam-iron or printing press, and thus squeezed, as with winepress, the essential juice out of them by turning words into ink-on-paper, in the process adding to the deforestation of Ireland (439.6-14) and to the consternation of an already print-swamped public (189.10). In part, the psychology at work is obvious: like Harpo Marx in *Duck Soup*, Shaun is angered by books because he can't read them. His signatorial X's, always at the letter's bottom, are after all the traditional mark of the illiterate; in the II.2 passage discussed above, it is during an abortive writing lesson that he delivers the "blast through his pergamen," partly no doubt out of that frustration and envy which we would expect from the character who in I.6 assigns to himself the part of the fox of sour grapes fame.

Shaun's problem—according to the *Wake*, Christianity's problem—is that for all the talk of the transcendent Word (e.g. at 167.28), that word remains dependent on, derived from, what Derrida has taught us to see as the scandal of writing. Shaun (apparently the "robot" of 219.23) needs that "scribblative" (189.10) "shem"—who throughout I.7, perhaps echoing the story of Rabbi Low's golem, he calls a "low" sham—to give meaning to his utterances, articulated differentiations to his blasts of wind; when he temporarily exorcises his brother, as at 426.2-4, he collapses, like a shemless golem, into incoherent blubbering followed by silent somnolence. He is, after all, whatever his scribicidal animus, a letter-carrier, a "Lettrechaun" (419.17)—alternately letter-carrying bottle, letter-bearing mailbox, and beer-barrel full of the product of Shemian fermentation—and the *Wake* repeatedly equates that letter with all letters in all senses, with the whole business of writing. So it is that Shaun, in his own conceit a pioneer of that twentieth-century return, via megaphone and radio, to the post-literate, post-linear communications culture announced by avid Wakean Marshall McLuhan, finds himself again and again reminded of his dependence on the shem-script referred to (462.16) as his "innerman" (a.k.a. "inkerman"—433.9) and "inmate friend" (523.23), the writer and "first liar" whose "indwellingness" is, as the questioning of 487.35-488.3 asserts and the questioning 419.11-424.13 reveals, the real source of his "Ondt and Gracehoper" fable. (And his "Mookse and Gripes" fable is a "translation" [152.12-13]).

As resident post- or ante- or rudimentarily literate orator, Shaun is the spokesman of that corner in every *Wake* reader who at some time or other feels like flinging Joyce's farrago of verbal spaghetti across the room and turning on the television to anything at all. His is the logocentric voice we hear when the text turns on itself and demands (292.31-32) that it draw the line somewhere (but drawing a line is the beginning of writing), that we can't stay here for the rest of our existence reading this stuff (187.20-24) and that the writer should just "Stand forth" and reveal himself in his true colors (but even in the middle of his indictment the accuser needs Shem's help to find the right epithet [191.1-4]). As the text often reminds us (19.20, 124.3-5, 172.9-10, 379.5-6, 424.13), "X" is the sign of ending, of finality—an old traffic signal for stopping, the sign of obituary and salutation, both for illiterate ("his mark") and pious ("yours in X"), the sign on the map marking the spot where the search ends, the purgings of exile, excommunication, and exorcism, the "axenwise" "Axe on thwacks" (19.20) which end the argument. And of course, for a Christian, it symbolizes the moment when the eternal and unchanging God rent the fabric of history, the sun stood still in the sky, and the old *megillah* of begats and bequests, the old cycles of falling-away and wrathful retribution and return to Yaweh, etc., was canceled with a seal of blood in the shape of a cross.

And that, finally, is why Shaun keeps smiting, X-ing, punching holes in, scribbling brother and letter and book—because he embodies what in *Finnegans Wake* is the specifically Christian impulse[14] to so to speak punctuate the "unbrookable script" (123.32-33) of time and scripture and *Wake* inherited from the dark abysm of the old faith. Time must have a stop, and before that a shape. As in the margins of II.2, his anti-Shemitism marks an impatient temperament given to capital letters, large or bold-faced (or red-lettered—50.31, 456.34) type announcing momentous events changing everything, versus Shem's italic "cursives" (99.18), letter connected to letter, arabesquing endlessly from hidden past to unseeable future.

Something perhaps there is in the gentile soul which recoils at, feels itself oppressed by, the Ulyssean patience of a people still waiting for the messiah, meanwhile spinning the infinite web that is Jewish scholarship. That, anyway, was something of my sensation when, awhile ago, I attended a friend's daughter's Bat Mitzvah, opened the book before me of excerpts from the Torah, was immediately reminded of *Finnegans Wake*, II.2, and was also struck by the visible sign of the Torah's endless braid of commentary: footnotes piled on footnotes about footnotes, exegesis of earlier exegeses. It is all, for someone used to the Bible and Book of Common Prayer, both impressive and dismaying. What it suggests is that Judaism has little of that Neoplatonically Christian anxiety about commentary, the sense that the more of it one does the farther one gets from the source, that from the Jewish point of view it is good that all this go on indefinitely, literally until the end of time. I understood how Shaun feels: Migod, there's no end to it! No red letters in comparison to which everything else is secondary, either prologue or aftermath. On the contrary, there is even a ceremony, the Simchat Torah (245.10), in which the last words of the Torah's last scroll are read and the first scroll begun again. (So it may not be coincidental that the *Wake*'s distinctively Hebraic Book I is, uniquely, circular—it ends with a running river and begins with "riverrun.")

The "the" to "riverrun" end-beginning of *Finnegans Wake*, doubling "Revelations" back to "Genesis," is its Simchat Torah, one which at the least runs counter to the book's Shaun-triumphant Jew-to-Christian progress. "A way a lone a last a loved a long . . . "—one can imagine a frustrated Shaun, waiting to hear the one syllable, "men," to complete the word of conclusion and end the show, wishing he could coach the mother as earlier he had (Issy: "ah ah ah ah . . . . / MEN! Juan responded . . ." [461.32-33]) the sister. But somehow or other these females and the low scribbler for whom they have a weakness keep drawing out what he had intended to be the last word or final sign, doubling his single X's, as he indignantly says of Shem (534.30), adding extra X's to his "cruciform postscript" and thus turning a symbol of fixity into something else altogether, the *basia* which are obviously inviting a response (122.20-22), a continuation of correspondence, ending not with "Amen" but "To be continued. Anon" (302.29-30). Book IV, in which, after the *Wake*-long warfare of "the young gloria's gang voices the old doxologers" (454.29-30), the former has finally triumphed on the day foretold in "Revelations," then lets the victory slip away simply because, like Old Man River (363.10-11), it "jest keeps rosing. He jumps leaps rizing. Howlong!" (How long, O Lord?) And with that unbrookable rolling is canceled what, probably, was Shaun's main idea in his campaign to convert the Jews by hook or crook, by lance, fire, or fork: that according to (curses!) scripture, once that is accomplished it is only a (short) matter of (finite) time before the voice of X will be heard again and for good, piercing through those heavens which are to be rolled up like a scroll, and the unsettlingly Wakean book of time will at last reach (not phoenix but finis) its last stop.

Notes

1. Jean-Denis Bredin, *The Affair: The Case of Alfred Dreyfus*, trans. Jeffrey Mehlman (New York: George Braziller, 1986), 79. A good deal of the following account of antisemitism is drawn from Drumont's *La France Juive*, an expansive and relatively lucid compendium of antisemitic lore with which Joyce was probably familiar. Much of the description of Shem at *FW* 169.11-20 seems to me to derive from Drumont's account of the Jewish physical type. See Edouard Drumont, *La France Juive: Essai D'Histoire Contemporaine* (Paris: Marpon & Flammarion, 1885), I, 34.

2. See Adaline Glasheen, *Third Census of Finnegans Wake* (Berkeley: University of California Press, 1977), 263.

3. James Joyce, *Finnegans Wake* (New York: Viking, 1939, 1958). Unless otherwise indicated, all citations in parentheses are to this edition of *Finnegans Wake*.

4. Joyce may have heard the same joke I heard many years ago—about the general who, having been told that Napoleon habitually wore a red shirt in battle so that if he were wounded in the chest the fact could be concealed from his troops, has his orderly provide him with a red shirt and pair of brown pants.

5. "*En tout ce qui touche a l'ordure, le Juif est passé maître . . .*" [the Jew is a past master at anything having to do with excrement]—Drumont, II, 455.

6. Apparently it was widely speculated among conservative nineteenth century French writers, among them Michelet, whom Joyce read and admired, that Napoleon was of Semitic origin. See Drumont I, 300-301.

7. "*Le Sémite est un terrien ne voyant guère rien au-delà de la vie présente; L'Aryen est un fils du ciel sans cesse preoccupé d'aspirations superieures . . .*" [The Semite is an earthling barely able to see anything beyond the present life; the Aryan is a child of the sky ceaselessly concerned with higher aspirations]—Drumont, I, 9. Compare for instance the "terricious" (114.29) Shem-written letter "unfilthed" (111.32) from a mound of mud and/or dung, and the "celestine" Shaun (191.15).

8. I don't know Yiddish—some Wakean who does should put together a glossary—but I can report that a pleasant afternoon spent with Leo Rosten's *The Joys of Yiddish* (New York: Pocket Books, 1973) called up all kinds of *Finnegans Wake* echoes, especially Shemian ones. Here, pretty much randomly, are some examples: "schmalz" (83.35), "shiddach," or arranged marriage—"shitateyar" (319.27); "shemozzl," or donneybrook (177.5); "nudnick" (395.17); "mish-mash" (466.12); "putz" (a Shemian judgment of Shaun—603.5); "dybbuk" (149.7); "gozlen," or swindler (233.12); "kaddish," or mourner's prayer (101.21); "kvell," to gloat over someone's defeat or destruction (37.16); "landsman," a fellow townsman (577.7); "mazik," a clever, mischievous child (565.21); "megillah," a prolix, confused history

(514.2); "melamed," a luckless incompetent (247.19); "plotz," to burst from extreme emotion, especially anger (231.14); "potchkeh," to fuss around inexpertly and inefficiently (184.18); "schmuch," literally a penis, figuratively a worthless fool (89.9, 337.2); "shamus," which 169.1 identifies as Shem's full name: the caretaker of a synagogue, a menial functionary, a private detective, a sycophant, a stool pigeon, the ninth candle of the menorah, used to light the others; "shnorer," a beggar or bum (37.12); "shnoz," a big nose (179.6); "shul," synagogue (149.8); "timtum," an effeminate man (463.1).

9. Rosten, 405-406.

10. See note 7, above.

11. The four old men of 397.7-398.30, trying out their voices to "sing a mamalujo," sound like a quartet preparing to sing a chorale, canonical or otherwise, but I can't hear it or any music in the song of 398.31-399.28. On the other hand, the finale of their performance at 140.15-141.7 certainly qualifies.

12. "*À l'Aryen . . . on peut tout faire; seulement il faut éviter de l'agacer. Il se laissera dérober tout ce qu'il possède et tout à coup entrer en fureur pour une rose qu'on voudra lui arracher. Alors soudan réveillé, il comprend tout, ressaisit l'epée qui traînait dans un coin, tape comme un sourd et inflige au Sémite . . . un de ces châtiment terribles.*" [You can do anything with an Aryan as long as you don't provoke him. He will let you have the shirt off his back and then suddenly be outraged if someone tries to snatch a rose from him. Then, suddenly aroused, he sees through everything, seizes as of old the sword which had been languishing in the corner, strikes like a sudden blow and inflicts on the Semite . . . a terrible chastisement] Drumont, I, 12.

13. "Golem," *The Jewish Encyclopedia* (New York: Funk and Wagnall, 1925), 37.

14. As for instance in the pranquean story: " . . . and she punched the curses of cromcruwell with the nail of a top into the jiminy . . . and he became a tristian" (22.14-17).

Joyce's "Blue Guitar": Wallace Stevens and *Finnegans Wake*

Albert Montesi

One method of approaching the monstrously difficult and oft-times indecipherable *Finnegans Wake* is to step into the circumambient ooze that surrounds its maker. Although one would believe from some recent scholarship that James Joyce was a totally original mind, speaking out of the blue skies as some sort of god-figure, he was, in fact, very much a product of his time.[1] Sharing this environment and compelled to respond to it aesthetically was, of course, a whole generation of literary artists. Some of these were of major significance to the age, among them such luminaries as W. B. Yeats, Ezra Pound, T. S. Eliot, Virginia Woolf, Gertrude Stein, and William Faulkner—all of whom were in some manner, large or small, influenced by the waves of protest and reaction to the rationalism and realism of bourgeois art.[2]

Symbolism, surrealism, dadaism, impressionism, expressionism, the decay of language, the search for new forms (new medias) by which to capture and express the modern sensibility, the breakthroughs created by Marx, Freud, and Einstein—all of these shook the timbers of the old house of European art and learning. A young artist starting out had to somehow respond to all these waves and demands. Among these was another major artist, seldom in any manner connected with James Joyce although confronting the same problems—both aesthetically and culturally—that Joyce had to face, and that was the American poet Wallace Stevens. Surprisingly enough, we find on looking at the record that Wallace Stevens was three years older than Joyce.[3] Seldom are the two related, but it might be helpful to look at some of Stevens's longer poems—not to try to demonstrate how Joyce might have influenced Stevens, but rather to examine how Stevens dealt with the same problems of form and substance that Joyce faced. In this exchange, we hope to illuminate some of the intent and mysterious design of *Finnegans Wake*.

Before attempting this, however, it might be helpful to set off a grid or screen by which we can examine *Finnegans Wake* with the angles of visions provided by new discoveries made into the areas of sleep and dreams. At the same time, we should retain all our old methods of looking at the bicameral consciousness and the cognitive processes of the mind. Let's draw up a schemata that appears something like Figure 1 and, in doing so, let us recall that we understand neither the mind nor sleep with even a minuscule of understanding. And we should remember as well that *Finnegans Wake* is, above all, an attempt to examine both night and day, dream and nightmare, cognition and knowledge in both the light of day and the dark of night. (Refer to Figure 1.)

In considering the schemata laid down in Figure 1, let us remember that James Joyce is finally a "bookish" writer, an academic baiter, who is more strongly attracted to scholarship and erudition than has been generally conceded. Like Ezra Pound and T. S. Eliot, he has laced his works with baits and leads that attract traditional scholarship. The commentary on *Ulysses* by Stuart Gilbert is very much like T. S. Eliot's notes appended to *The Waste Land* or Ezra Pound's parading of his knowledge of medieval, classical, and renaissance literature. Joyce loved academic debate, as we can well see in the Shakespeare dispute in *Ulysses*, for instance. But withal, he is hardly stuffy and pompous about his learning. He balances it out with his love of the nonsensical and erotical of his times. He is, perhaps, the most holistic writer of the European experience, encompassing as he does *le homme moyen sensual* with *homo faber*, *homo sapiens*, and *homme d'esprit*. Like Ernest Hemingway, F. Scott Fitzgerald, Thomas Hardy, Joseph Conrad, and D. H. Lawrence, Joyce was also a "life" writer, writing his works out of "living life" rather than out of books. For my generation at least, he was also a sexual evangelist, setting free those areas of erotic experience that needed so much to be understood rather than hid. He, too, dared to write about totem and taboo subjects that debunked and demythologized some of the sacred cows of the Victorian past. What we are attempting to explore here is how and why Joyce wrote the infinitely puzzling opus *Finnegans Wake*, and why he leaves ideation, thought, substance, conceptualizing, and preconceptualizing behind. How does Wallace Stevens's search for his own voice illuminate this question? This is what the following discussion will explore.

In our attempt to connect Joyce and Stevens, we must remember that Stevens works within certain conventional approaches to substance and form; he on most occasions does not attempt to separate form and content. Joyce, however, does seem to eschew all rational ordering of discursive communication. In *Finnegans Wake*, moving as he does from realism and symbolism to impressionism and, finally, to expressionism, he means for us to attempt to follow his creation of a new language, a new iconology, a new notation for experience. We must understand why. We must learn his new dream language, his new language of the night, in order to vindicate our great enthusiasm and love for his magisterial work *Finnegans Wake*. I believe that, in taking a look at Wallace Stevens's search for his own identity and his struggle to understand the relationship between the imagination and the real, between the poet and his world, will be helpful here. Is (as Stevens calls out in some of his aphoristic triumphs) Joyce really the ultimate "Emperor of Ice Cream," his imagination God, and *Finnegans Wake* the "supreme fiction" of our times?

With these comments and schemata before us, let us turn immediately to Wallace Stevens's famous poem on creativity and the artist, "The Man With The Blue Guitar." The poem was modeled, remember, after a Picasso painting during his blue period. We quote the first segment:

I

The man bent over his guitar,
A shearsman of sorts. The day was green.

They said, "You have a blue guitar,
You do not play things as they are."

The man replied, "Things as they are
Are changed upon the blue guitar."

And they said then, "But play, you must,
A tune beyond us, yet ourselves,

A tune upon the blue guitar
Of things exactly as they are."[4]

We can easily see similarities and analogues to *Finnegans Wake*, in particular, and to James Joyce, in general, in these lines. The guitarist is seen as artist, shearsman, entertainer, experimenter, obscurantist, tailor-pioneer, trail blazer, reality-creator, shaman, and visionary. One of the sanest and most balanced voices raised in the Babel of voices surrounding *Finnegans Wake* is that of Mrs. Adaline Glasheen, who writes in her prefatory notes of the *Third Census of Finnegans Wake*, "*Finnegans Wake* is a simulacrum of the machinery of God's creation. . . . Overthrow of memory is one of the 1001 silent, cunning devices by which Joyce exiles the reader from his rational mind and persuades him that *Finnegans Wake* contains as many possibilities of design and random effect as God's creation."[5] Also, consider the economium rendered Joyce by Samuel Beckett: "I welcome this occasion to bow once again, before I go, deep down, before his heroic work, heroic being."[6] Given this praise, what is there in Joyce (shaman, visionary, reality-creator) that he strums out on his "blue guitar"? Is there, in effect, something in *Finnegans Wake* similar to the "art god" of Richard Ellmann, or the post-Kantian belief that the truth relayed by literature is superior to that of rational science—that if we squeeze *Finnegans Wake* long enough, the godhead will pop out?

Looking further into the poem "The Man with the Blue Guitar," we notice that the guitarist is a "shearsman of sorts," a new sort of tailor who, in Carlyle's sense, is creating a new suit of clothes, a new exterior costume of a new age. He is also a tradesman who is shearing away the notions and styles of the past. He, of course, is again Joyce who, in *Finnegans Wake*, is creating for us a new icon by which we rid ourselves of all the incubala of past writing. For Joyce ultimately came to believe, like Jean-Paul Sartre, that the old-fashioned novel, bred and expanded in the eighteenth century—moving from Richardson's *Pamela* to Sterne's *Tristram Shandy*—from realism to surrealism, was exhausted. Built on ancient ideas and on the philosophies of Descartes and Hume, Jean-Paul Sartre, wanted to write a novel patterned after Heidigger rather than these older philosophers and thinkers.[7] Margot Norris in her *The Decentered Universe of Finnegans Wake* talks of the "novelistic fallacy" of the approaches to *Finnegans Wake*. Of the conventional novel, she writes:

> Ian Watt in *The Rise of the Novel* locates [its] philosophic roots in the subjectivism of eighteenth-century thought. He cites specifically the belief in the individual's claim to knowledge and truth through the senses, independent from the collective traditions of the past, as the cornerstone of realist epistemology. This view is manifested in the novelist plot, which portrays the individual's experience as the testing ground of reality and thereby justifies the exploration of everyday life in literature.[8]

Finnegans Wake, of course, refutes these conditions, and Joyce, in writing to one of his patrons, says quite openly that *Finnegans Wake* is not involved with a getaway plot or any of the structuring of past narratives. In truth, then,

Joyce is a "shearsman."

What then of Stevens's next quotation: "The day was green"? Surely, we can read here that the time was ripe, or green, to not only the possibilities of the new narrative, a rebirthing of the making of the novel, but (in the Viconian sense) a new turn of the cultural clock. Artists everywhere were shouting the need to annihilate the old and create the new. Pound insisted, "Make it new." In regard to the next line, people are concerned about this newfangled instrument "the blue guitar," for it has twanged out the obscure *Ulysses* and now the incomprehensible *Finnegans Wake*. It refuses to play the old game of the eighteenth century. Yet, it does play the old game of the family scenario: What is owed to the father? What is owed to the mother? If life hands one this family scenario and we are condemned to repeat its configurations, the debt to the mother conflicting with the debt to the father, the killing of the father, the Oedipal conflict—surely Joyce repeats his family story over and over again. However, he tells it differently each time.

Yet, in Stevens's next line, "They said, 'You have a blue guitar, /You do not play things as they are'," the "they" takes upon a certain subtle persistence, for it appears that "they" cannot stand too much of reality; they find that without art and new expression, life is intolerable. They live with the disbelief that life must have a design, a meaning, and that it can be found in art. They are incurably aesthetic in their religious pursuit of art, so they demand of the writer that he "must play, you must/A tune beyond us, yet ourselves,/A tune upon the blue guitar/Of things exactly as they are." Joyce responds to this with his *Finnegans Wake*, for in this book he presents things "exactly as they are." Whose "truth," you immediately ask, and whose reality?

To answer some of these queries and since, for Stevens, the blue guitar does not in this poem twang out the monumental answers, let's proceed further in Wallace Stevens's song bag, to seek our version of *Finnegans Wake* in it. Some of this might be provided in "Thirteen Ways of Looking at a Blackbird." The poem reads:

I

Among twenty snowy mountains
The only moving thing
Was the eye of the blackbird

II

I was of three minds,
     Like a tree
In which there are three blackbirds.

III

The blackbird whirled in the autumn winds.
It was a small part of the pantomime.

IV

A man and a woman
Are one
A man and a woman and a blackbird
Are one.

V

I do not know which to prefer,
The beauty of inflections
Or the beauty of innuendoes,
The blackbird whistling
Or just after.

VI

Icicles filled the long window
With barbaric glass.
The shadow of the blackbird
Crossed it, to and fro.
The mood
Traced in the shadow
An indecipherable cause.

VII

O thin men of Haddam
Why do you imagine golden birds?
Do you not see how the blackbird
Walks around the feet
Of the women about you?

VIII

I know noble accents
And lucid, inescapable rhythms;
But I know, too,
That the blackbird is involved
In what I know.

IX

When the blackbird flew out of sight,
It marked the edge
Of one of many circles.

X

At the sight of blackbirds
Flying in a green light,
Even the bawds of euphony
Would cry out sharply.

XI

He rode over Connecticut
In a glass coach.
Once, a fear pierced him,
In that he mistook
The shadow of his equipage
For blackbirds.

XII

The river is moving.
The blackbird must be flying.

XIII

It was evening all afternoon.
It was snowing
And it was going to snow.
The blackbird sat
In the cedar limbs.[9]

Under examination, we could easily call this, in our parallel fashion, Thirteen
Ways of Looking at *Finnegans Wake*. First off, in this poem about perspective,
we might be looking down on the very guts of life itself. As T. E. Lawrence
writes about the flogging of his own sexually aroused body: "the core of life
seemed to heave slowly up through the rending nerves, expelled from its body
by this last indescribable pang"[10] (the cry and being of, the "isness" of the
blackbird). Who, then, is our blackbird in *Finnegans Wake*? Is it, in fact, HCE,
Joyce, Anna Livia, or the eternal movement of the bird who, like the eternal
flow of events, is never ceasing, always giving way to change, to Viconian
"corso and recorso"? But it is simply not only the movement that stirs us here.
It is the rhythms of *Finnegans Wake*, the speech tunes—"the lucid, inescapable
rhythms," "the bawds of euphony crying out sharply,"—the three minds of the
teller (stories repeated over and over again, such as the Russian general, the
meeting of the cad in the park, the sexual life of Earwicker, and so forth). The
most revealing parallel, however, lies in the last verse of this scramble to
determine what do we see rightly. If change is protean, Anna Livia becomes as

she does, Mrs. Finnegan, the River Liffey, Mother Eve, and so on, how can we arrest and freeze time to "see" at all? So this oxymoronic closing exactly captures what we have to admit about reality. Its ambiguity, its opaqueness Joyce has neatly captured in his greatest book—a reality about which philosophers, preachers, and poets have sweated to define for eons.

We finally arrive at Stevens's major achievement, his masterful *Notes Toward a Supreme Fiction*. A longish poem (657 lines, 20 cantos), it is generally regarded as a capstone in his continual struggle to bring the imagination and reality to something like an alliance, to create, as he calls it, a theory of poetry that is also a theory of life.

The poem is written as a series of instructive notes to a generalized pupil (an ephebe, as he calls him) as to how he achieved a means by which he becomes a "total" person, and thereby a "total" poet. In order for us to deal with it in relationship to *Finnegans Wake*, let us briefly summarize its content.

Stevens divides the poem into three major sections as to what the modern poem should strive to be. A modern poem must be: (1) abstract, (2) it must change, and (3) it must give pleasure—all which, incidentally, describe the thrust and flow of *Finnegans Wake*. In the first panel of discussion, "It must be abstract," Stevens debates (with himself as well as his reader) the manner in which this might be achieved. This debate runs roughly in the following fashion:

The apprentice poet must first of all attempt to define "the real," the source of the poem as it, in some way, captures and mirrors the so-called "first idea," the "sun," the external world without the mediation of the intellect. This requires the thinking of the blood, rather than cerebration. It also negates the possibility of any teleological or divine plan in the making of the universe; in the death of one god, all other gods die. Nor should the ignorant apprentice retain any preconceived ideas as to how this otherness can be tagged or defined. In this manner, the beginner must dredge up out of his interiority, out of the inner self, the ability to express figuratively some sort of metaphor or "truth." (Stevens is at sea as to what the source of this *materia poetica* might be, whether Bergsonian, Freudian, or Emersonian.) The creation of metaphor must be done to provide for man a link with "real," without the intervention of the conceptualizing mind. This instinctual oneness, which we might dub a sort of Taoism, was first experienced by Adam and Eve. It is some primitive sense that they possessed while in Eden; but, before they acquired this kinship, there was the external world, the garden with all its objects. Expelled from the garden, they encounter a division between themselves and the external world. This separateness must be bridged by the poet in some leap so that he recaptures the primeval innocence, the instinctual bonding that animals experience, to become of the earth, earthy, to live in nature, not on it. The neophyte poet, however, is unable to make this leap. Because of his intellectual cocoon, he is unable to define and perform his nature. Nonetheless, the successful poet has developed an imagination which can contain this visible and invisible world (Wordsworth and Yeats, for instance). Through this great poet, men transcend their ordinary means of perception, tear down the veil, and touch a knowledge which transcends the intellect. However, the poet for Stevens is not the new priest of Baudelaire, who is able to find his way in a forest of symbols, nor is it the Wordsworthian romantic who erects his new altar over the ruins of Tintern

Abbey. He is a creature who, although he is uncommon, must in the last analysis retain his generic oneness with all men, with a large embrasure that takes in both his commonness and his uncommonness. Out of this unification comes the "ideal man" which the reader yearns so desperately to find. What Stevens seems to be attempting here is to reconcile our reptilian brain with our civilized cerebral cortex, or to reconcile that which is animal in us with that which is cultural and spiritual.[11]

In his generous way in *Finnegans Wake*, however, Joyce does realize that man is unfinished and undefined; that he is unable to make such a marriage of soul and body; that, as early as "Portrait of the Artist," man must live in himself as creature as well as idealist. Stephen (the pretentious idealist) becomes Bloom and Bloom, in turn, becomes Earwicker. Joyce knows that this romantic silliness about man without his limitations becomes an abstraction, not a reality. Therefore, in *Finnegans Wake*, Joyce does away with the intruding intellect and demonstrates man on a surer ground. A generation cliché, you'd say. Yeats said it many times: Man cannot know truth, but he can embody it, and writes lines to fishermen, and cannot tell the dancer from the dance, and selects Crazy Jane over the Bishop. Teilhard de Chardin said it with his omega point, where the flesh and the spirit become one.[12] What is so original about *Finnegans Wake*? For these answers, we must explore further still.

In the second segment of his "Notes," Stevens insists that the poem "must change," contending that the religionist of the past, with his system of atemporality, was dead wrong. There is, Stevens insists, no abstracted value scheme that transcends man and his world. In the sociology of man, nothing permanent obtains; since nothing there is that does not change, politics and art are as ephemeral as the rose and the briar bush. Greek art has all but disappeared; Shelley writes of Ozymandis, Keats of his melancholy. Is there, then, no absolute but change? Joyce is wonderfully positive here. He allows us through the Viconian circle to say that man will endure, that he will always have a second chance in that Anna Livia may become the sea, but later becomes reincarnated in Issy again and again. He does not, like Orwell, insist that man has in his cells an enzyme for self-destruct. He is blissfully Irish still in his capacity to say that man will not only endure—he can endure with humor, wit, and laughter. He has the rare capacity of the Irish, to survive with the pride of the tinker, to turn aside sorrow with a quick sally of wit, to laugh at misfortune. Joyce is saying in *Finnegans Wake*: If history is a comic joke, why does man take it so seriously?

To continue our discussion of Stevens, in his "Notes" on his second commandment, change, for Stevens, becomes the reconciliation of opposites. For man, the mediating force between creativity and hard reality is the imagination. Therefore, for Stevens, imagination is the essential tool for the new poet. He must be able to combine the forces of nature and the forces of his mind to touch not only the wellsprings of the *spiritus mundus*, but the *nota* of his world. The imagination somehow can unseat the mighty horse of reason of its old, tired rider and still retain the magnificent horse. Out of this process, the poet creates the ideal man that the ordinary man yearns to be. Although man scrambles and falters throughout history, he will not give up the dream of a utopia, of a city of graceful men; although he loves erotically and carnally, he still yearns to love lyrically and eternally. But this scaling between the dream and the reality must somehow be balanced out. The dream of the romantic—of ideality—must be counter-balanced by the awful limitations of his own psychology and his limited perception. Time, with its fluctuations and its alterations, is an otherness, an order that he can neither wholly understand nor freeze. It can only be tentatively bridged by the master-builder, the poet, to provide a synthesis through his magic skills, his imaginative leap. The poet is thus compelled to be a Darwinist, to witness change and to provide for brief moments a resting place from its eternal movement; this, then, is his art. He finds only in language the means to communicate this forever changing vision. Thus, the poem *Finnegans Wake* in time may well be considered the great epic poem of its age.

Even a brief glance at these notes will assure us that Joyce and Stevens are running along the same track here. The "yin and yang-ness" of Joyce, the reconciliation of opposites, the eternal mobility of *Finnegans Wake*, the constant blending of characters, the twinning of Shem and Shaun (Mrs. Glasheen has even included a long chart of the metamorphosis of each character; it is a long list). As for reality, the debris of history, Anna Livia's letter is finally indecipherable even to those cognoscenti such as Shaun. There is no letter to the world that will unriddle the mystery of man's biological and chronological history. Even the folk mind of Anna Livia cannot help us here. What other similarities of change do we detect in this paralleling? Surely no one in *Finnegans Wake* is made outsized or heroic. Everyone is mundane—gutsy, vulnerable, and unwashed. Yet, Joyce's tone and his attitude towards them is never harsh. He is, moreover (if in any sense he is a character of voice in this book), never judgmental or condemnatory. Shaun may speak nastily of Shem, but he is, of course, simply speaking in his own voice. The washerwomen at the ford, the four old men, the cad—all are providing their own angle of vision, their own point of view.

Turning now to the last segment of Stevens's instruction, "It must give pleasure," we can say by any scaling or measure that this is the main objective of *Finnegans Wake*. It becomes in the hands of this masterful puppeteer a triumphant peal of multi-sounding laughter—on occasion baritoned and lusty; in others, guffawed and hearty; in still others, silvery and lyrical. In it, we can hear the voices of Tolkien's elves as well as the bawdy notes of Rabelais's *Gargantua and Pantagruel*. It is at moments operatic and highly choreographed and orchestrated; at most times Wagner; at some others Puccini. Full of all sorts of noises, it may well be as highly poetic as any orchestra score, operatic scenario, or ballet book.

To continue our look at Stevens, however, since reality and any current expression of it soon deadens into custom-ridden familiarity, and since actuality is constantly taking on new hues and coloration, the poet must be forever inventive and innovative. The perpetual renewal of the earth and the poet's capturing of that renewal is, of course, one of the major motifs in *Finnegans Wake*. However, for Stevens, the marriage of the intellect and emotion is difficult to achieve, since Descartes's dualism seems to be enforced by our biology and our psychology. One method of mediating between these two disparities is the imaginative limit made by the poet in his leap toward an infinitude that transcends his own nature. This imaginative limit is controlled by man's incapacity to scale the skies, and his whole life is an effort to achieve those moments when he can transcend that limit. Thus, the poem ends with an epilogue addressed to a soldier who is, in effect, the poet and his neophyte, who stand in a perpetual war to fight the barriers that exist between the real and the ideal world.

At this juncture, Joyce and Stevens seem to part ways. Joyce seems to suggest that life might not have any pat formulas or solutions, that cause does not provoke effect in all instances, that certain human problems are beyond yes and no, that truth and knowledge may be impossible to achieve in any total or even partial fashion. He further suggests that certain matters do not have a one-to-one correlation; that they may better "play" with as/if, rather than neither/nor, or truth or falsity. Further still, he suggests that stimulus need not provide a perpetual response, that our life lines may be what Ibsen calls our life-lies. Art, Joyce insists, by its use of ambiguous counters repeats that our old mythologies need new coats, that our old ways of thinking and feeling may be leading us to moral and cultural entrapments, that we must take new risks and enter new portals of awareness, not stone the new that may be bringing new seeds to our old caves. Thus, Joyce's *Finnegans Wake* attempts to restructure the world, reinvent religion, and recreate God. Since language as we know it can be manipulated and contrived or utilized by dictators to distort and disorder reality and, in effect, fail us, Joyce attempts to create a new language in his *Finnegans Wake*, one that is so loaded with suggestion rather than statement, with indirection and ambiguity that it provokes ultimate thievery of our old stock of ideas and emotions.

The triumph of *Finnegans Wake*, however, is in its insistence that we learn its notation to discover the superior reality, the imp of the absolute, that obsesses us, that we are sure must exist in the novel, opera, or poem that *Finnegans Wake* must be. Joyce does not revert to the nihilism of literature, the glory of nothing, to the blank page, the willful disordering of the senses of the French symbolists, or Freudian symbolism, or the extremes of the surrealists or dadaists. He does not insist that we destroy our fallible language as it now exists, for that language is all that we have, duplicitous and vulnerable as it might be. What he does do is to ask us to plod relentlessly on through the pits, bogs, and traps of his *Finnegans Wake* so that our labor to find the design will make our tasks eternally young, to fulfill Wallace Stevens's adjuration that we must make art perpetually new. Joyce knows full well that we will never find that design, that pattern, that overarching unity that we think is in the labyrinths of *Finnegans Wake*, for at this moment and his—in our present state of consciousness and the split of the bicameral mind—it simply does not exist. There is no central design, no central statement, no secret totality of being in *Finnegans Wake*. Joyce knew full well that our hope that there is some grand design, some overpowering vision, will drive us on for generations to find it in our reading of *Finnegans Wake*. For Joyce has contrived in the *Wake* the most audacious cryptogram in the history of art. With each word, a little world made cunningly, each a puzzlement, and with thousands of these words to unravel, we will be at the task for eons. He knows, too, that we will be perpetually renewed by our search, that the expense of our greatness is to fail at unraveling this vast puzzle. This is the message that he twangs out on his blue guitar—a message that Stevens comes partially to understand, but which Joyce understood perfectly.

Areas of Consciousness

The *Rational* (Day)

Philosophy, history

1. Cognition and knowledge is treated in *Finnegans Wake*.
    a. Myth: history as a nightmare
    b. Theory: history as a joke.
2. History of mankind/history of Ireland
3. Popular and Formal Culture
    a. Music
        -Musical hall and popular song/ballads, Irish folk music
    b. Sports, boating, etc.
    c. Technology
    d. Science and cosmology
    e. Cinema and still photography

The *Irrational* (Night)

Pre-Sleep World (all the puzzling images that flash through our minds before we fall asleep).

Jungian, collective unconscious
Left and right sides of the brain
Id/ego/superego
Anima and Animus

Techniques of Tension: the circle, twinning, yang and yin of reconciliation of opposites, yoking, transmission into other areas of being, intertexuality.

Techniques of Style: Portmanteau words, punning, piling of one image upon the other, montage, doubling, etc.

The Language Trap: The tyranny of language
The betrayal of language
Rhetorical traps
Decay of language

Figure 1. Grid or screen by which to examine *Finnegans Wake*.

Notes

1. The canonization of Saint Joyce grows apace year by year. See, for instance, Jackson Cope's *Joyce's Cities: Archaeologies of the Soul* (Baltimore: Johns Hopkins University Press, 1981), where his works are "not unlike the unearthing of Troy or the discovery of Tutankhamen's Tomb." Or see the exchange of letters in *The New York Review of Books* in regard to the Hans Walter Gabler edition of *Ulysses*. Here *Ulysses*, once a saucy, scandalous book, is treated as if it were some sacred document that demands a "Biblical exegesis" (*The New York Review of Books*, March 30, 1989, 43-45). One wonders, with the invasion of Joyce scholarship by the hordes of linguistic and "new semiotic" researchers, whether their work is high scholarship or just plain Alexandrian decadence, or needless nitpicking.

2. This old scenario has been so well reported, repeated, and rehashed that I hesitate to rehearse it once more. But here goes: That Joyce knew quite well the nature of the period and its drift, confusions, shared ideas, its *Weltanschauung*, has been tirelessly recorded by generations of scholars. However, one need not have to catalogue the contents of a library to determine what books (read or unread) or whatever *onta* or movements of popular or serious thought might have influenced the young writer starting out. Most modern folk know Superman and Mickey Mouse, Elvis Presley and the Beatles, without anything to indicate in their letters or writings that these personages really existed. Joyce has tossed in *Ulysses* and *Finnegans Wake* such contemporary popular figures as Charlie Chase, Charlie Chaplin, and Peaches and Daddy Browning. Therefore, why do we constantly insist on a direct one-to-one relationship between the writer and his library?

    Joyce wrote essays on Ibsen's *When We Dead Awaken*, aped shamelessly from Dujardin's novel *Les Lauriers sont Coupes*, and listened to the trendy "art talk" and the tirades and protestations against middle-class art in the bistros of Paris, Zurich, and Trieste.

    Surely he had come first or secondhand to the slogans and the proclamations so much in the air when both *Ulysses* and *Finnegans Wake* were conceived —all declaring the decay and collapse of bourgeois culture. A more judicious evaluation of Joyce's debt to his times can be found in Danis Rose and John O'Hanlon's *Understanding Finnegans Wake* (New York and London: Garland, 1982), where Joyce is considered as a great synthesizer, a collector of debris and verbal exchange of any sort, as well as the erudite and serious works of the past and those of his times.

3. It might be helpful here to look at a biographical sketch of each writer:

Stevens (1879-1955)		Joyce (1882-1941)	
1909	Marries	1902	Leaves Ireland
1914	First Publication	1904	Union with Nora
			Barnacle
1916	Hartford Insurance	1905-1915	Trieste
1923	*Harmonium*, A.A. Knopf	1907	*Chamber Music*
	at 44		

1931	Second edition of *Harmonium*	1914	*Dubliners*
1934	Made Vice-President of Hartford Accident and Indemnity Company		
1935	*Ideas of Order*	1916	*A Portrait of the Artist as a Young Man*
1936	*Owl's Clover*	1922	*Ulysses* (Trieste, Zurich, Paris)
1937	*Man with the Blue Guitar*	1939	*Finnegans Wake*
1942	*Parts of the World (Notes toward a Supreme Fiction)*	1941	Death-January 13.
1946	National Institue of Arts and Letters		
1947	*Transport to Summer*		
1950	*Auroras of Autumn*		
1950	Pulitzer Prize		
1955	Death - August 2.		

4. Wallace Stevens, "The Man With The Blue Guitar," in *The Man with the Blue Guitar* (New York: Alfred A. Knopf, 1952), 3.

5. Adaline Glasheen, *Third Census of Finnegans Wake* (Berkeley: University of California Press, 1977), xi.

6. S. B. Bushrui and Bernard Benstock, eds. *James Joyce: An International Perspective* (Gerrards Cross, Buckinghamshire; Calvin Smythe, Totowa, N.J.: Barnes and Noble, 1982), vii.

7. Paul Johnson, *Intellectuals* (New York: Harper & Row, 1988), 228.

8. Margot Norris, *The Decentered Universe of Finnegans Wake* (Baltimore: Johns Hopkins University Press, 1976), 10.

9. Wallace Stevens, "Thirteen Ways of Looking at a Blackbird," in *The Collected Poems of Wallace Stevens* (New York: Alfred A. Knopf, 1961), 92-95.

10. Quoted in Joseph W. Bean, "Lawrence of Arabia," *The Advocate* (11 April 1989), 29.

11. My reading of Stevens's *Notes Toward a Supreme Fiction* has been influenced by Margaret Peterson, *Wallace Stevens and the Idealist Tradition* (Ann Arbor: UMI Research Press, 1983); Helen Vendler, *On Extended Wings* (Cambridge, MA.: Harvard University Press, 1969); Albert Gelpi, ed. *Wallace Stevens: The Poetics of Modernism* (Cambridge: Cambridge University Press, 1985); and Rajeer S. Patke, *The Long Poems of Wallace Stevens: An Interpretive Study* (Cambridge: Cambridge University Press, 1985).

12. See "Truth" in Stephen Maxfield Parrish and James Allan Painter, eds. *A Concordance to the Poems of W. B. Yeats* (Ithaca: Cornell University Press, 1963), 838.

PART II: JOYCE'S TEXTUAL SELF-REFERENTIALITY

Every Man His Own God: From *Ulysses* to *Finnegans Wake*

Alan S. Loxterman

After an initial gasp of astonishment over a text that looks like English yet seems to be in a foreign language, readers encountering *Finnegans Wake* for the first time may be even more daunted by popular handbooks on Joyce to which they turn for encouragement and explanation:

> Everything in the book ought to be information, but much of it continues to be noise, and perhaps always will be.[1]

> We have to remember not only the appearance of images but the appearance of individual words, and, individual though the words unquestionably are, this cannot be done.[2]

> Any set of standards that will account for the essential greatness of *Ulysses* must, I feel, find a certain sterility in *Finnegans Wake*.
> . . . In *Ulysses*, parody and satire have direction because they serve a moral vision; but in *Finnegans Wake* they turn in upon themselves and destroy their own foundations.[3]

An assumption which all these commentators share is that with *Ulysses* Joyce had already stretched his readers' skills to their limits. Therefore *Finnegans Wake*, despite some worthwhile passages, remains incomprehensible in that it far exceeds the capacities of even its most experienced and sympathetic readers to view it continuously as a whole.

Nevertheless readers continue to be fascinated by *Finnegans Wake*, and scholars keep trying to explain it. I would contend that we gain aesthetic as well as historical perspective by viewing the obstacles to understanding *Finnegans Wake* as an extension of those stylistic experiments which also make *Ulysses* problematic. In this way we can better appreciate how Joyce was working toward his ultimate achievement, an anomaly in the history of literature which expands the way we read. Today, and into our foreseeable future, *Finnegans Wake* survives not as the completed comprehensible entity which previous fiction (including Joyce's own) had conditioned us to expect. Rather it remains what Joyce first called it, a "Work in Progress," an artistic arrangement of words which requires continuous collaboration from its readers to make those words meaningful *as* a text.

Joycean commentators who do not recognize such continuity between *Ulysses* and *Finnegans Wake* tend to draw on *Ulysses* for contrast, as a means by which to measure the deficiencies of Joyce's final work. The most fully developed argument along these lines is that of S. L. Goldberg, who finds *Finnegans Wake* to be "neither life nor art" because "it cannot realise [its 'argument'] imaginatively," as does *Ulysses*: "I would invoke the support both of *Ulysses* and of the insight on which its achievement rests: that we understand life (or imagine truly) only as individuals, necessarily living in and by means of our particular circumstances."[4] Through its plot and characterization *Ulysses* provides sufficient circumstantial evidence for us to follow its characters to "the limits of their self-understanding." Then the author as arranger provides metaphors like the Homeric parallels to lead us "beyond [the characters], not rejecting their vision but transcending it."[5] Despite its obscurities and stylistic vagaries *Ulysses* expresses a moral and spiritual vision because its author maintains a classical control over character and plot which grounds us in life's particulars. *Finnegans Wake*, on the other hand, dissolves such particulars in a romantic flux of " '*formless* spiritual essences,' " giving the reader no sense of "a completed *action*" (Charles Feidelson, quoted in Goldberg, *The Classical Temper* 196-197).

One problem with Goldberg's comparison is that, in emphasizing the contrast with *Finnegans Wake*, it oversimplifies *Ulysses*. Goldberg finds an early indication of Joyce's moral/spiritual vision in the ship which Stephen Dedalus sees at the end of "Proteus." But his ship is more than a metaphor assuring us that Stephen too "is silently moving homeward" (*The Classical Temper* 163). Before he turns and sees the ship Stephen has melodramatically placed a piece of snot on a rock, declaring "For the rest let look who will."[6] Thus the narrative intrusion describing Stephen's glance at the ship as "rere regardant" may be phrased in the stiff, even precious, language of striking a heraldic pose to mock the pretentiousness of Stephen's self-dramatization. The ship itself appears to offer the promise of Christian iconography: "Moving through the air high spars of a threemaster, her sails brailed up on the crosstrees, homing, upstream, silently moving, a silent ship" (*U* 3.503-505). The "threemaster" (three crosses, or Christ as the "master" of the Trinity?) and the echo between "brailed up" and "nailed up" (especially in conjunction with "crosstrees") could suggest a funeral ship of crucifixion "homing" toward resurrection. But the sentimentality of Ireland's spiritual ideals is also questioned when the homing ship's actual cargo turns out to be mere earthy political ballast: bricks coming from England (*U* 10.1098-1099). At the end of "Proteus" it is impossible to distinguish between the reader's response to the consoling appearance of the spiritual ship which, in his earlier works, Joyce might have regarded as an epiphany and the author/narrator's mockery of such an epiphany as a reminder of Stephen's immature past. In its romanticized view of art as being sacred, the concept of epiphany seems well suited to a young man choosing between art and the priesthood in *Portrait*. But it is no longer adequate for what Stephen has become in *Ulysses*, a self-dramatizing apostate haunted by the ghost of his mother.[7]

Goldberg's characterization of Joyce's other main protagonist, Leopold Bloom, also becomes problematic when we look for textual support. Goldberg sees "the son-father relationship of Stephen's theory [about *Hamlet*] established" when Bloom bends to help the fallen Stephen and has a vision of his own dead son at the end of "Circe" (*The Classical Temper* 187). But the details of Bloom's vision do not foreshadow a future meeting between Bloom and Stephen; they satirize the past, Bloom's muddled aspirations for this son, Rudy. To fulfill what must have been the dream of Leopold's own parents, the ghost of the eleven-year-old dutifully scans a book. It is not identified as the Torah, perhaps because the grandparents' rabbinical aspirations get confused with Leopold's own knowledge of gentile ritual through freemasonry so that the boy reads "from right to left," yet "appears in the attitude of secret master." To fulfill the aspirations of Bloom in Ireland looking toward England for intellectual and social status, Rudy also wears an Eton suit. In fact, he has become a modishly decadent British esthete with "delicate mauve face," kissing the page as he reads, as if the book were Swinburne rather than scripture (*U* 15.4955-4967). The details of Bloom's vision gently mock his mixed aspirations for his son to be Jewish and Christian, Irish and English all at once—a "changeling" (*U* 15.4957) indeed. The satire implicit in Bloom's vision of possibility is milder than it was in Stephen's, as befits Bloom's greater compassion and ineffectuality. But the cumulative effect of these details does not seem, as Goldberg suggests, to foreshadow some father-son relationship with Stephen. Rather the future which Bloom had dreamed of for his own son is satirically depicted, being comically exaggerated and even contradictory—as parents' plans for their children are apt to become.

Goldberg argues that Stephen's sighting of a ship and Bloom's vision of his son constitute evidence for a moral and spiritual argument beyond the actions of characters in *Ulysses*. But I have shown that a counter-movement toward satire negates, or at least questions, that argument. Both in *Ulysses* and in *Finnegans Wake*, the satire "turns against itself," undermining the very principles and expectations being generated by plot and character. Therefore Litz's comment which I quoted at the beginning, a contrast between the two works on the basis of "parody and satire [which] serve a moral vision," seems overdrawn. Both works evince a comic skepticism toward even the most indirect moral conclusions, especially where theology and the supernatural are concerned, as in the visions associated with Stephen and Bloom. Contradictory conclusions reached by Joycean commentators on both works demonstrate that drawing moral conclusions or deducing spiritual consolation is as risky in *Ulysses* as it is in *Finnegans Wake*. To the extent that the language of *Finnegans Wake* continually disorients us, rendering all our preconceptions ambivalent, its satire does seem more comprehensive and unrelenting. But in both books "although Joyce claimed to be able to communicate whatever he liked with language, he also recognized that the complexity of life requires that any such idea must be played off against its opposite, the counterpoint serving to indicate the futility of the search for absolute truth in a universe ruled by relativism, randomness, and uncertainty."[8]

Another similarity between *Ulysses* and *Finnegans Wake* seems more fundamental in that it makes them seem more like each other than like any other fictions. Goldberg justly observes that "Joyce's streams-of-consciousness represent not the endless flux of subjective experience or the formless chaos of objective 'reality,' but the creative insight, the informing activity, that is the real subject of [Joyce's] aesthetic theories and the basis of his moral judgments" (*The Classical Temper* 37). Yet this observation applies only so long as the interior monologue remains grounded in those moral and spiritual values which Goldberg recognizes in terms of character and plot concerns. And I would claim that at least half of *Ulysses* diverts its readers' attention from plot and character to the activity of the author as arranger. A rapid survey reveals six chapters which clearly and consistently divert readers' attention from character and plot, with their attendant moral concerns, to each chapter's own stylistic pattern of organization : "Aeolus," "Wandering Rocks," "Sirens," "Oxen of the Sun," "Eumaeus" and "Ithaca." In four more chapters story and patterns of arrangement compete almost equally for readers' attention: "Proteus," "Nausicaa," "Circe" and "Penelope." Even when an interior monologue continuously represents a character's reflection, the author as arranger may become intrusive by implication. Long after we understand in "Proteus" that

Stephen interprets reality through a convoluted association of allusions to literature and philosophy, the details continue to accumulate until we wonder whether this is more the author's own obsession than his character's. The same happens in "Penelope," where we can savor the comedy of Molly's intuitively random associations only to the point where the pattern becomes obsessive in its inclusiveness, seemingly being indulged for its own sake. This I take to be a foreshadowing of the "total inclusiveness" in accretion of detail that Litz finds to be Joyce's method of construction throughout *Finnegans Wake*.[9]

A number of commentators have sought to justify the shift in *Ulysses* from story to organizational concerns by explaining how the various narrative styles perform the function of character and plot by indirectly developing the book's overall moral and spiritual argument. Nevertheless, the reader of "Scylla and Charybdis" who has been closely following Stephen's convoluted arguments about Shakespeare in order to find out more about Stephen's own temperament and circumstances is apt to find the fragmentary montage of the next chapter ("Wandering Rocks") to be diverting as a distraction, not as an entertainment. Throughout *Ulysses* the reader is deflected back and forth, from concern about what a chapter means to a stylistic preoccupation with its expressive arrangement.[10]

Of course the narrative style which seems to intrude on an otherwise conventional telling of a story in *Ulysses* becomes all-encompassing in *Finnegans Wake*. Here there is no consistent plot being generated by characters and no coherent system of parallels with other literary works, as there was in *Ulysses*. The structure of *Finnegans Wake*—which has variously been determined to be myth, metaphysical entity, and historical system—cannot be experienced immediately by the reader as a symbolic dimension of the plot. It can only be arrived at mediately, through critical explication.[11] *Finnegans Wake* can provide its readers with a more unified reading experience than *Ulysses* because the discontinuity which readers experience between the *Wake*'s characters and plot and its overall argumentative design is more uniform—in fact, more comprehensive—than in any previous work of literature.

Like *Ulysses*, *Finnegans Wake* has its multiple narrative voices. But in *Ulysses* these voices express a style dictated by the conceptual concerns of a particular chapter. The narrative voices of *Finnegans Wake*, on the other hand, seem more like each other than like the voices dictated by their particular narrative contexts since they are all composed of the same extraordinary language which sets any passage selected at random apart from any other passage ever written. From beginning to end the unique style of *Finnegans Wake* reminds its readers that this work is more about itself than about people or ideas.

That chapter in *Ulysses* which most clearly anticipates the self-referential style of *Finnegans Wake* is "Sirens." Here the very syntax of sentences is determined by abstract concepts, various musical techniques like polyphony and tonality, through which sound may be organized artistically. Verbal organization in "Sirens" is at its most abstract since its materials can be treated primarily for their sound values. If, for example, we compare it to "Oxen of the Sun," in that chapter words are still treated *as* words rather than sound, and must both parody their literary originals as well as proceed stylistically in chronological order.

Yet even in "Sirens" words are treated less abstractly than they are in *Finnegans Wake*:

> . . . Bloom. Old Bloom (*U* 11.49).
> Big Benaben. Big Benben (*U* 11.53).

Throughout the chapter Bloom's sound value (which he even gaseously generates himself by way of conclusion: *U* 11.1288;1293) is the middle letters of his name, a weak and regretful "Oo." This suits him because he *is* "Blue," depressed and feeling "Old" (*U* 11.230) from constant fretting over the impending assignation which he feels powerless to prevent between his wife Molly and her lover Blazes Boylan (*U* 11.639-641). Ben Dollard, in contrast, is introduced as "big" not only because of his actual girth but also by virtue of his vigorous and hearty disposition. His sound signature is doubled into two explosive "Bs" (Benben) because he is bursting with sexual energy. At least that is the way Bloom remembers Molly seeing Ben, laughing at tight trousers that put "all his belongings on show" during a concert (*U* 11.557). The sound of his name puts Ben in the category of that other double "B," Blazes Boylan, who is "Boylan with impatience" to get to Molly (*U* 11.289). Joyce's primary method for establishing a sound typical for each character in "Sirens" is onomatopoeia, the deliberate shaping of art to echo life in sound. Here Ben's name rebounds energetically (Benaben), like a big man on a bed. His verbal repartee in this chapter is predominantly sexual, and the repeated sound of this name joins all the other up-down, in-out, jiggling sexual rhythms of the chapter: the "Fro. To, fro" of the beerpull, a "baton cool protruding" (*U* 11.47), the "jumping rose" on the breast of a barmaid (*U* 11.181), the "rebound" of her garter (*U* 11.413), and the jingle of Blaze's jaunting car which anticipates another soon to follow of Molly's own jiggling bed quoits (*U* 11.304; 18.1130-1132). In itself onomatopoeia is a traditional device, and it poses difficulties for the reader in "Sirens" only because Joyce practices it so extensively with the concept of verbal music behind it. For example, the names just discussed appear in a verbal "overture" which exposes us to sound fragments of the motifs in isolation, before we can make sense of them within the context of the narrative that follows.

But whatever tenacity and ingenuity *Ulysses* requires from its readers, its demands seem reasonable in comparison to those of *Finnegans Wake*. Here, for the sake of comparison, are some other names cited in that text:

> not yet, though all's fair in vanessy, were sosie sesthers wroth with twone nathandjoe.[12]

As in the "overture" to "Sirens," the reading experience must be circular rather than linear; we must reread in order to read with any conceptual understanding. But since the plot and characters of *Finnegans Wake* are sketchy at best, and constantly shifting, the subsequent narrative establishes little of the dramatic context which helped us to interpret the sounds of "Bloom" and "Ben" in "Sirens." If we allow for spelling variations, we can begin by extracting some names from the text: Vanessa, Susie, Esther, Nathan, and Joe. The last four are Biblical, and this encourages us to discover a fifth Biblical name, "Ruth," which we can derive primarily from saying it and finding it to be a pun on "wroth" since the spelling distortion is greater than with the other names. But what about "saucy sisters," with its spelling distorted so that we can see both "Susie" and "Esther" embedded in the words and hear them as puns? By pronouncing "vanessy" with an accent on the first syllable, we can find another pun in it and rewrite the proverb of "all's fair in [vanity]," then see that "sisters" is being used in the feminist sense of women united in conflict between the genders. So, returning to our Biblical connection between the names, we have the meaning that younger women, like Susannah, Esther and Ruth, involved with older men are liable to be particularly temperamental with their lovers or husbands because their female vanity accentuates the generation gap.[13]

So far there does not seem to be too much difference between our interpretation of names in *Ulysses* and in *Finnegans Wake*, except of course that the latter is more complex, requiring many more mental operations. Both depend on sensitivity to sound values in language and the ability to find hidden associations by interrelating words (in this case names) with concepts and feelings derived from our own observations of human behavior. So far, demanding though they are, both texts nevertheless call upon skills which we might be expected to exercise to a lesser extent in reading other works of literature.

But *Finnegans Wake* requires more. We have two men's names to match with three women's; and if we use the Bible to try and associate them with those women in terms of love and war, we reach a dead end. The words "twone nathandjoe" exemplify a sort of orthographic onomatopoeia in that they look like what they are saying: "two" shares its "o" with "one" just as "nathan" shares its "an" with "and." Two-in-oneness. Could this be twins? Not if these are the Biblical Nathan and Joseph. Perhaps Vanessa, the remaining name which does not fit the Biblical context, needs to be connected with these men and the concept of twins in a different way. A literary Vanessa? Jonathan Swift's "twin" young loves, Stella and Vanessa! So "nathandjoe" is being used not primarily for the men's names but as the code word which Stella employed in private correspondence as "an anagram for Jonathan (Dean Jonathan Swift) split in two and turned head over heels by his two young-girl loves."[14] If, in this passage as quoted, we had not caught the arcane allusion to Stella's anagram, two earlier drafts of *Finnegans Wake* could have provided us with more overt clues: "twin sesthers" and "twone jonathan." [15]

Here we have an essential distinction between the interpretation of *Ulysses* and of *Finnegans Wake*. So long as "the integrity of the individual word" (Litz, *Art* 70) is retained, even the abstract concepts of sound and rhythm in "Sirens" become symbolically meaningful in terms of character and plot. The connotations of a word (Ben) in a plot context (Ben Dollard as lover and singer) are reinforced through onomatopoeia in terms of a particular tonality (Benben) to evoke some character or quality (Big). They then become like musical *leitmotifs* as they are repeated in other contexts, reverberating throughout the chapter. But in *Finnegans Wake* isolated syllables, both singly and in groups remain the primary source of meaning. Ultimately we can, of course, recognize a vital connection between the Biblical women and their elder loves, Swift and his girl-loves, and the main character Humphrey Chimpden Earwicker, whose guilt over his desire for his daughter Issy in her multiple guises runs throughout *Finnegans Wake*. Yet the puns, orthographic symbolism, and allusions are so demanding in themselves, and the plot and character seem so minimal by comparison, that we only experience a remote connection between that part of a sentence which we are decoding by syllables and the chapter which contains the sentence, much less the book as a whole. In this manner *Finnegans Wake* fulfills the self-referential implications of those chapters in *Ulysses* where the development of plot is obscured by stylistic and organizational features. Unlike

Ulysses it has little plot to be interrupted or undercut because it is organized at the smallest unit of discourse, not section or chapter or even sentence but the syllables of each word. All of *Finnegans Wake* is experienced by the reader as being less about Vico or myth or even relationships between characters than it is about itself, the generation of meaning through language.

Joyce's increasing preoccupation with language as a reflexive medium parallels comparable developments in other disciplines. Borrowing Joyce's own use of musical analogy, we might call *Ulysses* neo-Romantic because its passages of atonal composition serve to highlight by contrast those tonal harmonic combinations recognizable as melodies (plot and character generating theme). By comparison *Finnegans Wake* would be more difficult to listen to, sounding atonal and serial throughout because its intricate texture only permits plot and character to surface fragmentarily, directing our attention instead to the succession and blending of sounds, the compositional process itself.[16] Using the visual arts we could make a similar distinction. *Ulysses* seems visually challenging in itself, alternating between realism and a surrealism so highly organized (levels of narrative being analogous to visual planes) that most commentators call it cubism.[17] Yet *Finnegans Wake* makes even greater demands on an audience accustomed to mimetic modes of representation by being more abstract (non-representational) throughout.

With respect to scientific disciplines, the design of *Finnegans Wake* anticipates "complementarity," a fundamental principle of quantum mechanics that the observer actively *creates* meaning through the very act of mental attention rather than passively discovering it from physical stimuli perceived as external data.[18] In its systematic multiplicity of reference *Finnegans Wake* seems designed for complementarity, "an interpretation that is inevitably unstable, that (like our composite view of the universe) derives its sense of order only from a careful selection of those facts that support the hypothesis we have in mind at any time."[19] So *Finnegans Wake* exists in "no spatial time" (*FW* 358.5). The special/spatial pun reminds us that this work lacks the special sense of space and time which enables conventional fiction—including part of *Ulysses*—to imitate life through plot, that spatial sequencing of events which readers (using their linear sense of time) interpret as cause and effect.

Finnegans Wake anticipates another idea associated with complementarity and the subjective nature of our construction of events in space/time, one which is so speculative and to many physicists so unverifiable that it cannot be scientifically dignified as a hypothesis. If "what we experience is not external reality, but our *interaction* with it," then our very identity is provisional, a series of choices which might have been otherwise, even opposite. This leads to the Many Worlds theory that all of the choices we do not make continue to exist, but at other levels of reality. Of course we cannot verify the existence of these alternate realities because that very sequence of choices by which we exclude ourselves from them is also the way we construct our own reality from one moment to the next.[20]

The observer's constitutive role in making meaning which seems so central to the art and science of our own time has long been influential in philosophy. Joyce could have derived a philosopher's version of what some scientists now call the Many Worlds theory from the Italian Renaissance philosopher Giordano Bruno. The idea that "oppositions collapsed into unities at their extremes" led Bruno to conclude that "all identities were, therefore, provisional."[21] From this came Bruno's version of Many Worlds: "At one level of consciousness we claim an identity and stability both for ourselves and our objects of perception. But such identities can only be produced by a process of differentiation in which other identities are rejected."[22] We need only add to this the idea that all those rejected identities continue to co-exist in other, mutually exclusive, branches of reality and we arrive at the Many Worlds interpretation of quantum mechanics.

In *Finnegans Wake* it is not merely the shifting identities of the characters that dramatize the provisional nature of identity according to Bruno. The language itself branches into multiple realities whenever syllables of once-familiar words (our expressions of observed reality) are distorted through spelling changes and juxtaposed with other syllables in unfamiliar combinations. We can only hold in our minds one interpretation of such syllables at a time. Yet, as in the Many Worlds theory, we are also aware that other, perhaps equally valid, interpretations of that same syllable co-exist with ours, waiting for us to claim them as meaning. Through the satire often implicit in puns, these alternatives also qualify as Bruno's "oppositions collapsed into unities." Like reality itself in the Many Worlds theory, the text exists not merely as possibilities but as multiple realities which only require complementarity, interaction with our consciousness, to actualize them. Since *Finnegans Wake* is primarily language being re-read in circular succession, cause-effect interpretations of events in linear time no longer apply. Any given event may be interpreted as preceding the next one as well as following it.[23] With the disappearance of cause and effect, traditional distinctions of tense become inapplicable as well, as if the text could keep its readers in a perpetual present: "if we each could always do all we ever did" (*FW* 287.F2). But of course each encounter with the text must be sequential, remaining in linear time. Readers regard *Finnegans Wake* as observers relate to space/time, both being conscious of the fact that they are only able to descry a few letters of a continuously unwinding scroll on which totality has been inscribed. In *Finnegans Wake* such a totality is represented by the very density of its text which ensures that each reading experience will be more retrogressive than progressive. Inevitably readers follow the injunction to "Forget, remember!" (*FW* 614.22) by forgetting more than they can remember so that each reading will become, in effect, a new remembering: "all that has been done has yet to be done and done again" (*FW* 194.10).

The quotation above suggests another philosopher whom many commentators identify as having the greatest theoretical influence on *Finnegans Wake*. Parallels between Giambattista Vico's cyclical view of historical development and the organization of *Finnegans Wake* are usually cited as evidence for Vico's influence. Like Bruno, Vico also emphasized the role that observers themselves play in determining the nature of whatever they observe. Mario Valdés calls this "relational theory," and he traces its origins to Vico in the eighteenth century:

> If with Vico we accept the epistemological primacy of the man-made historical world, it follows that there is no absolute to which we can appeal as the basis of the truth. It follows therefore that man is in a unique position as both the subject and the object of history. He is making his historical world as he himself is already in history and subject to historical forces that antedate him and against which he has only the recourse of self-consciousness. Therefore it is in his history-making that man encounters his own historical reality.[24]

Except for typographical errors, the black letters on white paper which constitute the text of *Finnegans Wake* obviously remain unchanged. It is we who continually change the text by re-reading it cumulatively. But Vico's relational attitude is that, while we are able to verbalize entities like "text" or "history" as being independent, we cannot conceive of them apart from our own experience. In practice *Finnegans Wake* is no more static than history itself because each re-reading is a Viconian spiral of variegated attention, either to new details noticed each time around or to recollected details viewed in a different interpretive *Gestalt*.

With Vico, history is a making, man's imposition of concepts upon whatever is and has been happening around him; and with Joyce, literature is making, the reader's imposition of meaning upon a text through language. What Goldberg condemns as the relinquishing of authorial control and a consequent dissolution of meaningfulness, Joyce, as a Viconian, could defend as a deliberate distortion of familiar vocabulary to dramatize how reflexivity (knowing that we *are* reading while we do it) is an essential part of the creative process. As Valdés concludes, "In his history-making . . . man encounters his own historical reality."

From *Ulysses* to *Finnegans Wake* Joyce increasingly relies on language to enact the process of how meaning is being made before our eyes. The alteration of a single letter in *Ulysses* alerts us to characters as composites sharing parallel roles. Bloom loves his daughter Milly as "Silly [Milly]" (*U* 4.284), a diluted version (with its higher vowel) of Molly with her lower, more mature, sex appeal (a feminine parallel to the high and low-pitched Bloom/Dollard contrast already mentioned). A final draft of *Finnegans Wake* transforms "thouartpatrick" to "thuartpeatrick" (*FW* 3.10) and opposite possibilities emerge. Either this could be a celebration of Irish Catholicism, combining "peat-rick" (Litz, *Art* 87) with (Saint) Patrick, both puns being embedded in Peter, the Latin pun on which the church was founded as *petras*, a rock of ages. Or as "pea-trick" it could expose the whole Christian enterprise as a shell-game, the sort of sound-and-light show which both Mulligan and Bloom regard it to be in *Ulysses*.

Finnegans Wake differs from *Ulysses*, however, in the extent to which its language becomes self-referential. As plot and character recede in *Finnegans Wake*, referentiality of language more easily becomes self-referentiality, a linguistic transformation with no discernible meaning beyond rearrangement of the letters themselves. In *Ulysses* the inversion of the letter sequence within a word signals a duality of concepts, dog/God being the paradoxical material/metaphysical nature of the Trinity which confronts Stephen on the beach in "Proteus" (*U* 3.286-364) and which "dogs" Bloom's footsteps into nighttown in "Circe" (*U* 15.247; 15.633; 15.559-697). But in *Finnegans Wake* Tristan is inverted to "natsirt" (*FW* 388.3), Mark to "Kram" (*FW* 388.2), and Dublin to "Nilbud" (*FW* 24.1), seemingly to no other end than puzzlement or to create an amusing sound.[25] *Ulysses* offers us stream-of-consciousness, a representation of our simultaneous processing of internal and external information. But *Finnegans Wake* carries this interior exploration further, providing us with a matrix ("stream" sounds too linear) of the pre-conscious where mind becomes mind, the play of our identity as we begin to formulate our reality in words even before being aware of them *as* words.[26]

Being a recognized work of literature, *Finnegans Wake* has a potentially limitless history simply as text, "a continuity in time as a sequence of words" which invites an infinite succession of readers to respond in various ways.[27] We might regard *Finnegans Wake*, then, as the first work of literature to dramatize the relational implications of Viconian theory by treating text in terms of itself rather than as a transparent medium for constructing fictional realities or presenting ideas. To Litz, "it is a damning commentary on Joyce's method [of composing *Finnegans Wake*] that a study of earlier versions often provides important clues to the meaning of a passage in the final text" (Litz, *Art* 113). But if we look at *Finnegans Wake* as the first truly Viconian text, then its very lack of finality becomes its primary virtue. All of Joyce's drafts for it, and his comments to others about it, form a text which is itself merely a prototype for collective authorship by an open-ended series of subsequent commentators. The very difficulty of *Finnegans Wake* makes it continuously collaborative.[28] Joyce requires his readers to create their own words, constructing the meaning syllable by syllable. We are thereby constantly reminded that each word functions as a text in itself, accumulating its own interpretive history.

Litz sees Vico merely as a source for historical *schema* which became part of the design of *Finnegans Wake*. Using the various drafts of each composition, he demonstrates that Joyce wrote both *Ulysses* and *Finnegans Wake* from a "single image in his mind" which he established fairly early so that completing the rest of each work was a predominantly static process of filling in and elaborating details within a predetermined framework (Litz, *Art* 5; 19; 52; 86; 89; 101). But is the reader therefore obliged to try to reconstruct the author's intention in order to recover Joyce's original design? (Litz, *Art* 57). Anthony Burgess might believe so since he concludes that Joyce himself must be the dreamer of *Finnegans Wake*.[29] But surely this is an oversimplification. Joyce is not present there as a character, and a number of perspectival discontinuities make the representation of any single narrative stance problematic.[30] Rather than trying to reconstruct Joyce's intention or recover his design, we can more profitably view *Finnegans Wake* as it appears today in Viconian terms of collaborative authorship, the proliferating ingenuity of various conflicting theories about what the text means.

Post-structuralist critics have emphasized the openness and undecidability of Joyce's texts. But since they see all literature as exhibiting such qualities, they only perfunctorily distinguish between Joyce and other authors, or even among Joyce's own works.[31] But the reader without post-structuralist presuppositions is likely to find that an overview of Joyce's best-known works reveals striking contrasts. In comparison with what follows, *Dubliners* appears to be Joyce's most realistic work. The narrative is simultaneously so reticent and so selective that, on the whole, *Dubliners* leaves its readers with a naturalistic response of "pity or grief or outrage at inadequate human beings, largely self-condemned, who fail to understand the nature of power and oppression."[32] The realism of *Portrait* is more expressionistic in that its language begins to reflect Stephen's maturity, his growing awareness of his world and of his need to break away from those aspects of his environment which had trapped his predecessors in *Dubliners*. In *Ulysses* I have already noted how the narratives of Stephen and Bloom are halfway to *Finnegans Wake*. That is, both within and between chapters some episodes centered in character (either psychologically realistic or, as in "Circe," expressionistic) contrast with others where plot and character are obscured by narrative style and arrangement.

Once we regard *Finnegans Wake* as an extreme example of the narrative experimentation which Joyce was already pursuing in *Ulysses*, we see that this final work represents his ultimate achievement, a new world created through the merging of the microcosm of interior monologue with the macrocosm of exterior reality. Using his own fictional time and space, Joyce invents a language which more closely approximates music than the sound-language of "Sirens" because it has become even more abstract and self-referential. The godlike narrator begins with the *logos*, exercising both omniscience and omnipotence; and the development of his fiction is the reader's witnessing of a new world which he helps to create, syllable by syllable.[33] In the history of literature *Finnegans Wake* becomes the first work to make self-referentiality a fundamental characteristic of its overall design, beginning with every syllable of the text.[34] Yet it remains more than a closed circle, a completed imitation of the process of its own creation. To the best of our own more limited abilities as readers, *Finnegans Wake* requires us to assume Joyce's godlike power of creation ourselves, not through the assimilation of Goldberg's "argument" or "circumstance" but through collaboration with Joyce as creator, whenever we piece together each word for ourselves. *Finnegans Wake* seems more speech-gesture than imitation, a text which requires us not, as Litz implies, to understand it by attempting to replicate the mental processes that produced it, but to participate in making it a text by drawing on our own creativity, the construction of meaning through language. After all, the slip of Martha Clifford's typewriter in *Ulysses* has already demonstrated how, at any moment, "word"-making can become "world"-making (*U* 5.245-246).

So the most remarkable thing about *Finnegans Wake* is not Joyce's ego, which drove him to become a godlike author devoting over sixteen years to the creation of a world which no one else could comprehend, even though his labors pronounced it good. More remarkable is Joyce's generosity in conferring on his readers so much of his own godlike responsibility for making his creation meaningful. What is lost in the text's systematic open-endedness is the "sense of 'inevitability' or 'rightness' which is the sign of a controlled narrative structure" (Litz, *Art* 62). But there is also gain. More of what was previously under control of the author as arranger in *Ulysses* is transferred to the reader in *Finnegans Wake*. For Joyce, God is the artist himself, contemplating his own *logos* even as he questions it in comedy, so that at every point the reader is free to believe and/or not-believe. This contradictory (or at least opposite) view of meaningfulness and satire, together with self-referentiality in the language throughout, so distance the godlike creator of *Finnegans Wake* from his narrative(s) that readers are granted an unprecedented opportunity to recreate the text in their own ever-widening Viconian spirals of cumulative perspective.

Notes

1. Matthew Hodgart, *James Joyce, A Student's Guide* (London: Routledge and Kegan Paul, 1978), 132.

2. Sydney Bolt, *A Preface to James Joyce* (New York: Longman, 1981), 161.

3. A. Walton Litz, *James Joyce* (U.S.A.: Twayne, 1966; rev. ed. Hippocrene paperback, 1972), 118.

4. Samuel L. Goldberg, *James Joyce* (Edinburgh: Oliver & Boyd, 1962. Reprint. Grove Press paperback, 1962), 111-112.

5. Samuel L. Goldberg, *The Classical Temper, A Study of James Joyce's Ulysses* (London: Chatto and Windus, [1961] 1963), 152. Hereafter cited in the text.

6. James Joyce, *Ulysses*, ed. Hans W. Gabler, *et al.* (New York: Random House, 1986), 3.501. Hereafter cited in the text.

7. Post-structuralist critics might regard this as an example of the indeterminacy which they find everywhere in Joyce. But I would call it ambiguity in the service of characterization, a reflection of the ambivalence which Stephen ruefully acknowledges when Haines asks him whether he is "a believer": "you behold in me . . . a horrible example of free thought" (*U* 1.625-626).

8. Patrick A. McCarthy, "A Warping Process: Reading *Finnegans Wake*," in *Joyce Centenary Essays*, eds. Richard F. Peterson, Alan M. Cohn, and Edmund L. Epstein (Carbondale: Southern Illinois University Press, 1983), 51.

9. A. Walton Litz, *James Joyce*, 99.

10. Like Goldberg, Litz (*James Joyce* 99) underestimates this similarity in the experience of reading all of *Ulysses* and *Finnegans Wake*. When comparing the two he refers to symbolic elaboration in "the last episodes of *Ulysses*," as if only these were affected since by that time Joyce would also have been working on *Finnegans Wake*.

11. Clive Hart notes that "the more one understands of the detail [in *Finnegans Wake*], thanks to the continuing flow of explication, the more difficult it becomes to sustain a satisfying sense of the whole." As a compromise between overall *schema* and local textual details, he suggests "interrelationships of image and idea within a short paragraph, reread and pondered with a general if imperfect sense of the whole book in the background" (Clive Hart, "Afterword. Reading *Finnegans Wake*," in *A Starchamber Quiry, A James Joyce Centennial Volume 1882-1982*, ed. Edmund L. Epstein [New York: Methuen, 1982], 156-157).

12. James Joyce, *Finnegans Wake* (New York: Viking, 1967), 3.11-12. Hereafter cited in the text.

13. Joseph Campbell and Henry M. Robinson, *A Skeleton Key to Finnegans Wake* (New York: Harcourt Brace, 1944), 30.

14. Campbell and Robinson, 30.

15. A. Walton Litz, *The Art of James Joyce, Method and Design in Ulysses and Finnegans Wake* (London: Oxford University Press, 1961. Reprint. Oxford University paperback, 1968), 87. Hereafter cited in the text as Litz, *Art*.

16. Hodgart makes a broader comparison between Schoenberg's serial works and both *Ulysses* and *Finnegans Wake*, all of which are distinguished by "an elaborate hidden structure, which no reader[s] however attentive could possibly work out during [their]first reading" (Hodgart, *James Joyce, A Student's Guide*, 6). But Fritz Senn warns that all such musical analogies are inadequate in that they "cannot be kept up consistently, since in practice we shall hardly be able to . . . listen to the voices consecutively, as in a musical performance we could, even allowing for intervals" (Fritz Senn, *Joyce's Dislocutions: Essays on Reading as Translation*, ed. John Paul Riquelme [Baltimore: Johns Hopkins University, 1984], 87). Perhaps the most provocative comparison between Schoenberg and Joyce is the implied circularity of Joyce's self-referentiality. Theodore Adorno on Schoenberg: "Twelve-tone rationality approaches *superstition per se* in that it is a closed system . . . . The legitimacy of the procedure in which the technique fulfils itself is at the same time merely something imposed upon the material, by which the legitimacy is determined. This determination itself does not actually serve a purpose. Accuracy or correctness, as a mathematical hypothesis, takes the place of that element called 'the idea' in traditional art" (Quoted by Jean-Michel Rabaté, "Lapsus ex Machina," in *Post-structuralist Joyce, Essays from the French*, ed. Derek Attridge and Daniel Ferrer [Cambridge: Cambridge University Press, 1984], 80).

17. The most complete analogies between cubism and Joyce's narrative are in Max Halperen, "Neither Fish nor Flesh: Joyce as Picasso," in *New Alliances in Joyce Studies*, ed. Bonnie K. Scott (Newark: University of Delaware Press, 1988), 93-101.

18. Gary Zukav, *The Dancing Wu Li Masters, An Overview of the New Physics* (New York: 1979; reprint. Bantam paperback, 1984), 93.

19. McCarthy, 49.

20. Zukav, 83.

21. Colin MacCabe, "An Introduction to *Finnegans Wake*," in *James Joyce: New Perspectives*, ed. Colin MacCabe (Bloomington: Indiana University Press, 1982), 33. [Editor's note: This essay is reprinted in this volume.]

22. MacCabe, 34.

128   James Joyce's *Finnegans Wake*

23. David A. White, *The Grand Continuum: Reflections on Joyce and Metaphysics* (Pittsburgh: University of Pittsburgh Press, 1983), 49.

24. Mario J. Valdés, *Phenomenological Hermeneutics and the Study of Literature* (Toronto: University of Toronto Press, 1987), 24.

25. Fritz Senn, *Joyce's Dislocutions: Essays on Reading as Translation*, ed. John P. Riquelme (Baltimore: Johns Hopkins University Press, 1984), 88.

26. Sheldon Brivic anticipates further investigation of the dynamics of mind represented through the fluidity of Joycean language, critical "attempts to present Joycean mentality in cybernetic terms" (Sheldon Brivic, "Joycean Psychology," in *Joyce Centenary Essays*, eds. Richard F. Peterson, Alan M. Cohn, and Edmund L. Epstein. [Carbondale: Southern Illinois University Press, 1983], 107).

27. Valdés, 38.

28. Valdés, 15.

29. Anthony Burgess, *ReJoyce* (New York: Norton, 1968), 192.

30. White, 16-20.

31. To post-structuralists everything is literary that "refuses and resists the scientific model of knowledge . . . by being an event and not an argument or truth-claim." Joyce's texts, in particular, are open to being literary in this way because in his comedy "the ruling principles of scientific knowledge can be tested against themselves, can be made to reveal their dependence on the aleatory, the exluded, the counter-rational, and the contingent" (Derek Attridge, "Criticism's Wake," in *James Joyce, The Augmented Ninth: Proceedings of the Ninth International James Joyce Symposium, Frankfurt, 1984*, ed. Bernard Benstock [Syracuse, New York: Syracuse University, 1988], 85).

    After Jacques Derrida proclaimed his debt to Joyce ("Two Words for Joyce," in *Post-structuralist Joyce, Essays from the French*, ed. Derek Attridge and Daniel Ferrer [Cambridge: Cambridge University, 1984], 145-161), his followers found Derrida's own most distinctive traits in Joyce so that he could join Homer and the rest of Western civilization, who of course were already there: "Joyce . . . preinscribes Derrida" (Christine Van Boheemen-Saaf, "Joyce, Derrida, and the Discourse of 'the other,'" in *Augmented Ninth*, 88).

    So perhaps this article could be regarded as an initial attempt to implement the same author's call for an approach to "Joyce's *oeuvre* as the reflection of one continuous development from a primarily text-external (referential) approach to the nature of fiction to a primarily text-internal semiotics" (Christine Van Boheemen-Saaf, "Deconstruction after Joyce," in *New Alliances in Joyce Studies*, ed. Bonnie K. Scott [Newark: University of Delaware Press, 1988], 35).

32. Phillip F. Herring, *Joyce's Uncertainty Principle* (Princeton: Princeton University Press, 1987), 203.

33. Seeing Joyce's art as some sort of substitute for religion is, of course, commonplace. For the most extended application of the analogy through all of Joyce's life and works see Sheldon Brivic, *Joyce the Creator* (Madison: University of Wisconsin Press, 1985).

34. With respect to self-referential design, at least, Joyce may have felt that *Finnegans Wake* did have a literary predecessor in *Tristram Shandy* (McCarthy 48). Twentieth-century predecessors include Gide, *Les Faux-Monnayeurs* (1925) and Gombrowicz, *Ferdydurke* (1937) (Ihab Hassan, "(   ): *Finnegans Wake* and the Postmodern Imagination," in *Light Rays: James Joyce and Modernism*, ed. Heyward Ehrlich [New York: Horizon, 1984], 101).

Joyce's Nonce-Symbolic Calculus: A *Finnegans Wake* Trajectory

by

David W. Robinson

What exactly does Joyce carry over from a source, or from one of his earlier texts, when he reuses a plot, a character, or an abstract configuration in *Finnegans Wake*? Critics have long questioned the use of terms like "parallel" or "parody" to describe Joyce's use of Homer and other sources, and I will generalize their point: the meanings we can assign to Joyce's borrowings always remain radically local and *ad hoc*. They remain what can be called, with an anti-essentialist pun, "nonce symbols," that is, significant structures whose meaning is tied to a particular usage by Joyce and a particular reading by us. The meanings of a putative symbol or motif vary from one use to the next according to new opportunities opened by new contexts; Joyce jettisons previous details or connections when they grow confining for him. Readers, attempting to assemble and reapply these very details elsewhere in a text, are starkly confronted with a dialectic of sense and nonsense that all reading inhabits, but which Joyce's writing specifically exploits. Joyce did not base late texts on what preceded them, so much as he rereads his early texts in light of later ones, crediting what came first with containing seeds of what was to follow. My calculated example of this procedure, a demonstration of the literary potential of the equation $3 + 1 + 1 = 5$, begins with *Finnegans Wake* Chapter I.4 and works backwards through a derivation based on the *Dubliners* story "Grace."

FW I.4 is the final installment of the four-part HCE saga, in which the hero's origins, fall, death, and resurrection are repeatedly and contradictorily narrated. It describes primarily HCE's interment and rumored return, with digressions into the reasons for his fall and the consequences of his absence. The chapter's surface structure appears to follow from the attack on the pub, narrated in the previous chapter beginning at 69.30, where HCE barricades himself inside the pub to avoid his abusive visitor. In I.4, shortly before HCE's situation is transformed into residence within a heavily fortified tomb, the dream-narrator speculates about what the trapped HCE may be thinking: perhaps "the besieged bedreamt him stil and solely of those lililiths undeveiled which had undone him"[1] or perhaps "he conscious of enemies, a kingbilly whitehorsed in a Finglas mill, prayed, as he sat on anxious seat" (*FW* 75.15-16) —appropriately, since the seat on which he sits is no doubt a toilet seat, and the sin in Phoenix Park may have as easily been scatological as sexual. It shortly becomes apparent, however, that HCE is really dead, at least in the opinion of the narrator ("Let us leave theories there and return to here's here" *FW* 76.10), and the remainder of the chapter proceeds from this assumption. Focusing principally on a version of HCE's crime or encounter in the park, and a court trial ensuing from it, the major (if confusing) action of the chapter is diagrammed in Figure 1.[2] Thematically, the chapter concentrates on *sin* (using the mythic examples of Adam, Parnell, and HCE himself); *falling* (Adam, HCE); *false denunciation* (Parnell/Piggott, HCE); *resurrection* (Finn, Christ, Parnell, HCE); and *burial/immersion* (Finn, Christ, Parnell). It resolves itself in the newly explicit role of ALP as preserver and regenerator, the force behind the eternal cycles, figured in the waters of babble-on (Egypt and Babylon being equivalent as biblical lands of exile) at either end of the chapter.

Among the more puzzling aspects of this chapter are its numerous allusions to the *Dubliners* story "Grace," Joyce's harshest indictment of Irish Catholicism.[3] "Grace" tells of Tom Kernan's fall while drunk down a set of lavatory steps, and of his restoration to spiritual good health through the plottings of four friends, Martin Cunningham, Jack Power, Mr. M'Coy, and Mr. Fogarty, who induce him to attend a religious retreat. The densest set of allusions to "Grace" occurs on pages 83-84, the conclusion of the Cad/Cropatkin's encounter with HCE, a context apparently sharing nothing in common with the events of the short story: the narrative sense appears to be that HCE's adversary turns friendly after receiving a sum of extorted money. The many references, signalled by "grace" (*FW* 83.23) and "gracies" (*FW* 95.4), point to Tom Kernan's fall, his injury, the discussion in his bedroom, and the events at the religious retreat. There are specific allusions to Kernan's hat (*FW* 83.28, 36), which was damaged in the fall down the steps, to his injured tongue (*FW* 83.10-11, 16), to the motto "*Lux upon Lux*"[4] spuriously ascribed to Pope Leo XIII during the sickbed conversation (*FW* 83.9, 25), and to Father Purdon, the retreat preacher (*FW* 83.11, 17, 28-30). Kernan is surely present in the description of "this poor delaney" (*FW* 84.8) with "the white ground of his face all covered with diagonally redcrossed nonfatal mammalian blood . . . bleeding in self defience . . . from the nostrils, lips, pavilion and palate . . ." (*FW* 84.19-22). Other "Grace" allusions abound, including, of course, Martin Cunningham's feminized presence as "Minxy Cunningham" at *FW* 95.9.

To show that the chapter contains allusions to "Grace" says little, of course, about *why*. The "plot" of *FW* I.4 (if one can use such a word in reference to *Finnegans Wake*) has almost nothing in common with the plot of "Grace"—both texts contain a metaphorically suggestive "fall," but the same could be said of every chapter of the *Wake*. The characters themselves appear to have forgotten their earlier functions, HCE/Kernan receiving his bloody face from a fight rather than a fall, and Martin Cunningham appearing as somebody's "dear divorcee darling" (*FW* 95.10). The principal theme of "Grace," corruption in the Church through a debased, simoniacal, businessman's theology (articulated by Father Purdon) may be echoed in the scene where the Cropatkin extorts money from HCE (it is simony for HCE to buy "pardun" [*FW* 83.29]) but the details of the original plot are wholly absent, along with the theological and historical discussions which make up the bulk of "Grace." It appears as though the allusions to "Grace" serve no purpose other than to establish the short story's presence. Its significance of which must function, if at all, on a level other than one-for-one correspondence between plots, characters, themes, or even verbal surface.[5]

After leaving the confines of *Finnegans Wake* to search for meaning in "Grace," the reader has no reason not to regress further and consider the sources of "Grace" as well: an angle of vision taking in further texts appears to be the only hope to escape this abyss of unmotivated intertextuality. This is true despite the fact that the most convincingly identifiable sources seem merely to augment the short story's themes and to show little promise for future reworking. Based on internal evidence, these include the Book of Job and Swift's *Tale of a Tub*.[6] Job, like Kernan, follows a cyclic progress from prosperity, through adversity, to regained prosperity. Kernan's friends

(Cunningham, Power, M'Coy, and Fogarty) match Job's comforters (Eliphaz, Bildad, Zophar, and Elihu) in number and arrangement, with the initial three in both cases being joined by an argumentative latecomer; on a theological level, both sets of comforters believe in "a direct connection between virtue and material prosperity."[7] Finally, the voice of God speaking from a whirlwind is parodied in Father Purdon. Swift, whose *Tale of a Tub* will show up in *FW* I.4 dressed in a "padderjagmartin tripiezite suet" (*FW* 86.2), is directly alluded to in "Grace" by the mention of "yahoos" (*D* 161), but more intriguingly in the spectacle of four fools discussing theology: Swift presents the three sons Peter, Martin, and Jack judging at a remove their father's (theological) intentions, with Swift's "Modern" narrator, a latecomer like Joyce's Fogarty and Job's friend Elihu, completing the parallel.[8]

Now, in light of these examples, another comes to mind for any reader of Joyce. The four old men in *Finnegans Wake*, Matt Gregory, Marcus Lyons, Luke Tarpey, and Johnny MacDougall (so named at *FW* 384.6-14), also customarily occur in a 3 + 1 configuration, with Johnny trailing behind. This derives in part from the distinction between the three Synoptic Gospels (Matthew, Mark, and Luke) and the final Gospel of John, which lagged behind in date of composition. As the author of John suggests, the common task of all four Evangelists is to elucidate, in a special sense, the Word; this is also the task of Joyce's four old men in their guise as four philologists struggling to make sense of the words of ALP's letter.[9] The common task of all these quadripartite groups is to interpret and judge, sometimes to accuse as well, and it is specifically as "four justicers" (*FW* 92.35) that the Four preside over the trial of Festy King. Despite all changes in immediate circumstance, and retaining an association with judgment, the numeric configuration of 3 + 1 + 1 = 5 has survived in transit between "Grace" and the *Wake*. Like the four men in Job and the four in "Grace," the Four in the *Wake* accuse, admonish, historicize, and interpret with respect to a fifth, central figure. This pattern, which in "Grace" was only an arbitrary, incidental detail of a specific occasion of parody, recurs in *Finnegans Wake* as an essential structuring principle, a peg on which to hang the guilt that permeates HCE's dream. What matters to Joyce, retrospectively, is the convenient association of a clear human situation with a simple structure, regardless of his own original intent. As nonce symbol, the equation recurs with an accumulating repertoire of possible meanings, only some of which may be relevant at any given point in the text.[10]

None of this explains yet why one of the four friends in "Grace," Martin Cunningham, figures so prominently in *FW* I.4 (where he is the only one clearly named) and elsewhere in the *Wake*. Another set of accidents is suggestive: the history of the real person after whom Cunningham was originally modeled, John Joyce's friend Matthew Kane. Kane, like Cunningham, was an employee in Dublin Castle, had a drunkard wife, and died of drowning off Kingstown on July 10, 1904.[11] These biographical details contribute to Martin Cunningham's longest guest appearances in *FW* II.4, "Mamalujo," where the Four reminisce about his death:

> . . .[Johnny section] and then there was the drowning of Pharoah and all his pedestrians and they were all completely drowned into the sea, the red sea, and then poor Merkin Cornyngwham, the official out of the castle on pension, when he was completely

> drowned off Erin Isles, at that time, suir knows, in the red sea and
> a lovely mourning paper and thank God, as Saman said, there were
> no more of him. And that now was how it was. The arzurian deeps
> o'er his humbodumbones sweeps. And his widdy the giddy is
> wreathing her murmoirs as her gracest triput to the Grocery
> Trader's Manthly.   (*FW* 387.25-35)

. . . .

> Marcus. And after that, not forgetting, there was the
> Flemish armada, all scattered, and all officially drowned, there and
> then, on a lovely morning, after the universal flood, at about aleven
> thirty-two was it? off the coast of Cominghome. . . . (*FW* 388.10-
> 13)

Besides the allusions to Kane's life, these passages contain several echoes from
"Grace." "Poor Merkin Cornyngwham" recalls "poor Martin Cunningham" (*D*
157), although the sympathy in the original story concerns Cunningham's marital
troubles; "gracest" recalls "Grace"; "widdy the giddy" refers to Cunningham's
inebriated wife; and the detail that Mr. Fogarty is a grocer leads to "Grocery
Trader's Manthly." In death, Cunningham has become (like Finn) the Irish
landscape ("off the coast of Cominghome") and HCE's name is approximated in
the first passage by "humbodumbones," which recalls the Humpty Dumpty story,
always emblematic in the *Wake* of *the* Fall, and a dual symbol of death and
birth. The same resurrection motif emerges from the distortions of
Cunningham's name, "Cornyngwham" suggesting a fall, "Cominghome"
(obviously) a return.

"Seadeath, mildest of all deaths known to man" (*U* 3.482-483) is the
dominant mode of death in *FW* I.4, where HCE sinks beneath various bodies of
water, and in *Ulysses*, Stephen Dedalus linked it with resurrection. Stephen
imagines during his beach walk a perverse resurrection when he envisions the
bloated corpse of a drowned man bobbing to the surface, eaten by minnows, an
image foreshadowed in "Telemachus," shortly after a similar reverie about "a
swollen bundle to bob up, roll over to the sun a puffy face, saltwhite. Here I
am" (*U* 1.676-677). Martin Cunningham's function in *Finnegans Wake* thus
appears to build on the earlier theme of death (especially drowning) as a
"seachange" (*U* 3.482), as suggested by the distortion of his name in "There you'll
fix your eyes darkled on the autocart of the bringfast cable but here till youre
martimorphysed please sit still face to face" (*FW* 434.30-32). Cunningham is
allowed to range free as a suggestion of certain themes and relations, but not
necessarily one position within those relations.

This, however, is still not the end of the matter, because the funeral of
Matthew Kane, attended by John and James Joyce, served as the model for
Paddy Dignam's funeral in *Ulysses*.[12] Joyce's attitude toward his raw materials
emerges from this proof that Paddy Dignam and Martin Cunningham share a
common source—the transformations between characters in *Finnegans Wake* are
nothing new, for as early as the "Hades" chapter of *Ulysses*, analogous divisions
and redistributions of source material were already taking place. Matthew Kane
gives rise to *two* characters, one of them, Martin Cunningham, alive; the other,
Paddy Dignam, dead. This division, and its conflation, are among the most
dominant themes in both *Ulysses* and *Finnegans Wake*, so it is altogether

appropriate that Martin Cunningham should serve in the later book as one manifestation of the multiple-natured HCE. Joyce apparently was willing to mine his own earlier work with the same ruthless detachment about original intent, context, details, and so on, that governed his use of other writings. Martin Cunningham takes on value as a paradoxical symbol of life and death because of an earlier artistic decision made for local, specific artistic purposes. Joyce did not *plant* all these correspondences in the early works; they become correspondences only when we *mis*-read the earlier works according to Joyce's own example.

To proceed with just such a misreading of "Grace" and "Hades" from the anachronistic perspective of *Finnegans Wake*: What can be made of the fact that Cunningham is again part of a group of *four men* when depicted on his way to Dignam's funeral? "Hades" opens with first Cunningham, then Mr. Power (whom we also know from "Grace"), and next Simon Dedalus entering a funeral carriage. Once these three are seated, Cunningham urges, "Come along, Bloom" (*U* 6.8) and Mr. Bloom gets in. As in "Grace," not to mention *Finnegans Wake*, 3 + 1 = 4, and the fifth figure, the center of attention, the object of commentary, is naturally Paddy Dignam, who out of necessity rides in a different coach.[13] The assemblage seems only superficially to resemble that of "Grace," the greatest coincidence (a weak one) being that both groups are engaged in religious missions; but it very strongly foreshadows *Finnegans Wake*, where the Four tell stories and jokes, insult each other, gabble about the past, and generally carry on like the occupants of this funeral carriage. (The later book is supposed to be a wake, after all.) It is altogether appropriate that Martin Cunningham should serve there as one particularly fortuitious participant in it, after having already been an accuser in "Grace" and both mourner and mourned in *Ulysses*.

With the help of Figure 2, which represents schematically all of the texts discussed, other correspondences appear. The benevolent project of the four friends in "Grace" was to raise a fallen comrade, one who fell, in fact, because of his devotion to drink, a peculiarly Irish form of drowning. Kernan's fall was a perverse baptism also in that he fell down into a *lavatory*, a place where one washes dirt off oneself, though usually not sins, and spends certain moments laved in "ooze"; he also gets baptised in his own blood, an unpromising sort of ritual. To lift Kernan out of this mess is, literally and figuratively, what his friends set out to do. Hence it seems significant that in "Hades" the mourners, in the course of "waking" Dignam, relate the story of Reuben J. Dodd's son:

> —Reuben J and the son were piking it down the quay
> next the river on their way to the Isle of Man boat and
> the young chiseller suddenly got loose and over the
> wall with him into the Liffey.
> —For God' sake! Mr Dedalus exclaimed in fright. Is
> he dead?
> —Dead!   Martin Cunningham cried. Not he!   A
> boatman got a pole and fished him out by the slack of
> the breeches and he was landed up to the father on the
> quay more dead than alive. (U 6.278-284)

(For which service the rescuer received the award of a florin.) From a *Wake*-reader's perspective, Reuben J.'s son has been transformed into yet another avatar of HCE: dead, "buried," and resurrected, all within the scope of a story told by a character who springs from a genuine drowned man, and whose own future drowning is retroactively assured by the logic of *Finnegans Wake*. Opportunistic to the end, Joyce successfully merged all the previously unrelated aspects of a character named "Martin Cunningham," as well as those that *were* foreseen, such as the familiar 3+1 pattern (though questions of intention like these lead into a hall of mirrors and reversed chronologies which, apparently, pleased Joyce greatly). When HCE is thus revealed as an amalgam of characters present in Joyce's writing from the start, the now-commonplace observation that all the characters in the *Wake* bear shifting, exchangeable identities takes on new force. It is only slightly more remarkable that the same basic, even schematic relations among characters appear so early and persist so long: for a writer unfazed by inconsistency and constant re-vision, a single structure can accommodate any number of meanings. For the effect to come off properly, however, the reader must be as unconcerned with pre-conceived orderings as Joyce was in his self-reinterpretations.

One of the reasons that "Grace" makes it into Chapter I.4 is doubtless a thematic one, the idea of grace itself, versus perversions of it, as suggested by the contrast between the inquisitorial nightmare acted out by the Four, and the life-giving waters of Anna Liffey that lap on either end of the chapter, circumscribing the narrower views between. But the chapter's structure and the particular turns taken by its narrators owe more to borrowed structural patterns than to any such thematic inferences we may make. The theme of grace, like other clever extrapolations we might wish to make about Joyce's texts, is finally an imposition on the text, not a fact nestled within it from the start. Just as Martin Cunningham takes on significance because of earlier artistic accidents, from decisions made for local purposes, so Joyce's life work takes on structural cogency when read retrospectively, through *Finnegans Wake*—and we all end up following Joyce's example and reading him in this anachronistic manner. In practice, however, Joyce disregarded the limits on meaning set by his own past uses of characters, plots, or motifs. His symbols are nonce-symbols, filled with meaning (by Joyce, by us) on a provisional basis. The arithmetical pattern I have been discussing is typical not just in its aloof distance from intrinsic meaning, but also in its efficacy as a structuring device *because* of that aloofness. The reader is tempted by two conflicting approaches to reading these texts—to totalize them individually and as a corpus, or to see them as deformations of various conceivable totalizations.[14] In his ruthless detachment when rereading himself, his dismissing original intent in favor of literary opportunism, Joyce holds out to his readers and critics a vertiginous model of interpretive self-reliance.

Figure 1. Outline of *Finnegans Wake* I.4.

76.10 - 78.6	Description of HCE's coffin, grave and funeral.
78.7 - 78.14	Interlude on Viconian themes.
78.15 - 79.13	Wars ensuing from HCE's departure; speculation on his current hibernation.
79.14 - 79.26	Sexual behavior in ancient times.
79.27 - 80.36	Kate Strong dumps her load in Phoenix Park; Jove's voice interrupts the fighting.
81.1 - 81.11	Recollection of gigantic heroes.
81.12 - 84.27	Attack on HCE by the "cropatkin," and its aftermath.
84.28 - 85.19	Crimes committed in Phoenix Park.
85.20 - 93.21	The Trial of Festy King.
93.22 - 94.22	Letter written in response to trial.
94.23 - 96.24	The judges rehash the trial and crime.
96.25 - 97.28	The Fox Hunt.
97.29 - 101.1	HCE's cyclic recurrence; his present existence; his imminent return.
101.2 - 103.11	Inquiry shifts from HCE to ALP.

Figure 2. ". . . the four justicers laid their wigs together, Untius, Muncius, Punchus and Pylax . . ." (*FW* 92.35-36).[15]

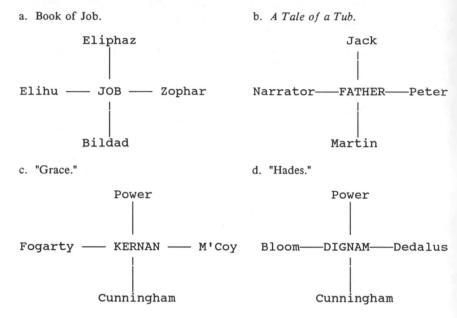

a. Book of Job.   b. *A Tale of a Tub.*

```
        Eliphaz                                   Jack
          |                                         |
          |                                         |
Elihu ── JOB ── Zophar          Narrator────FATHER────Peter
          |                                         |
          |                                         |
        Bildad                                   Martin
```

c. "Grace."   d. "Hades."

```
        Power                                     Power
          |                                         |
          |                                         |
Fogarty ── KERNAN ── M'Coy       Bloom────DIGNAM────Dedalus
          |                                         |
          |                                         |
      Cunningham                               Cunningham
```

e. *Finnegans Wake.*

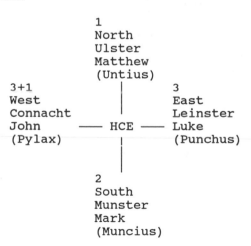

```
                              1
                              North
                              Ulster
                              Matthew
                              (Untius)
        3+1                      |              3
        West                     |              East
        Connacht                 |              Leinster
        John        ── HCE ──                  Luke
        (Pylax)                  |              (Punchus)
                                 |
                              2  |
                              South
                              Munster
                              Mark
                              (Muncius)
```

Notes

1. James Joyce, *Finnegans Wake* (New York: Viking Press, 1939), 75.5-6. Subsequent abbreviated references are to this edition.

2. See Adaline Glasheen's somewhat different synopsis of the chapter (*Third Census of Finnegans Wake: An Index of the Characters and their Roles* [Berkeley: University of California Press, 1977], xxxiv-xxxvii).

3. These allusions were first pointed out by Virginia Mosely in "The 'Coincidence' of 'Contraries' in 'Grace,'" *James Joyce Quarterly* 6 (Fall 1968): 2-21.

4. James Joyce, *Dubliners*, ed. Robert Scholes in consultation with Richard Ellmann (New York: Viking Press, 1967), 167. Subsequent abbreviated references are to this edition.

5. Mosely argues rather implausibly that Vico underlies not only *Finnegans Wake*, but "Grace" as well. Attempts to chart a line of development among Joyce's works often stumble unknowingly on anachronisms of which the author was fully aware—Joyce never hesitated to regard his prior accidents as providentially guided.

6. For an early discussion of the Job connection, see F.X. Newman, "The Land of Ooze: Joyce's 'Grace' and the Book of Job," *Studies in Short Fiction* 2 (1966): 70-79. A similarity between "Grace" and *Tale of a Tub* is noted by Mosely (12). Stanislaus Joyce describes in detail the real-life models for the events in "Grace," and reports that the story is also a parody of Dante's *Divine Comedy* (*My Brother's Keeper* [London: Faber and Faber, 1958], 223-226). However, his brother James clearly misled him if he mentioned *only* Dante, who is a relatively unconvincing indebtedness.

7. Newman, 74.

8. Swift even supplies the names for two of Joyce's comforters, *Martin* Cunningham and *Jack* Power, and perhaps for M'Coy as well. Like Fogarty, M'Coy possesses only a surname in "Grace," but Joyce later supplies him with initials: "Just C.P. M'Coy will do" (*Ulysses*, ed. Hans Walter Gabler, et al. [New York: Random House, 1986], 5.176; subsequent abbreviated references are to this edition). We later learn that the first initial stands for "Charley" (*U* 6.884). What can the "P" stand for but Peter?

9. Clive Hart stresses the Viconian significance of "3 + 1" and discusses Joyce's reasons for superimposing this and other numeric configurations on one another (*Structure and Motif in Finnegans Wake* [Northwestern University Press, 1962], 62-63).

10. Viewed with hindsight, the deployment of the five men as a "quincunx" (*D* 172) in "Grace" is startlingly irregular; the central figure should be Kernan, yet here it is M'Coy. I interpret this as proof that Joyce realized only later the pattern's full potential. As Sheldon Brivic argues, the quincunx gains significance at the *conclusion* of an evolution of Joyce's formal experiments (*Joyce the Creator* [Madison: University of Wisconsin Press, 1985], 5).

11. The facts about the Kane/Cunningham biography used here are drawn from Robert M. Adams, *Surface and Symbol: The Consistency of James Joyce's Ulysses* (New York: Oxford University Press, 1962), 62-63.

12. Adams notes that when Matthew Kane drowned in 1904, he left behind five children, his friends subscribed for a fund to send them to school, and his funeral cortege crossed Dublin from southeast to northwest—all details of Dignam's funeral as well.

13. Taking care of his own, Joyce sees to it that John Power, Thomas Kernan, and C.P. M'Coy are also listed as mourners in Dignam's obituary (*U* 16.1257, 1259,1260-1261).

14. This is true of all Joycean texts, but particularly the last one as John Bishop argues in *Joyce's Book of the Dark: Finnegans Wake* (Madison: University of Wisconsin Press, 1986): "[A]s soon as it [*Finnegans Wake*] provides a reader with 'meaning' through the letters and words apparent on the line, it takes the meaning away and leaves him with . . . puzzles to solve . . ." (313).

15. The *Finnegans Wake* portion of this table is based principally on *FW* 140.8-141.7, *FW* II.4 ("Mamalujo"), and on Joyce's letters. The arrangement of the Joycean comforters follows as far as possible the pattern finally arrived at in *Finnegans Wake*. I have followed Glasheen (*Third Census* 66) in connecting Cunningham with Mark.

The Female Word

Kimberly J. Devlin

In Joyce's waking worlds, the attempts by men to envision women writing betray unmistakable limitations in the male imagination. Bloom, for instance, thinks of female letter writers as a potentially intriguing sight, as a visual lure that would easily promote the sale of commercial goods. He has recommended to Wisdom Hely, his former employer in the stationery business, an advertising gimmick featuring "a transparent showcart with two smart girls sitting inside writing letters, copybooks, envelopes, blottingpaper. . . . Smart girls writing something catch the eye at once. Everyone dying to know what she's writing" (*U* 8.131-35). The ad pretends to think female subjectivity ("Everyone dying to know what she's writing"), when in fact it only sees it as a convenient mystery to be commercially exploited; instead of thinking female subjectivity the ad actually negates it, insofar as the women have been reduced to provocative visual objects—they are "smart" only in the sense of being stylishly dressed, not mentally acute. Exactly what they are writing does not matter at all—it is clearly only the image, the simulacrum of female writing, that is needed to make the ad work. When Bloom shares this idea with Stephen in "Ithaca," the young artist transforms it into a sexual drama that perfectly reveals the scotoma frequently afflicting his vision of the female:

> What suggested scene was then constructed by Stephen?
> Solitary hotel in mountain pass. Autumn. Twilight. Fire lit. In dark corner young man seated. Young woman enters. Restless. Solitary. She sits. She goes to window. She stands. She sits. Twilight. She thinks. On solitary hotel paper she writes. She thinks. She writes. She sighs. Wheels and hoofs. She hurries out. He comes from his dark corner. He seizes solitary paper. He holds it towards fire. Twilight. He reads. Solitary.
>
> What?
> In sloping, upright and backhands: Queen's Hotel, Queen's Hotel, Queen's Hotel. Queen's Ho . . .
> (*U* 17.611-20)

Stephen's constructed scenario here is connected to that moment in "Scylla and Charybdis" when he briefly espies a young woman in the library, logically presumed to be Emma Clery: "Is that . . . ? Blueribboned hat . . . ? Idly writing . . . ? What? . . . . Looked . . . ?" (*U* 9.1123). The man in Stephen's sexual drama shares its author's curiosity here about the female text, a text that creates in the male psyche an intellectual lacuna, signified through proliferative ellipses and question marks. In "Ithaca" Stephen fills that lacuna with the most facile of sexist clichés: forced to think female subjectivity in the form of a letter, he can imagine only bored and mindless scribblings.

The imaginative paucity that plagues male attempts in waking life to think a female text disappears in the Wakean nightworld where the female writer returns in varying guises. The dreamer envisions ALP chronicling his past in a personal biography ("her murmoirs" [*FW* 387.34]), a newspaper ("our national rooster's rag" [*FW* 220.22]), or —most consistently—the ominous nightletter ("Her untitled mamafesta memorialising the Mosthighest" [*FW* 104.4]). ALP is linked to the letter in various capacities—as its commissioner, its discoverer, its hider, its interpreter, and as one of its creators. Sandra M. Gilbert and Susan Gubar have argued that because women in patriarchal societies lack "the pen/penis that would enable them to refute one fiction by another, [they] have been historically reduced to mere properties, to characters and images imprisoned in male texts . . . generated solely by male expectations and designs. . . . As a creation 'penned' by man, moreover, woman has been 'penned up' or 'penned in.'"[1] The Wakean female is similarly confined, figuratively the creation of a male dreamer, literally the creation of a male author; but rather than being "pen-less" as well as "penned in," she is imagined writing from her unique vantage point, always perplexing, often subversive.

The opening of the letter chapter (I.5) of *Finnegans Wake* records a psychic effort to get in to the *content* of ALP's text, to penetrate to a site of female writing, to go beyond those limited waking visions of mere sights of female writing. The specific and proliferative titles of ALP's "mamafesta" replace those ellipses marking Stephen's response to Emma's writing, that provocative blank at the center of Bloom's eye-catching ad, or those vacuous doodles in Stephen's elaboration of it. The absence in the waking works returns as superfluous presence in dream, when HCE tries to imagine the female testament that may save or ruin him. Reflecting his deepest hopes and fears, some names for the document augur praise ("*The Best in the West*") or redemption ("*The Augusta Angustissimost for Old Seabeastius' Salvation*"), while others allude to the threat of filial conspiracy ("*How the Buckling Shut at Rush in January*") or scandal in the form of a woman's exposé of a man's sexual performance ("*In My Lord's Bed by One Whore Went Through It*"; "*He Perssed Me Here with the Ardour of a Tonnoburkes*"). Some promise a resolution of the issue of sexual responsibility for the dreamer's fall, albeit with predictably contradictory results: through a reference to *Macbeth* ("*Look to the Lady*"), one title suggests a concession of female guilt, pointing to the wife who spurs her husband on to fatal ambitions, though another blames the man himself ("*Siegfield Follies and or a Gentlehomme's Faut Pas*" [*FW* 104-106]).

Under the transformative logic of the *Wake*, ALP's multiple possible letters become her litter of multiple children (her "superflowvius heirs" [*FW* 526.25-26]) or her multiple gifts, catalogued by the washerwomen in I.8. ALP's seemingly generous distribution of Christmas parcels takes on unsavory overtones when we remember that on a naturalistic level Anna Livia is the anal Liffey of "dear dirty Dublin": her presents may be the trash people have thrown into her which in flood she vengefully returns to them ("like Santa Claus at the cree of the pale and puny . . . with a Christmas box apiece for aisch and iveryone of her childer, the birthday gifts they dreamt they gabe her, the spoiled she fleetly laid at our door! On the matt, by the pourch and inunder the cellar" [*FW* 209.23-30]). Like the tidings offered in her letter, her tidal offerings are ambiguously valenced, possibly injurious or rehabilitating: the river's effluvia may be the source of illness ("a cough and a rattle and wildrose cheeks for poor Piccolina Petite MacFarlane"[*FW* 210.9-10]), but its benigner properties may offer cures ("spas and speranza and symposium's syrup for decayed and blind and gouty Gough" [*FW* 211.24-25]). The contradictory nature of ALP's "gifts," both physical and textual, betray the dreamer's uneasiness about what sorts of medicine—for body and psyche—she has to offer a dying man.

The *Wake* invites us to read this female bearer of gifts and letters as the return of at least two female figures from Joyce's earlier fictions, the first being Maria from "Clay." In her provocative reinterpretation of the short story, Margot Norris has demonstrated how cruelly Maria is treated by those around her, how vulnerable she is in an androcentric culture that marks aged and unmarried women as insignificant and undesirable.[2] In the Wakean dream this devalued female has her revenge when residues of her character resurface in inverted form in the images of ALP as an elderly domestic. In "Clay," for instance, Maria is treated shoddily in the cakeshops she visits; in dream she retaliates as "Hanah Levy, shrewd shroplifter" (*FW* 273.11). The forbearing old woman becomes the plundering outlaw, her yashmak and apron—the visible signs of her sexual oppression—turning into a bandit's mask ("with a naperon for her mask" [*FW* 11.33-34]). Norris argues that when the children insert the saucer of clay into the Hallow Eve's game, they hope Maria will interpret it as "shit" and recoil with embarrassment, betraying her own dirty mind;[3] in the *Wake* ALP in the guise of Kate pays back in kind, offering to others "*Shite*! will you have a plateful?" (*FW* 142.7)—this is the anthropomorphic version of the river's gift to the city of its own detritus and sewage. In dream the elderly woman returns with a malicious and rebellious spirit, implicitly protesting her mistreatment in the waking world of androcentric Dublin.

This female deliverer of suspect litter and letters can also be conceptualized as a dream vision of Molly, who contemplates writing an exposé of Bloom's anomalous impulses in a moment of exasperation with her quirky spouse ("he wanted to milk me into the tea well hes beyond everything . . . if I only could remember the 1 half of the things and write a book out of it the works of Master Poldy yes" [*U* 18.578-80]). In *Finnegans Wake* the dreamer envisions what Bloom would fear if he had access to some of his wife's schemes and suspicions, as he pictures ALP actually embarking upon such a slanderous enterprise, recording for posterity in a succinct and frank letter his questionable transactions with "apple harlottes" and "Honeys [who] wore camelia paints" (*FW* 113.16-17): a dream allusion to a wife who knows that her spouse has been visiting the brothel district. The image of the female writer in the nightworld is frequently not so much a provocative eye-catcher, material for an ad campaign, as it is a paranoiac threat, material for a smear campaign. In her most disturbing guise, ALP appears as "Cowtends Kateclean, the woman with the muckrake" (*FW* 448.10), who in the course of her scavengings in the midden discovers "the fairest sin the sunsaw" (*FW* 11.26). The vision makes sense as a dream transmogrification of a wife in the role of domestic detective, searching her husband's belongings for signs of transgression—a role Molly sounds thoroughly familiar with ("first Ill look at his shirt to see or Ill see if he has that French letter still in his pocketbook I suppose he thinks I dont know deceitful men all their 20 pockets arent enough for their lies" [*U* 18.1234-37]). In the consoling dialectical reversal of this vision, the wife is represented burying or erasing any damaging evidence, or—even better—shredding testimony she never even bothered to write: "she, of the jilldaw's nest who tears up lettereens she never apposed a pen upon" (*FW* 276.6-7).

The compromising version of the letter that appears in I.5 may be a written testimonial derived from the fragmented artifact gleaned from the dump, as Shari Benstock has suggested: "like a good critic, [Biddy/ALP] has come up with a 'reading' of the letter (or some bits of it) that bears little—if any—resemblance to the original document."[4] Because the connection between the two texts remains opaque, we are left to wonder if the hen's report records or constructs HCE's "feebles," dutifully transcribes or scandalously exposes them by filling in the gaps of the initial litterish document. Within the dream's dualistic structure, the female letter is at points the by-product of the male fall, the text constructed from his remains, at others the cause, the text that has reduced him to his shattered state. There are hints that the woman in the act of writing subverts patriarchal origins and critiques patriarchal authority, bringing down the father through her story, forcing him to read his own guilty desires—hence we hear "About that original hen" (*FW* 110.22). In I.5 the dreamer tries to reassure himself that the ominous challenge the female critic/author offers to the father's word, the androcentric logos, is only an unsubstantiated rumor: "No, assuredly, they are not justified, those gloompourers who grouse that letters have never been quite their old selves again since that weird weekday in bleak Janiveer . . . when to the shock of both, Biddy Doran looked at literature" (*FW* 112.23-27). But elsewhere associated with the noxious contents of Pandora's box ("All that and more under one crinoline envelope if you dare to break the porkbarrel seal. No wonder they'd run from her pison plaque" [*FW* 212.22-24]), the message of ALP's letter threatens the welfare of the dreamer, just as the effluvia of the river's litter threaten the welfare of the city. One of Issy's provocative footnotes tellingly represents female writing as transgression, as a violation of a forbidden textual domain: "Dear and I trust in all frivolity I may be pardoned for trespassing but I think I may add hell" (*FW* 270.F3).

ALP's final long letter in Book IV is highly equivocal, oddly schizophrenic. It sounds exculpatory in its attestation that the male has not mistreated the female ("Item, we never were chained to a chair, and, bitem, no widower whother soever followed us about with a fork on Yankskilling Day" [*FW* 618.24-26]) and trusting in its disbelief of HCE's detractors ("What those slimes up the cavern door around you, keenin, (the lies is coming out on them frecklefully) had the shames to suggest can we ever? Never!" [*FW* 615.34-36]). Yet reference to the father's homosexual buggery is compromising, his potential fate inauspicious, and the description of him highly unflattering: "Meaning: one two four. Finckers. Up the hind hose of hizzars. . . . Conan Boyles will pudge the daylives out through him . . . . The big bad old sprowly all uttering foon!" (*FW* 617.2-19). The text also contains a sinister announcement of an impending funeral, clearly the father's own ("His fooneral will sneak pleace by creeps o'clock toosday" [*FW* 617.20-21]). Disturbingly duplicitous, the nightletter is often envisioned as not only a distinctly feminine work of art, but also a by-product of female artfulness: "The letter! The litter! And the soother the bitther! Of eyebrow pencilled, by lipstipple penned. Borrowing a word and begging the question and stealing tinder and slipping like soap" (*FW* 93.24-27). The missive may be evidence of the female's "stealing tinder," of her creation of the document from her foragings, or of her usurpation of the male verbal prerogative, the father's word—evidence, in short, of her stealing his thunder. The form of this female text is protean, elusive ("slipping like soap"), its message often distrustfully censored, elided ("begging the question"). But it frequently also resembles—in part or in total—a letter copied from a writing manual: chattily banal, properly formulaic, totally unoriginal ("borrowing a word"), questionably sincere.

The tension in the female letter becomes clearest in the practice letter Issy writes during the homework lesson. Shari Benstock has pointed out that "as Issy learns to write letters (following the model set forth by her mother's letters) she retraces her father's sin, remembers an act in which she was a complicit witness; her writing is the return of represses, it is the 'trace' of desire."[5] The daughter's role as witness and transcriber, I would emphasize, is a threatening uncertainty, a psychic fear rather than a known actuality. But in contrast to the provocative insinuations of Issy's text, both its format and the gestures she makes as she composes it are conventional, contrived, a series of verbal and physical posturings.

Joyce received from Nora a well-known letter that a friend suggested was taken from a letter-writing book (see *JJII* 167). Ellmann speculates that "the notion of her pathetically adopting so much artifice in the face of his own attempt at sincerity gave Joyce a hint for the amorality of woman, to be invoked later in force" (*JJII* 168). Although this interpretation of Joyce's response may be true, I suspect he also started to see the cultural pressures on women that drive them to such artifice—the pressures to be "proper," to please men in socially endorsed forms. In "Penelope," after all, Joyce represents Molly recalling how during courtship she had to fake a sort of mental virginity, feeling socially compelled to say the correct things in response to Bloom's queries about the level of her sexual knowledge: "he wrote me that letter with all those words in it . . . after when we met asking me have I offended you . . . and if I knew what it meant of course I had to say no for form sake dont understand you I said" (*U* 18.318-25). (This female confession of feigned verbal ignorance may call into question the authencity of Martha Clifford's coy request, "Please tell me what is the real meaning of that word?" [*U* 5.245-46].) Envisioning the female letter in the dream, HCE often reads the subtext beneath the prescribed formalities—the slurs, the desires, the sinister prophecies, the damaging revelations (one of which has a distinctly Mollyesque ring to it—he "kissists my exits" [*FW* 280.27]). Alternately conventional and challenging, respectful and irreverent ("Dear. And we go on to Dirtdump. Reverend. May we add majesty? [*FW* 615.12-13]), the hybrid female nightletter reflects the dreamer's ambivalence towards the writing woman, his uncertainty as to what he would like to hear—polite formalities, potentially duplicitous, or blunt truths, potentially disquieting.

In the final monologue of the dream, HCE imagines ALP as the authoress of two letters, one written on his behalf, the other for herself. The first has been crafted with great care and labor and comes from across the sea, "the site of salvocean" (*FW* 623.29), with a promise of redemption. This letter is a version of the flattering "murmoirs" HCE dreams his wife will write about him after his death: "The arzurian deeps o'er his humbodumbones sweeps. And his widdy the giddy is wreathing her murmoirs as her gracest triput to the Grocery Trader's Manthly. Mind mand gunfree by Gladeys Rayburn!" (*FW* 387.32-35). The second more personal document records ALP's *own* desires and violates androcentric law. She has buried this letter at the sound of the thunder, the signifier of patriarchal interdiction, but thinks that some day the lost transcript of her hopes will return: "When the waves give up yours the soil may for me.

Sometime then, somewhere there, I wrote me hopes and buried the page when I heard Thy voice, ruddery dunner" (*FW* 624.3-5). This final bifurcation of ALP's letter along gender lines hints that female writing within androcentric structures is inevitably a double document, containing both an official and repressed text: the former speaks the language of male desire, telling the father what he might like to hear, while the latter tells a different story, one that is at odds with patriarchal imperatives and concerns—or perhaps has nothing to do with them at all. This dualistic letter mentioned within the final monologue is a miniature of the monologue as a whole, for ALP's speech is indeed a double document, uttered in conflicting tongues as it were.[6]

Joyce's waking fictions often record a male resentment of female discourse, an implicit desire to censor it, a preference for the voiceless female visual object seen most patently in an early portrait of the artist: "Stephen sat down beside one of the daughters and, while admiring the rural comeliness of her features, waited quietly for her first word which, he knew, would destroy his satisfaction" (*SH* 46). When women are permitted to speak, are actively sought out as participants in ostensible dialogues, males try to control what they say. Martha Clifford's missive, for instance, can be viewed as the perverse counterpart of the proper copybook letter, insofar as much of her writing sounds prescribed, artificial. Bloom clearly attempts to control the female voice, manipulating his correspondent into uttering the language of his particular masochistic brand of male desire. Bloom's need to be the "dictator" of female psyche and speech resurfaces in his own recollection of an encounter with a prostitute ("Girl in Meath street that night. All the dirty things I made her say. All wrong of course. My arks she called it" [*U* 13.867-69]) and in Molly's disgruntled account of a sex game he makes her play, during which she is asked to speak the words that will allow her husband to cuckold himself and to turn her into a whore ("who is in your mind now tell me who are you thinking of who is it tell me his name who tell me who the german Emperor is it yes imagine Im him think of him can you feel him trying to make a whore of me what he never will" [*U* 18.94-97]). In the *Wake* this urge to control the female word at least partially disappears: in the irrepressible and often subversive footnotes of Issy; in the spontaneous singing, chattering, and laughing of ALP; and in the proliferative and compromising discourse of the ordinarily marginalized washerwomen, who imitate the rhetorical mode of the "gossipaceous" riverwoman (*FW* 195.4) they describe.

But male subjects in Joyce's waking and night worlds alike are plagued by a recurrent sense that women have access to an "other" language, often audibly silent, a language comprehensible only to other females and implicitly threatening to the excluded—and effectively deaf—male listener. Bloom feels that Molly and Milly understand and communicate with each other in elusive and perhaps nonverbal ways—through "a preestablished natural comprehension in incomprehension" (*U* 17.2289-90). In the margins of the nightlesson, Issy and her addressee are glossed as "*Procne, Philomela*" (*FW* 307L), the sisters who subvert the censoring powers of the male tyrant by inventing an alternative mode of discourse—the visual text of weaving. Even the imagined voice of ALP, the vehicle for one of the clearest speeches in the dream, is occasionally marked as the incomprehensible, as a string of mere fragments of sense ("With lipth she lithpeth to him all to time of thuch on thuch and thow on thow. She he she ho she ha to la. Hairfluke, if he could bad twig her!" [*FW* 23.23-25]). Joyce adumbrates—almost as a present absence, as it were—a linguistic space beyond male discourse; in his representations of men who try to listen to this alternative female language but still fail to understand totally what they hear, he inscribes the potential limits to his own auditory forays into that terrain.

Notes

1. Sandra M. Gilbert and Susan Gubar, *The Madwoman in the Attic: The Woman Writer and the Nineteenth Century Literary Imagination* (New Haven: Yale University Press, 1979), 12-13.

2. Margot Norris, "Narration under a Blindfold: Reading Joyce's 'Clay,'" *PMLA* 102 (March 1987): 206-215.

3. Norris, "Narration," 212.

4. Shari Benstock, "The Genuine Christine: Psychodynamics of Issy," in *Women in Joyce*, eds. Suzette Henke and Elaine Unkeless (Urbana: University of Illinois Press, 1982), 185.

5. Shari Benstock, "The Letter of the Law: *La Carte Postale* in *Finnegans Wake*," *Philological Quarterly* 63 (1984):176.

6. See my essay "ALP's Final Monologue in *Finnegans Wake*: The Dialectical Logic of Joyce's Dream Text," in *Coping with Joyce: Essays from the Copenhagen Symposium*, eds. Morris Beja and Shari Benstock (Columbus: Ohio State University Press, 1989), 232-247.

PART III: PERFORMANCE

"Group drinkards maaks grope thinkards or how reads rotary" (*FW* 312.31):

Finnegans Wake and the Group Reading Experience

David Borodin

I am reading [*Finnegans Wake*] now, and, though I meet many allusions, the book is very high over my head. A friend here (a painter) and I often read it (or try to) together; and I, it is fair to say, am better than he, and lead him into many a laugh and into the midst of wander and wonderland. It is an amazing book; and hardly to be understood in a year, much less in a day.

So wrote Sean O'Casey to James Joyce in May of 1939, within only a month of the publication of *Finnegans Wake*.[1] And here we see in its infancy a tradition of reading Joyce's great last book that was gradually to be embraced the world over: the custom of reading *Finnegans Wake* communally.

The idea of sitting around in a group—be it of two or twenty—to read a work of prose fiction is perhaps an uncommon one, but a book that so stubbornly resists being read from any one perspective is probably one best read from a multitude of perspectives. And a good way of sustaining a plurality of views in the reading of *Finnegans Wake* is to read the book in a group.

One precedent for reading the *Wake* communally is the practice sometimes accorded to the reading of religious texts, namely group monastic readings of scripture in the Middle Ages. It may be appropriate that the profane work which probably comes closest to continuing this tradition is *Finnegans Wake*, a work apparently conceived of, modeled on, and developed as a kind of surrogate for the sacred scripture. The *Wake* is permeated with references to the world's great religious texts, and even identifies itself with a religious manuscript: *The Book of Kells*. James Atherton, in *The Books at the Wake*, points to Joyce's romantic conception of himself as artist-God as the very basis of *Finnegans Wake*:

There was a medieval theory that God composed two scriptures: the first was the universe which he created after having conceived the idea of it complete and flawless in his mind; the second was the Holy Bible. What Joyce is attempting in *Finnegans Wake* is nothing less than to create a third scripture, the sacred book of the night, revealing the microcosm which he had already conceived in *his* mind. And as the phenomenal universe is built upon certain fundamental laws which it is the task of science and philosophy to discover, so the microcosm of *Finnegans Wake* is constructed according to certain fundamental axioms for which Joyce is careful to provide clues, but which it is the task of his readers to discover for themselves.[2]

Finnegans Wake is bigger than all of our attempts to reduce it. Just when we think we have the key to some secret storeroom of *Wake* explication, we arrive only to find that it had been open for us all along, and its shelves lined with fresh copies of the *Wake*. Yet, many long-term readers find that their eyes do eventually adjust (somewhat) to the dark, and that their ears, too, have been sensitized by the climb up Joyce's tower of babble. Today, half a century after the publication of *Finnegans Wake*, it is not uncommon to find groups of readers convening on a regular basis in cities throughout the world—groups of academics and amateurs alike with no more of an agenda than to read aloud, ponder, discuss, and enjoy Joyce's great enigma.

The Philadelphia *Wake* Circle is an example of a community of readers that has allowed the demands of reading Joyce to subject us to the ritual of regular meetings. This group was begun by Richard Beckman in the early 1970s and—allowing for a couple of interruptions—has been reading the *Wake* communally ever since. However, the group has changed gradually through the years. Participants come and go, bringing and taking with them an eclectic range of expertise in the fields of literature, language, philosophy, history, music, and the visual arts. If we were to choose as our agenda the goal of never finishing the book, we would not be selecting a difficult one. All we would have to do is read the *Wake* from morning till night for the rest of our lives and we would easily not finish it. Even if we were to read rapidly enough to rearrive on page 3 every year or two, we would still find a new book before us each time in light of all that we have lived and learned (and forgotten) in the meanwhile. But at such a fast clip the landscape goes by us in a blur; and there are countless stones there waiting to be turned over.

Our group approach, therefore, has been that of a "close" reading, a term now meaning different things to different people, but used here in its more traditional sense to suggest a slow, careful reading that would permit us to stop for what we stumble on. At a maintained cruising speed of about a half a page per three-hour session, we have allowed ourselves the opportunity for a word-by-word scrutiny that can often reveal much about the book's overall design. One often finds the biggest concepts mirrored in the smallest details. Of course, the trouble with the world-in-a-grain-of-sand approach is the relatively small stretch of beach one has time to examine in an afternoon. And since the intricate architecture of the book emerges only gradually through repetition—while informing the reading of the smallest details all along—it might be ventured that anyone not planning on living beyond, say, a century might miss a great deal of the book's special beauty. The practical solution, therefore, appears to be the augmentation of our close-up group reading with that of the wide-angle variety on our own (that is, concurrently reading the book at two different speeds) so that we may ultimately attempt to keep one eye focused on the road while the other surveys the vast landscape before us.

I. "the beast of boredom, common sense"[3]

Before we discuss the problems inherent in group readings of *Finnegans Wake* it may be helpful to prepare by taking a brief look at some of the problems faced by a single reader of this book. After spending a third of our lives unconsciously exploring the strange terrain of sleep, what do we do now when we wake to find it in our reading material as well?   How do we recapture, consciously, the frame of mind that safely steered us, nightly, past the wandering rocks of rational thought?   We spent our childhood learning to give up the remnants of this consciousness in favor of a practical taste for facts, and have consequently allowed the banal encumbrances of time, space, movement, gravity, and the belief in progress to blunt our senses.

Enter James Augustine Joyce, Jesuit-trained apostate, worshipful iconoclast, wordman, wordlover, drawer of words, who devoted his life to the invigoration of the English language before finally putting it to sleep. For, if the dark, metaphoric world of man's unconscious is ever to be surveyed in language, it is evidently not to be done with words of concrete, but with words as fluid and changeable as their subject. Under Joyce's direction, word becomes "woid" (*FW* 378.29) in an exhilarating assault on our complacent trust in words as factual correlation. No longer can we expect to see words as the sharp-edged blocks of graven images they largely have been for us before. Joyce put them to sleep for their relative resistance to an essential ingredient of the imagination: *ambiguity*. Michael Patrick Gillespie addresses Joyce's use of ambiguity quite succintly:

> To counteract the impulses of Enlightenment empiricism which still influence our response to experience, Joyce urges the acknowledgment and even the pursuit of ambiguity as a means of opening one's consciousness to the mystery inherent in art. Ultimately in *Finnegans Wake* the problem does not turn upon a resolution of contraries but upon a reconciliation with them.[4]

Ambiguity is an essential aspect of the dreaming mind, both in sleep, and in the conscious imagination. We turn to sleep for what is probably our most effective release from the relentless, hard-edged confines of factual certainty. The ambiguity inherent in the condensation and displacement phenomena of the dreamwork provides an escape from the rigid particularity of conscious perception.[5] We have consciously sought daytime entrance to this refuge via myth, art, and imagination; though even here we often find ourselves trapped in the tyrannical clutches of certainty. Consider how we search through notebooks, drafts, sketches, and letters for insights into a work of art, often finding less about the finished work of art there than about the notebooks, drafts, sketches, and letters.

Understandably, it is rather disconcerting, after years of trained submission to the despotic authority of fact to read in *Finnegans Wake* what we have all nightly understood: that 1 + 1 is sometimes 3. To read the *Wake*, therefore, we probably should learn first to unread a few thousand years of literature. Hugh Kenner aptly described for us our sleep at Joyce's *Wake* when he declared: "Joyce worked seventeen years to push [*Finnegans Wake*] away from 'meaning' adrift into language; nothing is to be gained by trying to push it back."[6]

We can't say that we weren't warned. We are probably given everything we need to know about the *Wake* right in the text itself. If the universe of *Finnegans Wake* operates according to its own principles (as any good universe should), it also comes complete with the owner's manual of operating instructions dispersed throughout its pages: "Thus the unfacts, did we possess them, are too imprecisely few to warrent our certitude" (*FW* 57.16-17); "What can't be coded can be decorded if an ear aye sieze what no eye ere grieved for" (*FW* 482.34-36). Such suggestions should be expected in a book predicated on the "gossiple" (*FW* 38.23) truth, where the fine line between the grapevine and the history book is usually blurred or absent. Conversely, however, we are warned against reading sheer nonsense out of this nonsense. Just when we think we're looking at a mere riot of blots and blurs and bars and balls and hoops and wriggles we read, "No, so holp me Petault, it is not a miseffectual whyacinthinous riot of blots and blurs and bars and balls and hoops and wriggles and juxtaposed jottings linked by spurts of speed: it only looks as like it as damn it" (*FW* 118.28-31).

Anyone who has followed Joyce through the *Ulysses* episodes of "Cyclops," "Nausicaa," and "Eumaeus" knows better than to trust implicitly the objectivity and accuracy of the narrational voice. But, in our attempts to see through their prejudices and incompetence, we run the risk of holding out for an ideally knowable ("real") story line behind the language of its presentation, or, in other words, of looking for a different book beneath its pages.[7]

This dilemma is compounded ten-fold in the *Wake*, where we don't even usually know who's doing the talking, or to whom, or about whom (let alone what is being said!). In a book where a five-member suburban Dublin family permutates into endless social configurations encompassing all of mankind, and where the texture appears modeled on the sound (and consequence) of gossip, it might be safe to conclude that *Finnegans Wake* is the one book that cannot (must not) allow clear traditional distinctions between the roles of the characters, the reader, and the writer. Therefore, the question of how much authority we should invest in these supposed authorial reader-promptings will presumably remain debatable.

In light of the infamous reading dangers inherent in Joyce's "*worldrenownced*" (*FW* 341.19) "farced epistol to the hibruws" (*FW* 228.33-34), we may be tempted to ask the obvious question: just how much abuse is a reader expected to endure? The answer to this question is probably to be found in a closer examination of the question. Is there any reason to insist that Joyce would have really envisioned such a book being read by a single reader? Have you ever been the sole participant at a wake? Would not a sole participant at a wake be the corpse itself?[8] In the lookingglass world of Wakean identity we might just as well assume that the reader is the dreamer who dreams of the writer dreaming our wake.

A quick look at the history of *Finnegans Wake* from its evolution as *Work in Progress* through the publication and critical reception of the finished work might provide a clue as to just how many people constitute a reader of a text like this. Let us begin with the creator himself. Joyce masterminded a group effort to defend *Work in Progress* with the publication of *Our Exagmination round His Factification for Incamination of Work in Progress*. This book of essays was published in May 1929, long before any one reader on his or her could have been expected to digest the serially published segments of the then unfinished work. Evidently predicated on the belief in the power of numbers, this group of twelve "disciples" was directed by Joyce like a team of specialists attacking a newly discovered scientific phenomenon, and might enjoy a distinction as the primal ancestor of our modern *Finnegans Wake* reading groups. That he paid them little tribute in the finished work—"Imagine the twelve deaferended dumbbawls of the whowl abovebeugled to be the contonuation through regeneration of the urutteration of the word in pregross" (*FW* 284.18-22)—should not discourage us from divining Joyce's approval of the group effort method. That was perhaps just his way of saying thank you.

Just a couple of months after the publication of *Our Exagmination*, Joyce gave another hint of a company policy toward the *Wake* when he suggested that the book might need to be finished by someone else. His eyesight quickly diminishing along with the patience of his readers, a dispirited Joyce, still obsessed with the importance of his mission, formally proposed that his countryman James Stephens oversee completion of the book if and when it became necessary. As we know, it didn't, but Joyce even went so far as to contemplate the aesthetic value of their combined initials, *JJ* and *S*, under the title of the book. Such a remarkable gesture might suggest a belief in the author as medium rather than creator—where the writer's job is only to make visible a work that was here among us all along.

Already by 1940—only a year after the *Wake*'s publication—there emerged an example of the *Finnegans Wake* reading group as we know it today when William York Tindall of Columbia University gathered together a small group of graduate students to pursue the *Wake*. Though Tindall eventually took up reading the book on his own as well as in the group, he believed that the pooled resources of varied learning and languages would go further than any one individual might. And nearly thirty years later, in the introduction to his 1969 *A Reader's Guide to Finnegans Wake*, Tindall acknowledged his indebtedness to this group effort for much of what he learned about the book, and eventually published.[9]

In 1962 another concentrated, long-term, group effort at surviving the *Wake* appeared with the publication of *A Wake Newslitter*. This journal was founded to provide an arena for the quick exchange of ideas throughout the Wakean world, and opened its premier issue of March 1962 with the understatement: "*Finnegans Wake* needs to be read communally." And like a Wakean motif this battle cry has been heard, in various guises, echoing from the various parts of the known world. The following year Clive Hart wrote these words again (though never too often) in the introduction to that most primary of secondary works on the *Wake*, *A Concordance to Finnegans Wake*, adding the modest appraisal: "I doubt whether any one person can ever see enough of Joyce's linguistic panorama."[10]

But we could just as easily justify the necessity of group reading using the opposite approach from that above. It could be argued that the only thing more limiting to an individual's grasp of the *Wake* than the inevitable limits to one's erudition is one's inevitable erudition. In such a book as *Finnegans Wake*, where world literature, history, philosophy, art, and science constitute the very fabric of the text, it is indeed impossible to ride one's hobby horse off into the proverbial sunset, never to be heard from again (excepting, of course, in an occasional *James Joyce Quarterly* article). Joyce may have used the *Encyclopedia Britannica*, 11th edition, as a source book for the *Wake*, but he did choose to leave a few things out. We might go so far, then, as to see the communal reading as a sort of group insurance, where the individual readers are protected from their own worst enemies: themselves. The collective conscience of the group usually has the effect of gently curbing excesses, and constraining even the most exuberant imaginations to soar within the Wakean universe. We all come to the *Wake* with our own agendas, whether we like to admit it or not. Even the least eventful of reading groups are conspicuous by the gentle whir of axes grinding. This is probably nothing so unnatural in the context of a book that warns us to use "The soft side of the axe!" (*FW* 433.28).

Hugh Kenner once described *Finnegans Wake* as "a multiplicity of voices being misapprehended by a collectivity of ears."[11] In my experience, this would also serve as an excellent description of almost any communal reading of the book.

The peculiar texture of the writing translates easily into the experience of reading it together. To sit among a circle of intent *Wake* readers of various backgrounds, pondering the possible significance(s) of an impossible passage is often like attempting to keep your story straight on a telephone party line.

Those who have never tasted the pleasures of a group reading may turn to *The Finnegans Wake Experience*,[12] where Roland McHugh includes a transcribed tape recording of the "European Finnegans Wake Study Group" of 1970/71. However, something of the same experience can be gotten simply by opening up a copy of his *Annotations to Finnegans Wake*.[13] As a compilation of margin jottings from the pens of various expert readers, the *Annotations* lives up to its name. It is a bewildering array of "once current puns, quashed quotatoes, [and] messes of mottage" (*FW* 183.22-23) dragged into daylight, labelled, and keyed to a text which isn't there. These strange, jumbled pages take on the look of a palimpsest of Joyce's book—a fitting commentary on a book that looks in some ways like a palimpsest of the *Encyclopedia Britannica*, 11th edition! Or maybe they resemble more the heaps of unusable, wide-awake language that Joyce discarded—arranged here like the tagged and numbered harvest of an archeological dig. The important factor concerning these collected readings is their inability to coalesce into a focused, privileged reading. Here in the lap of ambiguity we can find something of the real atmosphere of the group reading—allowing, that is, for a conspicuous telegraphic simplicity. You see, to read the *Annotations* is to witness, not to participate; and it is well known that *Finnegans Wake* is not a spectator sport. For those used to the luxury of reading with real people, the effect of reading the *Annotations* can be more like peering over various shoulders than hearing over various views. There can be something disconcerting in forfeiting the opportunity of staring an Annotator in the eyes while weighing his or her contribution, in that the source and context of a comment often helps gauge the grain of salt needed. On the other hand, a danger inherent in group reading is learning to perfect the fine art of tuning out, a survival tactic acquired early in childhood wherein opinions from unauthorized sources are blocked by the static of one's own ideas.

Perhaps the way to have the best of both proverbial worlds in this case is simply to enter the group session with the *Annotations* tucked under your arm. It is not unknown for readers to record their valued findings directly into the pages of the *Annotations*. This practice saves the trouble of bringing the mountain to Mahomet, and tends to keep the *Annotations* the fluid, everchanging book that any secondary work to a text like the *Wake* must be. There are still many blank areas along these closely-printed pages; the inevitable question arises as to "what happens when I fill them?" (i.e. when there is no room for more; not when there is no more to room). One of the primary dangers of using a book like the *Annotations* is that of inadvertently falling victim, even momentarily, to an unqualified belief in that which is found in print. It is somehow easier to trust the impersonal upper and lower case of the printed page than that which is personally recorded in the "scribblative" (*FW* 189.10) case. If we don't believe everything we read in *Finnegans Wake*, why should we be expected to in the *Annotations*? We will all presumably find curiosities, contradictions, and even outright errors in this book (as we do in that great Ur-book for it—*Finnegans Wake*). However, this book has been found by many to be a helpful tool, and has been used by our group as a point of departure in our conference presentations so that the audience may be spared the boredom of being present for the unearthing of old findings.

II. "two or three philadelphians" (*FW* 572.25)

The 1988 Venice Symposium was the Philadelphia *Wake* Circle's third opportunity to bring an old Philadelphia *Wake* tradition before the people.[14] The only thing consciously planned about its presentation was the choice of the passage to be read and the avoidance of anything consciously planned. The goal was not a concert piece of polished explication (anyone can do that!), but rather an unrehearsed example of just what goes on at home. Its members came equipped with their own "readings" of the assigned passage and a necessary willingness to sacrifice their great ideas to the omnivorous god of group (mis)interpretation. A straight line of observation often gets bent by our circle into a convolution not unlike the narrative structure of the *Wake* itself. The book really comes alive at these readings, and we're often left with the strangely satisfying sensation of having fully digested an untouched meal.

Due to the peculiarly fluid, elusive nature of this mode of idea-exchange, any attempt at a precise reconstruction of Muta and Juva in Venice would probably end up reading not unlike the Muta and Juva of pages 609-610. Notetaking at a session like this could be safely compared to bailing out a sinking rowboat with a spoon. In the heat of explication I confidently committed cryptic messages to my margins which, next morning, refused to yield their secrets to me. For example: next to "fundementially theosophagusted" on the first line of page 610 I was luckily able to reconstruct the words, "theological stomach problems=Luther/Berkeley-M." Nice, but who's "M?" M̲artha Davis . . . M̲ike O'Shea? . . . M̲ort Levitt? . . . Tim M̲artin? . . . me? . . . M̲uta? . . . maybe? . . . MERDE! In light of a few minor technical difficulties, therefore, I will concentrate on evoking the spirit of the session at the expense of the whosaidwhatwhenishness of it, and, simply introduce all contributions with an identifying "R" for reader or "A" for audience.

SILENCE

Act drop. Stand by! Blinders! Curtain up. Juice, please! Foots! (*FW* 501.6-7)

Shoot (*FW* 610.33)

R.1: Where's Shoot?

R.2: What Shoot?

R.1: That Shoot . . . there, at the end!

R.2: That's the beginning . . .

R.1: What . . . ?

R.2:   . . . of the next section!

R.1:   No, that's the last word of this one . . . supportable, I believe, on several grounds. First of all I think of *Hamlet*. In a dialogue between two people pondering the significance of cloud formations, I find it difficult not to think of Hamlet and Polonius', "Do you see yonder cloud that's almost in shape of a camel?" "By th' mass and 'tis—like a camel indeed," etc. Well, I'll get to that in a second, but I'd like to point out that *Hamlet* ends on the word "shoot": Fortinbras', "Go, bid the soldiers shoot." Now, we know how pervasive is the presence of Shakespeare in the *Wake*, and we can see it behind this very passage; I would like to argue that Shoot belongs here as an ending to our passage . . .

R.2:   But, R.1, "Shoot" sounds very much like a film director's order to a cameraman, and suggests to me the beginning of something, not the end.

R.1:   Right, the signal to start filming/reporting the confrontation between Patrick and the Archdruid that follows this. I think that's true as well . . . but I want to pursue the Hamlet theme a moment more. I find the image of these two watching smoke clouds to be comparable to Hamlet and Polonius except where they seem here to be seeing in them some sort of archetypal contenders . . . like the contenders who will soon confront each other in our next passage.

R.3:   You know, I cannot help listening to Joyce quite literally here when he calls for "puffs" of smoke that "roll out of the lord." Someone, years ago, observed a theme of papal conclave in the *Wake*, at the same time citing about a dozen references throughout the book to Pope Celestine I. Now, Celestine died in 432, the year of Patrick's rearrival in Ireland. A new pope had to be elected, as happened that year with the election of Sixtus III. So, maybe the smoke that Muta and Juva observe is, on one level at least, the smoke rising in the square from the stove pipe of the Vatican chapel during conclave. The current tradition allows the populace assembled out in the piazza to learn of the success of a majority vote by the burning of the voting papers with dry straw, making a cloud of white smoke (as opposed to the black smoke made by the addition of wet straw, signalling a failure of majority vote). Now, whether or not this tradition goes back very far does not, in my opinion, damage the beauty of the metaphor. And as proof of Joyce's conscious use of the theme, look at line 15 of page 100 where "the infallible spike of smoke's jutstiff punctual" announces the mysterious resurrection of the disappeared HCE. In my opinion, it looks like the smoke clouds which Muta and Juva see are ultimately a signal of the spiritual future of Ireland. And this reading would enable us to view this entire dialogue as a foretelling of the awakening of the sleeper by way of a metaphor of an Ireland awakening from the drugged sleep of druidic mysticism.

R.1:   Yes, "infallible spikes of smoke's jutstiff" certainly sounds papal . . .

R.4:   But there is also the sense of smoke rising from the Earwicker house as breakfast is prepared, as has been observed . . .

R.1: I don't see that . . . do the rest of you see a breakfast going on here? I've had trouble with that reading.

R.4: Well, maybe Muta is reprimanding against smoking before breakfast.

R.2: Yes, it used to be that you couldn't have breakfast before going to communion.

R.5: We don't know whether these two see steam, clouds or smoke, really. And it seems to me that there are different kinds of smoke. There's smoking as in "may I smoke?"; and then there's smoking as in "you may burn for all I care!" Perhaps the use is ambiguous here.

R.1: But in any case, this smoking is used by Joyce throughout the *Wake* . . . by way of the pipe and the cigar . . . as a symbol of arrogance and pride . . . as a symbol of authority . . . of God.

R.4: But this might be any number of gods. "Old Head of Kettle" might just as well be the Buddha . . . head in clouds . . .

R.1: Right . . .

R.4: But it is followed by language suggesting the Eddas and Scandinavian mythology. Maybe a plurality of gods is intended here to suggest that particular religions come and go, but Ireland remains . . . like the phoenix arising from the ashes, or Quinet's flowers surviving the destruction of civilizations.

R.5: Yes, when Laoghaire bets on which god will win out, he doesn't take any chances, and so bets on all of them!

R.1: As far as I can see, Juva's idea of God—Joyce's for that matter—is almost always expressed anatomically or meteorologically. Here it is the latter, with the suggestion of volcanic eruption.

R.6: Yes, don't forget that Jove was associated with emanations from the sky.

R.1: Good, yes, I see a lot of Jove or Jupiter here. And, while I'm on the subject, the spirit of Jupiter is conjured up on line 30 with "An I could peecieve . . ." when we remember Aristophanes' crack about rain being caused by Jupiter peeing through a sieve.

A.1: Yes, that's echoed on page 451, line 36 with Jupiter, the god of rain, given to us as "shoepisser pluvious."

R.1: Nice!

R.3: Before I forget this, I'd like to backtrack, briefly, to the interesting comment before about Juva's meteorological expression of god, and the godlike quality of the volcano image. The Eddic flavor of Muta's "He odda be thorly . . ." seems to me to confirm this connection, in that the Völuspà describes the end of the world—the wrath of God—in terms curiously close to contemporary accounts of the eruption of Mt. Hekla.

R.7: Yes, and in reference to these issues as issues of authority, I'd like to point out the Shem/Shaun correspondence with Muta and Juva: Muta, like Shem, seems to be the one asking the questions, while Juva, like Shaun, remains the authoritarian. It seems that the creative ones are those who ask the questions. But this correlation with Shem and Shaun I find particularly interesting. Line 30 of page 609 has Muta declare, "An I could peecieve. . . ." Now, if we read the "an" as a Shakespearean "if" and the "I" as an "eye," modifying the meaning to, "If an eye could perceive . . .," we get the sense of one possible self ("an I"), and a description of the process of perception . . . an interaction of two eyes—Muta and Juva/Shem and Shaun—two lobes of the one brain . . .

R.1: But aren't you actually forcing Muta and Juva to conspire to form one perception like some sort of friendly, cooperative effort? They seem, rather to be continually at each other's throats. I see this rather as a struggle for the paternal inheritance—in this case Laoghaire's—which is an underlying theme in the brother confrontations.

R.4: But Laoghaire stands above the two rival halves, observing them as a whole . . .

R.3: Rivalry leads to overthrow, which might be relevant to the possibly prophetic aspect of the smoke—so, do you mind if we go back to the smoke? One aspect we haven't touched on yet that I find essential to this passage—as well as to the book—is that of Sechseläuten, the Zurich spring fertility rite that Joyce was so interested in. This ceremony—"the ringing of six o'clock"—celebrates the burial of winter with a ritual burning of a huge stuffed white cotton dummy representing the winter demon, whose limbs blow off one by one as the implanted firecrackers ignite. It's a potent image for the *Wake*, encompassing the central themes of the overthrow of the father, and the dismemberment of Osiris. If we skip ahead a second to line 14 of page 610, we see a permutation of the word when we read "Skulkasloot!" For me the significance is clear when we view Muta and Juva as shadow extensions of Shem and Shaun: Muta and Juva watch the smoke of a burning dummy as the Earwicker sons watch the overthrow of the father.

A.2: Yes, all very interesting, but aren't we leaving out a few of the obvious readings? For instance, Muta's statement about smoking before the high host seems to me as well a reference to the lack of respect involved in [a Britisher] smoking before the high (royal) *toast* (i.e., before the health of the King or Queen has been drunk to).

R.6: Or, a reference to smoking before the raised Eucharist (i.e., in church). Also something one does not do.

R.3: But it seems to me primarily referring to Patrick's disrespectful lighting of the paschal lamp before King Laoghaire, his *host*. And, it seems clear that Joyce would have known that one of the chief differences in Patrick's day between the Roman and Celtic rituals was the calculation of Easter which changed in Rome in 463 from the old Roman/Jewish cycle of 84 years to 532 years. Since the Irish did not adopt this method until about two centuries after Patrick, Joyce might just be suggesting that the invader is brazen enough to celebrate Easter before his host, maybe long before. And this reminds me, by the way . . . the other major difference between the Roman and Celtic ritual at that time may shed some light on 610.11-13, where Laoghaire has evidently bet half his crown on Patrick, and the other half on the Archdruid. Since the word "crown" can refer to a pate as well as a coin, it is not unlikely that Joyce was also making a reference to the distinctly different types of tonsure worn by Roman and Celtic priests. As opposed to the coronal tonsure of Rome, the Celts drew a line from ear to ear and shaved half their head. And since the Greek church had a tonsure different from either of the two, he may have had reason to distinguish the "Generalissimo" as "Eurasian." At any rate, for me the meaning is clear: the identification of East and West as hostile contenders for an inheritance is made synonomous with the gambling theme that ultimately underlies, symbolically, the spiritual fate of Ireland. Joyce uses the gambling/horserace motifs as tools of deflation here.

A.1: But before we leave the smoke alone, I would like to bring to your attention a meaning I think the author of *Ulysses* was sure to have thought of: when Odysseus is first seen in book VI of the *Odyssey*, he is at the end of Calypso island, looking for smoke coming from his home.

Many R's and Several A's: Ahh!

III. "No Sturm. No Drang." (*FW* 300.L2)

The group went on in this manner, line by line, peeling back layer after layer of meaning until there was nothing but the next meeting to look forward to. Plans were made immediately upon the closing of the session for a "closer" reading of the passage back in Philadelphia.

But, as the title of this essay suggests, there is more to the reading group experience than the mere exchange of great ideas. "Group drinkards maaks grope thinkards . . ." (*FW* 312.31) may or may not be true, but it does hint at the similarities between Joyce's *Wake* and any other Irishman's wake, where drink flows freely and death is the life of the party. They are each a living relic of the great Celtic traditions of oral transmission and drinking together. There is an intense life throbbing through these pages, and if you pay close attention, you might notice the celebrants at Joyce's *Wake* demanding to be heard aloud: "Loud, hear us!" (*FW* 258.25). For, as in any celebration, the *Wake* is better when enjoyed aloud—when the sounds evoke sense that the eye is not looking for. Joyce's prose behaves more like poetry than most of that which we are accustomed to calling prose, and group readings of the *Wake* tend to keep alive this necessary sense of sound.

In an essay in the 25th Anniversary collection of *Wake* critical essays, *Twelve and a Tilly*, J. Mitchell Morse describes the group reading experience in a manner just as relevant 25 years later:

> For reading *Finnegans Wake* is a collective enterprise
> of no ordinary kind: what takes place is no mere

quantitative gathering and mechanical assembling of parts into larger units, but a blending of objective and subjective elements—a kind of communion—in which one person's information calls up from another's subconscious an inference that validates the conjecture of a third. Joyce has revived the magical function of the old bards and shamans, in what by convention we consider a most unlikely place, the seminar room. If it should suddenly begin to rain in the room, I suppose we would all be surprised; still it just might. Certainly we generate something in the nature of a ritual atmosphere.[15]

And, Professor Morse concludes his essay with the observation, "In the reading of *Finnegans Wake*, everybody teaches everybody else."

Of course, no one type of reading gives us the whole book, and group members usually want (need) to read the book on their own as well as in the group. Therefore, we should not look at this book as an experience prescribed by membership requirements. But, no matter which way we choose to tunnel into the mighty mountain of the *Wake*—be it together or alone—we would do well to stop and read the warning engraved over the entrance in the creator's own consoling words: "It is night. It is dark. You can hardly see. You sense rather."[16]

Notes

1. Richard Ellmann, ed., *Letters of James Joyce*, vols. 2 and 3 (New York: Viking Press, 1966), Vol. 3, 442. O'Casey's letter, dated 30 May 1939, was written to Joyce on the occasion of an announcement of the publication of *Finnegans Wake* in the *Irish Times*, wherein O'Casey was credited with its authorship. According to Ellmann, neither of the writers was fully persuaded that this was an accidental misprint, and not some prank. O'Casey's continued enthusiasm for *Finnegans Wake* is well documented in letters of the 1940s and 1950s. See *The Letters of Sean O'Casey*, David Krause, ed., 2 vols. (New York: Macmillan, 1975; 1980).

2. James S. Atherton, *The Books at the Wake* (London: Faber and Faber, 1959), 28. Also see Sheldon Brivic, *Joyce the Creator* (Madison: University of Wisconsin Press, 1985), for a fine and exhaustive inquiry into the subject of Joyce's conception of the artist as God.

3. James Joyce, *Finnegans Wake* (New York: Viking Press, 1939, 1958 with the author's corrections incorporated into the text; rpt. New York: Viking, 1960), 292.28.

4. Michael Patrick Gillespie, "Raiding fur Buginners: *FW* 611.04-613.04," *JJQ* 24 (Spring 1987): 321.

5. For an excellent, in-depth inquiry into the mechanics of sleep as it pertains to the conceptual basis and texture of *Finnegans Wake*, see John Bishop, *Joyce's Book of the Dark: Finnegans Wake* (Madison: University of Wisconsin Press, 1986). And for an equally fine discussion of Joyce's use of the "condensation" and "displacement" phenomena of Freud's "dreamwork," also see Margot Norris, *The Decentered Universe of Finnegans Wake: A Structuralist Analysis* (Baltimore: Johns Hopkins University Press, 1974 and 1976), particularly chapter 5.

6. Hugh Kenner, *Dublin's Joyce* (Bloomington: Indiana University Press, 1956), 304.

7. For an excellent discussion on this subject, see Brook Thomas, *James Joyce's Ulysses: A Book of Many Happy Returns* (Baton Rouge and London: Louisiana State University Press, 1982), 14-17.

8. Once again, the reader should see John Bishop's book for an in-depth treatment only hinted at here. The issues of identity, at sleep and awake, are discussed masterfully in his book.

9. William York Tindall, *A Reader's Guide to Finnegans Wake* (New York: Farrar, Straus and Giroux, 1969), 24.

10. Clive Hart, *A Concordance to Finnegans Wake* (Mamaroneck, N.Y.: Paul P. Appel, 1974), "Introduction," n.p. *A Wake Newslitter* has ceased publication.

11. Hugh Kenner, *A Colder Eye: The Modern Irish Writers* (New York: Alfred A. Knopf, 1983), 220.

12. Roland McHugh, *The Finnegans Wake Experience* (Berkeley: University of California Press, 1981).

13. Roland McHugh, *Annotations to Finnegans Wake* (Baltimore: Johns Hopkins University Press, 1980).

14. The Philadelphia *Wake* Circle is chaired by its founder Richard Beckman. The other members of the group were David Borodin, Sheldon Brivic, Martha Davis, Morton Levitt, Timothy Martin, and Michael O'Shea. [Editor's Note].

15. J. Mitchell Morse, *"On Teaching Finnegans Wake,"* in *Twelve and a Tilly: Essays on the 25th Anniversary of Finnegans Wake.* Jack Dalton and Clive Hart, eds. (Evanston: Northwestern University Press, 1965), 67.

16. Mercanton's recollection of this conversation with Joyce can be found in Jacques Mercanton, "The Hours of James Joyce," trans. Lloyd C. Park, in *Portraits of the Artist in Exile: Recollections of James Joyce by Europeans.* ed. Willard Potts (Seattle: University of Washington Press, 1979), 233.

Notes for the Staging of *Finnegans Wake***

David Hayman

James Joyce may well have envisaged a drama or, as Stuart Gilbert suggests, a film based upon one or both of his later novels: *Ulysses* and *Finnegans Wake*. In both works we find sections written in dialogue form and complete with stage directions. But, of the three plays thus far drawn from Joyce's novels, only one, *Ulysses in Nighttown*, can be classified as a successful adaptation of Joyce's work. The other two are instructive failures.

Allan McClelland's *Bloomsday* was produced at Oxford under admittedly unfavorable conditions in the winter of 1958. It represents an attempt to condense a complex 767-page book into two-hour's entertainment, a difficult enough job when you are working with, say, Maugham, an impossible one when Joyce is the subject. The author, an English actor, has demonstrated both his awareness of theatrical values and his rather limited acquaintance with *Ulysses*. Using Joyce's words wherever possible, he has cut the action to the bone sacrificing in the process all but one of the book's themes and destroying its structural balance. Understandably, the play emerges a varied, but shallow, naturalistic drama, lacking in continuity and point, racing relentlessly through an elaborate series of more or less disconnected sequences: a theatrical version of the motion picture that was played too fast.

Ulysses in Nighttown (New York, 1958) was first presented at the off-Broadway Rooftop Theater and later taken on tour to London and the continent. Introductory material has been taken from two of the book's early episodes; but the adaptor, Marjorie Barkentin, draws most of her material from a single chapter, the "nighttown" or "Circe" sequence. Like Mr. McClelland she omits much that is extraneous to the conflicts treated, but she does not distort Joyce's meaning or change the mood of the chapter, the most vivid and stageworthy in the entire book. Elsewhere in the novel we find only brief snippets of existence contributing to a larger progression. In this chapter there is a clear dramatic development; there are easily defined conflicts, complex character interrelationships; and there is a satisfactory if ambiguous resolution. Elsewhere, the effects hang on literary techniques alien to the stage, and the drama takes place mainly within the minds of the protagonists. Here the content of the brains of the two exhausted heroes, their inner drama is projected in the form of dialogue and mime against the tawdry substance of the night world with its witches' sabbath of whores and males in rut. Secret meditations and hidden urges become overt, if almost surrealistically conceived, activity. Nowhere else in *Ulysses* are the internal and the external aspects of events so thoroughly integrated; nowhere else are action and reaction so mingled as to make visible all facets of behavior. It is here that the themes meet and interlock, that the essence of the day's experience is reconstituted and given point.

** This essay originally appeared in Marvin Magalaner, ed., *A James Joyce Miscellany*, 3rd Series (Carbondale: Southern Illinois University Press, 1962), 278-293. Permission for use granted by the Southern Illinois University Press.

Working within the relatively narrow compass of this ideally constituted chapter, the adaptor and the director were able to create a convincing spectacle. The production emphasized the language and tonal qualities of the original, its imagery and the implied rhythms, the dreamlike effects which lend themselves best to expression through dance and the mime. Initiation was not a prerequisite for enjoyment.

Finnegans Wake, a less accessible work, has thus far found no comparable champions. One major play, Thornton Wilder's *The Skin of Our Teeth*, shows the influence of Joyce's book. But while we discover here the *Wake*'s basic situation, the existence throughout the ages of an archetypal family, Mr. Wilder's play uses neither Joyce's words nor his structural devices. There remains Mary Manning's version, published under the title *Passages from Finnegans Wake* (Cambridge, 1957) and produced at the Poet's Playhouse in Cambridge (1955). I have heard from friends who were present at the early performances and from Nora White Shattuck, the choreographer, that the production was well received and that both the cast and the audience made contact with Joyce's book through the medium of the spoken word, the gesture and the dance.

Unfortunately, Miss Manning, like Mr. McClelland, overstepped herself by purporting to take as her domain the whole of *Finnegans Wake*'s rather ponderous bulk. Given the nature of her material, the density of its language and the complexity of its organization, we need hardly be startled to find Joyce's dreambook of mankind distorted by this adaptation. As any reader of *Finnegans Wake* will see, the stage version resembles nothing more than a paste and shears job; it brings more mud and new confusion. Lines are attributed to the wrong characters, actions are misinterpreted, while whole passages are lifted out of context for reasons which are suspect. Miss Manning pays much attention to characterization, drawing heavily upon the first and third sections of the *Wake* for random lines and sequences. But the characters she creates are only partially Joyce's and the more coherent sequences from book II are virtually ignored. Even more than Mr. McClelland's play, this spectacle tends to demonstrate how easily Joyce's values can be misrepresented by a broadly generalized adaptation of his work. Here meaning, substance, balance and dramatic consistency are all sacrificed to the carnival spirit. Though the act of bringing Joyce's words and some of his humor before an audience is in itself worthy of praise, the atomization of his characters and structure in the name of his creation is not.

The Harvard production, good vaudeville and bad Joyce, constitutes a useful precedent, but perhaps there is a more valid approach to the staging of this book. My suggestion would be to follow the lead of the *Nighttown* adaptation and concentrate on the one segment of the book which best lends itself to staging: the pub scene from section II with its detailed account of the tragi-comic degradation of the Hero. But before entering into a discussion of the dramatic possibilities of this chapter, I should like briefly to resume some of the principal aspects of *Finnegans Wake*.

II

A compendium of man's experience, *Finnegans Wake* treats of the night and apparently takes place in a dreamer's mind. The story told is simple, elusive and redundant. According to the theory upon which the book is based, history repeats itself with predictable regularity; each man is the universe in small and every event of his life reflects the form of the whole. Like *Ulysses*, the *Wake* is cyclical and its people are archetypes or lowest common denominators for mankind. But in the latter, little emphasis is laid upon the contemporary level. Even place is as uncertain as it is multiple. The past, present and future here merge kaleidoscopically, and Man's experiences become as the notes, motifs, themes and as the overtones of a complex piece of music. Instead of individuated or rounded characters Joyce creates an archetypal family in an archetypal locale: the family Earwicker of Dublin, father-mother-sons-and-daughter or HCE-ALP-Shem-Shaun-and-Issy who give their identities to countless individuals past and present, fictional and real; to parts of the landscape; to planets and stars in the sky, animals and birds, etc. Most remarkable of all are the wordplay and puns which permit him to evoke not only all sorts of actions but all sorts of reactions and moods simultaneously, to provide his readers with a perspective that shifts elusively as we bring it into focus, that adapts itself to the individual reader's mind and even to the individual mood.

Here in its broad outline is Joyce's plot: With the sunset, man falls under the spell of the female or instinctual. During the night, he must redeem himself by means of a quest, must refresh his powers through sleep which takes him beyond himself into a world without definition. Man's goal is lucidity or the day: a fresh awakening. But the quest itself carries him through all history and his own individual past, present and future. Beyond that it engages him in the female stuff of his (mankind's) subconscious. It is the female medium that dominates the *Wake*'s language. It is also the females' activity that motivates fully one half of the book.

For the purposes of this discussion we may call the *Wake*'s four major sections childhood, maturity, senescence and death. Book II, or the second section, treats of the most vital part of a man's existence: the period during which his activity bears its fruit, the peak of his development in the post-fall or night world. But each subdivision of the *Wake* is logically a microcosm of the whole. Hence the four chapters of book II contain treatments in this order of childhood or the children at play; adolescence or the young at their studies; maturity and decline or the males at the tavern; and finally, old age and death with overtones of rebirth.

It is the third chapter of this section which is concerned with the most dramatic phase of the vital second period of human development. Occurring at the structural center of the *Wake*, this chapter is the only compact unit with a stage-worthy dramatic organization and a significant denouement. It contains in fact several such dramatic units, as Joyce, predictably enough, divides the chapter into four "tales," each with its own development and climax, each with its four parts. Within the larger context and through a progression that is at once subtle, lucid and consistent, the tales make manifest the steps of the mature hero's dissolution.

Joyce's plan is such that an abridged adaptation *can* reproduce the major facets of II.3's action, which is in turn complex and varied enough to convey the implication of the *Wake*'s language to an uninitiated audience. Also in the chapter's favor are its unity of theme, its orderly and conventional plot development, plus of course the complete integration of part with part, aspect with aspect and character with character. All of these qualities are available elsewhere in smaller quantities, but nowhere else is the theatrical potential so evident.

This chapter deals directly with the tragi-comic circumstances of the hero-figure or all-father HCE, Humphrey Chimpden Earwicker, in our times a pub-keeper or *host* in the small suburban village of Chapelizod, on the outskirts of Phoenix Park, home of the Dublin Zoo and the Wellington monument. The location is significant. We are outside the Garden of Eden or alongside the Phoenix' pyre in the company of post-fall man living in the memory of the fall and the primal sin. Like man, the day has fallen; dusk is deepening; and though the female is not present in this turn-of-the-century pub with its roistering rout of male drinkers, her spirit hovers over the proceedings and colors the action. For the night world is traditionally female, unconscious or instinctual. Standing behind his bar, the pub-keeping hero dispenses drink to his twelve clients in a manner reminiscent of Christ serving wine to the twelve disciples, Odin feasting the dead heroes, and King Roderick O'Conor entertaining his dissatisfied nobles. His physical movements are, however, minimal. Once he leaves the tavern to visit his privy. At other times he is seen counting coins or uneasily picking up bits of his client's conversation. Furthermore, his role is a mute one until halfway through the chapter when, faced with growing antagonism, he feels called upon to defend his present position as server of drink, leader of men and bestower of grace.

At this point, by attempting to justify himself before his guests, he lays himself open to the covert judgment of custom or of public opinion. He is saved only when, at pub-closing time, the reluctant drinkers are expelled from the pub by the old manservant, Siggerson. Once out of doors the angered clients raise their voices in drunken revelry reaffirming their condemnation of HCE to the tune of the scurrilous HCE lampoon, "The Ballad of Persse O'Reilly" (or *perce oreille*: earwig), the death hymn of the hero's reputation. Now the exhausted host accepts his fate or succumbs to it by drinking his guests' leavings and falling into a drunken slumber.

In terms of a posited contemporary night, the hour is nearing midnight. In terms of social history, the autocrat has abdicated in favor of popular rule. In terms of archetypes, we are witnessing the tragedy of the masterful leader or father-figure gone to seed. What follows after II.3 is his theophany, or the rise of his somewhat etherealized spirit in the form of the dream son or new leader, the successor in whom the heroic past reigns as the sign of authority.

III

In the stage version HCE's place is behind the bar until the customers have left, but he should have a silent helper or counterpart in the management of his establishment: Siggerson or the hero grown old. This personage has a clear dramatic function. He embodies the true condition or fate of the Hero as opposed to the illusory one evidenced by the vital bar-keeper. Siggerson, whose Scandinavian name identifies him as a debased descendant of the original Viking rulers of Dublin, is occupied serving drinks, cleaning tables, keeping order and finally clearing the house. It is in this role or as a latterday counterpart of Siggerson, the worn-out King Roderick O'Conor, that HCE finally falls under the influence of drink. The two should metaphorically blend into one at the end of the play. In all events, Siggerson is an ironic constant, a mirror image of HCE; and the narrowing of the gap which separates master from servant is part and parcel with the tragic development illustrated by this chapter. It calls to mind the conversion which takes place at the end of *Oedipus Rex* where the king becomes the equal of the blind seer, Tiresias. Characteristically, in Joyce's book the same progression may be interpreted as comic; for there is much that is ridiculous in the fate of an aging and perhaps paranoid pub-keeper who, having rid himself of antagonistic guests, proceeds to finish their drinks while dancing a tipsy jig. On the surface everything in the *Wake* is hilarious. This paradox was intended by Joyce. Its nature can be made clear to an audience with the aid of cleverly manipulated language and perhaps also with the aid of masks suggestive of the ritual origin of drama.

Till now I have paid scant attention to the action taking place in front of the bar. Here, along with the host's sterile future or Siggerson, we find the above-mentioned twelve clients: the king's subjects, the worshippers or disciples of the scapegoat hero, the hours of his day or the months of his year. They are also a cross-section of the useful trades, a group of citizens in the act of getting drunk or surrendering to some primeval urge, that is, coming into contact with their universal or archetypal heritage. Hence we may equate them with the ritual audience or the chorus of a Greek play. In terms of the pub-keeping present, this group of ordinary citizens is occupied drinking, quarreling, telling barroom tales and listening to the pub radio. Its components are an aspect of the mass mind, hardly worthy of differentiation, but capable of making rough and ready distinctions and of acting with violence when aroused. As Joyce says, "Group drinkards maaks grope thinkards" (*FW* 312.31).

These clients occupy a middle plane in the stage version of the chapter. They are not brought into clearer focus until the penultimate scene. However, the action of the chapter, which may best be envisaged as taking place mainly in the pub-keeper's brain, is capable of expression partially through the medium of their reactions. Filtering through the Hero's consciousness, their behavior evokes deep sensations raised from the primitive or shared substrata of experience: guilt feelings associated with the Hero's past or feelings of inadequacy linked to his present. Cast in narrative form, these are projected onto the stage through the medium of a mirror group of clients whose substance and behavior are ultimately more convincing than are those of the primary set of drinkers. Ideally both the primary HCE and the primary set of twelve along with the "real" or "temporal" level of the action should serve as a backdrop for the mental activity of the hero-figure. In the night world, what we normally perceive as real becomes bidimensional or flat. But, given the limits of the stage and of the audience, we can only approximate this condition by placing in the foreground or in front of the basic barroom scene physical embodiments of the pub-keeper's fantasy.

There are a number of ways in which the scene could be reproduced. The primary level might be projected on a scrim; it might be portrayed by actors placed directly behind, to one side of or even above the mirror group. It might include a primary HCE with a primary bar or it might not. This would depend upon physical factors. What is important however is that the audience understand the nature of the dramatic situation and the locus of the drama. It must be reasonably evident that, as Joyce says in his "Scribbledehobble" notebook, the "characters exhibit to terrified protagonist their dream malevolence." Given this knowledge, the theatergoers will be equipped to appreciate the humor of the *Wake* and the pathos and irony which filter through that humor. The swift pace of the action and its multiplicity make it necessary that these qualities be gently affirmed by means of such devices as the animated backdrop.

Joyce may have thought of the entire chapter as a single tale narrated in a single voice, a frame story in the tradition of the *Decameron* or of *The Thousand and One Nights*. The sub-tales, four in number, each contribute to the coherence of the major unit, and taken together, the chapter and its parts represent an account of the progression of the oral tradition and of the short-tale form through the ages or from historical period to historical period. Narrators are therefore an essential part of the stage version. The voice of the frame tale might emanate from among the primary group of clients. For dramatic effect his identity could be withheld until in the final sequence a spotlight reveals him to be none other than HCE's double, Siggerson. This "mystery" narrator should be heard only at the beginning of the chapter and in the intermissions between the acts or scenes. Each of the individual scenes has a voice and locale of its own and in each case the narrator should speak from the level on which the particular tale originates.

Taken separately, each of the stories gives a differently modulated account of the Hero's fall. First, there is the capitulation to woman or the procreative act; then, the fall at the hands of the progeny or a usurpation of function; third, comes dissolution or the loss of position or face before inferiors; and fourth, the acceptance of age, inanition and death. Viewed as a part of a rational framework these tales form a logical and coherent progression.

As the chapter opens, we are told how a certain Norwegian Captain made three raids on the Irish coast or three visits to the port of Dublin, each time taking something without paying for it. On the fourth and final visit he is apprehended by his landlubber counterpart, baptized and married off to the daughter of Ireland. Visit by visit, the figure of the captain becomes increasingly civilized, until, in the last sequence, the buccaneering Viking is very like a Dutch sea captain, a peaceful merchant. The Captain's story is among other things a record of Dublin's maritime history, of colonization and conquest and of commerce. It is the tale of man's coming or the taming of the sea and of man's subjection to woman and the social necessities. It concludes on a note of childbirth or fruition. The next tale takes up somewhat later and records the experiences of the Irish in the church or at war: that is, serving stranger lords. In it an Irish "wild goose" (soldier or missionary monk) reports how he (or someone with whom he identifies) has shot or otherwise embarrassed the scapegoat, a Russian General in the Crimean War surprised while answering the call of nature. After commerce and seamanship, war and religion, come politics and law, which Joyce treats by describing the trial and conviction of a public figure. It is HCE in his role as pub-keeper and conscience-ridden public citizen who stars in this segment of the "story of the house of the hundred bottles." The last tale takes drunkenness, the favorite Irish vice, as one of its themes and defeat as another when the rollicking King Roderick O'Conor, last high king of Ireland, tipples his way into eternity with a heavy heart.

If we are to preserve the structure of our models, the staging of the first tales must be elaborate. Thus the Captain's tale will be presented as though in a flattened-out three ring circus. At least three levels of activity are implied, though attention needs be focused on only one level at a time and on only one aspect of that level. From his position behind the bar HCE broods upon the implications of the tales being told in the pub and creates in his mind the second scenic level with its mirror clients. On this second level the tale is told by a second set of clients, but its action must be mimed and acted, partially at least on a supplementary level by actors perhaps in stylized period costumes. Much broad fun can be had through the presentation of the Captain's comings and goings, the rage of the repeatedly outwitted landsmen, and the final jubilee celebration on the occasion of the marriage to ALP, pathos can be conveyed through the mimed reactions and the general behavior of the Host: "the pilsener had the baar" (*FW* 313.14-15). There should be evident physical resemblances between the Host, the principal landsman (or "Ships Husband") and the Captain; for they, like the Russian General and King Roderick, are all aspects of HCE. As the action progresses in this and the following tales, the clients on both levels show signs of increasing drunkenness. The group ushered out by Siggerson in the third tale is almost out of control, in open revolt; here, it is full of latent chaos in anticipation of what is to come.

The second piece follows after an interlude designed to recall the pub-keeper's married state. Materializing from behind a calendar picture of the "Charge of the Light Brigade," the "television" skit reenacted by Butt and Taff is a manifestation of the dramatic or ritualistic impulse in man. The narrators of the tale are counterparts of other antagonistic couples appearing throughout the *Wake*: Mutt and Jute, Cain and Abel, Jacob and Esau and of course Shem and Shaun: the twin sons or two sides of HCE, his inner and his outer consciousness. Here, the two men may be variously seen. In one sense they are soldier-veterans (wild geese) reminiscing about the Crimean War and the Battle of Sevastopol. The tale they tell or rather the tale Butt tells, for he claims to have witnessed the event, is of one Buckley, a common soldier, who surprised a wild goose Russian general in full regalia praying or relieving himself in the wood. According to this account, Buckley was at first taken aback, then disgusted by the sight. Clearly he acted under provocation, but his action is equivalent to parricide. Butt and Taff may also be seen as penitent and priest of the Catholic faith, as two friars or jackpriests, as priests of some pagan fertility rite, as the sons of Noah, or as two music-hall clowns. In the detailed stage directions which precede each of their dialogues, Joyce evokes their posturing. Actually the tale of Buckley's behavior is told mainly through the gestures of Butt; its significance is made clear by those of Taff. Unfortunately, only a fraction of this can be dramatized. But with tact the actor's staging effects can convey more than the "gist."

The dramatic situation involves the two clowns more intimately than it does the protagonists of the tale they tell. In a social context these two sons of the land are preparing to accept the responsibility for overthrowing the leader, mesmerizing themselves into action. We are moving from an autocratic to a democratic period; the plebes are banding together. In the course of the narrative therefore subtle changes take place. Butt, who plays the penitent and identifies with the voyeur-killer, Buckley, begins by describing the event. His description becomes a boast and then a confession; and Taff, whose sympathies at the start are with the victim, gives vent to feelings of outrage. But gradually, as the tale advances, Taff finds his sympathy wavering, falls under the spell of the narrative and joins in the condemnation of the General, thus implicating himself in the murder. At the end of the recital, the two clowns are of one mind and are indeed joined in their rather timorous hatred of the semimythical hero-figure—the ineffectual leader or the aging father. A new age, that of the people and the sons, is dawning within the larger context of the chapter. Only at such a time would the pub-keeper feel compelled to identify openly with the overthrown and discredited Russian.

The staging of the dialogue should be relatively simple. As though projected upon a television screen, the two men play their provocative skit on a small spotlit area located somewhere between the mirror group and the primal group of clients. Though their appearance is heralded by comments from the mirror group only, their exit elicits chorused remarks from both sets of clients. The behavior of Buckley and the General is presented entirely through the mime of the brother pair. The two clowns should be broadly music hall—their dialogue is accompanied by much attitudinizing, by an occasional two-step, by blows and falls; while in the background we hear medleys of cheap tunes. Joyce had for one of his models for the chapter and particularly for this dialogue the traditional Dublin Christmas pantomime as he remembered it from his own childhood. It must be borne in mind, however, that every aspect of *Finnegans Wake*, every scene, action and gesture reverberates through the ages: The music-hall mime is for example a debased form of religious ritual. Its formulas are timeless. The skit is punctuated by interludes designed to point up and deepen the action: a horse race, the General's last rites, the "abnihilization of the etym" (*FW* 353.22). On the stage these effects might best be produced with the aid of film strips.

The two remaining episodes are more closely linked to the Hero's present, that is, to his status as an enfeebled ruler. We have left the realms of the folk memory and the heroic and autocratic past: HCE is judged and condemned not by some shadowy storytale figures but by his own guests, his former subjects, now his peers. In this connection it is interesting to explore the etymology of the word "host" which Joyce applies both to his hero as scapegoat-pub-keeper and to his hero's enemy, Hosty, the author of the "Ballad of Persse O'Reilly."

The action of the third tale is varied: While HCE, his position having been exposed by his own testimony, looks on in dismay, his judges and jury hear new evidence through the medium of a radio broadcast reaffirming the circumstances of his crime. Once again he feels obliged to speak, this time in defense of his own character rather than that of the Russian. His plea of "guilty but fellows culpows" (*FW* 363.20) leaves him at the mercy of the underdogs, who, after Siggerson expels them from the pub or locks them in the jury room, deliver their verdict amidst overtones of Old Testament law and the popular justice of Hosty's ballad.

The staging of this episode involves a subtle diminution in the number of the characters on stage and equally subtle changes in the aspect of the hero. As the story progresses the mirror group of clients mixes in with the primary group to form one set of twenty-four people (or hours), all accusing the hero. But before pub-closing time, their number will have dwindled to twelve, so that the group expelled by Siggerson suggests a jury. Only two people are left on stage at the end of this sequence: HCE and Siggerson. Also in the building and audible, though not visible, are the four old men or Mamalujo, whose presence on the premises after closing time suggests paradoxically that HCE, like Noah, is selected for individual salvation. Though there is a considerable amount of choral dialogue in the third tale, most of the action is mimed with descriptive comments from either the on-stage narrator or an anonymous radio announcer. The verdict of the clients, for example, is pronounced off-stage and broadcast over the pub radio which also carries the tale of the (mock) execution of the victim. With the aid of such mechanical devices, the complex behavior of the democratic personae can be made clear to a theater audience.

It is Siggerson who openly introduces and recounts the final narrative or fourth tale against the sound of rain heralding the deluge and of distant thunder signaling the theophany of the Hero and the advent of a new age. Throughout the second half of the chapter HCE is aging rapidly, taking on aspects first of the Norwegian Captain, then of the Russian General or of a Noah betrayed by his sons, then of a fallen politician, and finally of King Roderick O'Conor broken by the disaffection of his vassals. This last figure is of an age with Siggerson whom he resembles closely though the Viking serving-man must wear some item of clothing reminiscent of the costume worn by the first Norwegian Captain. King Roderick's demise takes place on a dramatically empty stage, littered with vestiges of the night's feast. HCE's part should be completely mimed. Here, amidst the props of his past, he is seen dissolving his misery in drink, succumbing at last to the night or the spirit. A feeble vestige of male power, he is drowning his consciousness.

The final curtain falls. HCE as mankind has relived his past, faced his present and been transported into his future. The chapter that opens with the statement: "It may not or maybe a no concern of the Guinnesses but" (*FW* 309.1), closes with a reference to the eternal repetition of types and events, a return to beginnings and the night: "As who has come returns . . . Now follow we out by Starloe!"(*FW* 382.30).[1]

Afterwords

Though several attempts have been made to film and stage *Finnegans Wake* and though I have seen three of them and read about the remainder, I stand by my prescription for the staging of this stage-resistant text. Some of my production ideas, which seemed radical in 1960, have become workable if not conventional in the wake of the spectacles of Robert Wilson and Philip Glass to say nothing of the rock operas. I am not certain, however, that elaborate staging is the key to aesthetic success, nor do I know how well anyone could convey theatrically the multilayered ambiguities and the rich comic and poetic texture of Joyce's languaged meditation on the universal experience. What is clear to me is that grab-bag and patchwork approaches are doomed to fail and that Chapter II.3 is potentially a dramatizable unit.

The *Wake* is not a novel with plot and characters, and in any reading and certainly in a stage version of the book, novelistic conventions must remain in the background, to be disclosed only as an indeterminate and shifting subtext. Still, we can demonstrate that there were from the start certain coherent strands of what might be called thematic/narrative upon which a performance could build without fear of undermining Joyce's accomplishment. This is one of the things that serious manuscript study, along with a careful reading of the *Wake* and a consideration of its genesis makes amply clear. Thus, despite current received opinion, frequently as dogmatic as that of the 50s and 60s, we can and should expose a human drama of sorts behind the scrim(s) of the "nightmare" of history while reproducing as many of the text's moods, genres and modes as possible. Ideally, this should be done in such a way as to preserve some of the essential language play while surrounding the not too completely "lost in the bush" viewer with a field of implications.

My original proposal was skeletal, an idea waiting for an interpreter. Its success or failure will hang on production decisions. In rendering Joyce's language as action, the interpreter would be obliged to make radical and, one hopes, judicious cuts. Not only is there no way to preserve all of the effects, there is in fact no point trying to do so. Informed editing, performed in the light of earlier drafts, could turn the theatrical text into a significant reading of the chapter and the book. Though any and all cuts and alterations do violence, there is a sense in which relatively little of the *Wake*'s text is actually available to a given *reader* on any given reading. It is in the nature of the reading process that readers of *Finnegans Wake* constantly miss and omit important aspects of what they read. True, what is not focused is peripherally experienced, but then, if properly handled, that peripheral wealth of experience could be partially accommodated by the staging. It can be also argued that we are all partial readers and enactors of any text. There is a place for an effective and professional dramatic rendering that makes no claim to reproducing the *Wake* but that manages to convey a sense of the text's coherence while clothing it in well-chosen and well-delivered language.

Ultimately, the language would have to be a major factor, supported by the voices and gestures of speakers capable of delivering a verbo-visuo-vocally satisfying experience. At the same time, it should be clear to initiates and uninitiated as well that only a fraction of what is heard and seen need be fully apprehended, and that only fleetingly, that it is best to think of the *Wake* as a "collideorscape." Though there is a plot line of sorts and though the words and actions may convey a range of attitudes, a great deal of stylized behavior is necessary. Joyce himself might have conceived these performances in what would now seem a dated fashion. For all his inventiveness, he was a man of his times. But a contemporary dramatic rendering, like so many renderings of Shakespeare, could strive for contemporary effects.

Having said this, I must mention a fine recent study which, after giving all documented productions a hearing, attacks the very notion of staging Joyce's last book. Josè Lanters' *Missed Understandings: a Study of Stage Adaptations of the Works of James Joyce* (Amsterdam: Rodolpi, 1988) has generously taken my modest proposal seriously, and freely rejected it along with the others. Though I find her objections to the idea of plot and character a bit too trendy, I respect and have tried to respond to her objections. Her complaint that my project relies too heavily on the concept of the well-made play may be more to the point; however, given the seeming opacity of the *Wake* and the current tendency to make Joyce into a precursor to deconstructionism, it may be healthy to show just how conventional at least one chapter of his last book actually was . . . beneath its layers of active/reactive wordplay.

My own problems with this conception, meditated on over the years, stem mostly from my sense that my projected version is too big in scale and scope for a single production and too arcane for the audience that would be needed to make such a production viable. It is, in short, a corrective dream scenario for a dream book. Over the years, however, the concept has helped me visualize Chapter II.3, that most difficult and rewarding of all the *Wake*'s chapters. Most recently, my choice of a chapter to stage has been reenforced by the discovery that this chapter, the last to be written, may actually have been the first to be conceived, that, along with the early sketches, it may have served as the (physically) absent armature for the book in progress. There is evidence in the "Scribbledehobble" notebook that Joyce not only began with a conception of the stories for II.3 and II.4[2], the essence of his Irish (Pub) Night's Entertainment, but that he had in mind from the start the situation of the beleaguered and "terrified" dreamer, presumably the precursor of the pub-keeping HCE. I would maintain that those very basic materials were never abandoned, that readers and would-be adaptors should attend to them.

Notes

1.   This essay dates from 1962, though it was written two years earlier.
      Understandably, it bears the marks of its period and of my own readings
      of the *Wake*. At that time none of the current critical and scholarly
      supports existed and I had little more to fall back on than my knowledge
      of the manuscripts and ten years as a reader and critic of the *Wake*. If I
      were to rewrite it now in the light of current research, certain details of
      presentation would be altered, but the overall plan would remain the
      same.

2.   See *Notebook* VI.A, 21, under the heading "THE SISTERS." There we
      find a list that includes something approximating the "Norwegian Captain"
      tale, along with the tale of the pub-keeper with his "house of the hundred
      bottles," the Buckley story and the "Tristan and Isolde." Under "EXILES
      (III.)" there is a single and telling entry: "characters exhibit to terrified
      protagonist their dream malevolence" (VI.A, 331). The earlier acts of
      Exiles elicited a detailed and largely parodic investigation of the "Tristan"
      tale. It is remarkable that through the years of gestation during which
      Joyce altered many aspects of his book, he appears to have retained these
      components of his central argument. I have dealt at length with both the
      early sketches and the history of the "Tristan" theme in *The Wake in
      Transit* (Cornell, 1990), but the question just raised is of a different order
      and merits further study.

Mary Ellen Bute's Film Adaptation of *Finnegans Wake*

Kit Basquin

In 1958 the award-winning independent filmmaker Mary Ellen Bute saw *Passages from Finnegans Wake*, Mary Manning's stage adaptation of James Joyce's text. Fascinated by the novel's cinematic metaphors and structure and its musical qualities, although aware of its textual difficulties, Bute determined to create a screen adaptation of Manning's play. In 1965 at the Cannes Film Festival it won a prize for best first feature by a director.

For Bute, who had devoted twenty-six years to pioneer forms of synchronized music and abstract animation, Joyce's musical language and unique imagery were irresistible. She quoted his cinematic metaphors to persuade potential backers of his interest in film and of the appropriateness of a cinematic interpretation of his work.[1] She said in an interview with Vincent Canby of *Variety* that Joyce's literary technique was "essentially cinematic."[2] Assisted by Mary Manning, she abstracted language from the text to create dialogue. After winning the Cannes prize, she added subtitles to her film to reinforce Joyce's focus on language and to emphasize the word play that interwove the audible with the visible.

Although some critics have praised Bute's visual and creative success in capturing the humor and spirit of *Finnegans Wake*, some charge that she muted the erotic overtones that permeate the text, substituting flirtation and sentimentality for frank sexuality, and departed too much from Joyce's text. But if Bute's inhibitions influenced her selection and presentation of bodily functions and sexually explicit scenes from the text, they did not affect what first attracted her to the novel and what she regarded as its central metaphor, filmmaking.

Bute's responses to specific portions of the text cannot be determined exactly. She left few marks in her copy of the novel, although she heavily annotated Manning's play. Her film begins with summarizing words that roll silently in front of the viewer, combining text and circulatory movement into a metaphor reflective of film rolling from reel to reel in a projector. Reinforcing this visual trope, the next image of the River Liffy is accompanied by a voice-over quoting the opening lines of *Finnegans Wake*: "riverrun, past Eve and Adam's, from swerve of shore to bend of bay, brings us by a commodius vicus of recirculation back to Howth Castle and Environs" (*FW* 3.1-3).[3]

Cinematic allusions that Bute could have used for promoting her film abound in the text, reinforcing themes, expanding the language, and relating cinema to other media. Specific cinematic terms such as "movietone" (*FW* 62.9), "Longshots" (*FW* 221.22), and "film folk" (*FW* 221.21) testify to the intentionality of Joyce's cinematic references. Cinematic words and word combinations, chosen to reflect themes of circularity and seeing, repeat incrementally, presenting in microcosm the structure of the book in which the text circles, beginning by completing the sentence that ends the novel. They reappear with variations, as if circling back to their original form. A real/reel interplay starts as "the real Us" (*FW* 62.26) which evolves into "reel" in the circular song: "And roll away the reel world, the reel world, the reel world!" (*FW* 64.25-26), eventually becoming "reeled the titleroll" (*FW* 134.9) in conjunction with "Silver on the Screen" (*FW* 134.10). And "flickerflapper" (*FW* 266.31) evolves into "circumflicksrent"(*FW* 298.15), and then "fickers" (*FW* 298.17).

Words that relate visual experience of life to visual experience of art include "seene" (*FW* 52.36), "fading out" (*FW* 226.11), "doubleviewed" (*FW* 296.1), "fickers" (*FW* 298.17), and "screen" (*FW* 134.28). Events in the text appear and reappear, narrated from different points of view. An incident in the park is rumored (*FW* 38.25-27, 34.17-29); HCE's version of the incident is televised (*FW* 52.18); the populace talks about the crime (*FW* 58.26-29); Festy King is accused and tried for an indiscretion in the park (*FW* 85.23-31); HCE defends himself (*FW* 532.6-26); and the park scene of HCE's indiscretion is recalled (*FW* 606.23-25). Differences in presentation and variations in cinematic allusions raise the question woven throughout the text, "What was seen?"

Cinematic words that could have attracted Bute to the text operate on several levels, expanding the text and contributing to the humor of the novel. "Screen him" (*FW* 134.28), for example, can be read as "seeing him as if on a screen" or as "judging him." Similarly, "exposure of him" (*FW* 57.24) can be read as a film developing process, a revelation of what had been hidden, and indecent exposure. "Loan of a lens to see" (*FW* 112.1-2) suggests the use of eye glasses as well as the employment of a camera lens.

These double entendres convey a sense of simultaneity, which is achieved on film by double exposure or split screens, the showing of two different scenes side by side. Bute constantly uses double exposures of water and ALP to associate the two, although she does not employ split screen effects. Critic Sarah Smith said that Bute could not express simultaneity in specifically cinematic terms.[4] However, double exposure is just such a cinematic device. In the text, simultaneity is accomplished by extended metaphors, as in the following example of intercourse verbally disguised as a ride in a boat:

> O, leave me my faculties, woman, a while! If you
> don't like my story get out of the punt. Well, have it
> your own way, so. Here, sit down and do as you're
> bid. Take my stroke and bend to your bow. Forward
> in and pull your overthepoise! Lisp it slaney and crisp
> it quiet. Deel me longsome. Tongue your time now.
> (*FW* 206.20-25)

As was mentioned, Bute avoids such explicitly sexual imagery. In another example of simultaneity in the text, lovers talk during lovemaking;

> If I am laughing with you? No. lovingest, I'm not so
> dying to take my rise out of you, adored. . . . Ever so
> sorry! I beg your pardon, I was listening to every
> treasuried word I said fell from my dear mot's tongue
> otherwise how could I see what you were thinking of
> our granny? Only I wondered if I threw out my
> shaving water. Anyway, here's my arm, pulletneck.
> Gracefully yours. Move your mouth towards minth,

more, preciousest, more on more! (*FW* 146.2-3, 26-
31)

Only the final two innocuous lines are used in the film.

Time in both Joyce's text and Manning's play is not realistically
chronological, but fabricated, as it is in cinema. In Bute's film, montage editing
juxtaposes different time frames into an integrated pattern, justified in the text
by the simulation of montage that appears in such phrases as: "seein as ow his
thoughts consisted chiefly of the cheerio, he aptly sketched for our soontobe
second parents (sukand see whybe!) the touching seene" (*FW* 52.34-36).
Speakers' thoughts and actions belong to the present, but the audience—
"soontobe second parents"—is in the future. Joyce's simulated cinematic
structural techniques, adapted by Bute, employ television, photography, and
conventions of the stage to manipulate time.

To convey aboriginal links with Shem and Shaun, Bute shows the
mourners at the wake watching the twins dressed as cave men on television. By
means of such techniques, Bute incorporates distant past into present, portraying
Shem and Shaun as human archetypes. Her creative interpretation of Joyce's
non-linear concept of time is a major achievement of her film.

Bute also uses photographs for temporal effect. The mourners at the
wake study an old picture of HCE's family. The past invades the present, as in
dreams, and in Joyce's text. Bute makes a similar use of stage presentations.
ALP and Shem, dressed in costumes that reinforce time differences, enact on
stage the medieval romance of Tristan and Isolde.

Costumes also help Bute visualize changes in point-of-view in the text,
as characters become different people, changing names and roles (e.g., HCE's
daughter, Issy, becomes Isolde; Shem becomes Tristan). By casting the same
actress as ALP, Issy, and Isolde, Bute reinforces the link among these different
personalities. Thus, she creates a visual experience of the fractured nature of
the characters in Joyce's text. Her consolidation of cast reinforces the idea of
incest apparent throughout the novel. When Isolde embraces Tristan, who is
also Shem, she is also Issy and ALP, embracing both brother and son as lover.
Telescoping the cast serves the additional practical function for Bute of limiting
production costs, always a problem for an avant-garde artist for whom funding
is a continuous struggle.

Discussing production costs, Zack Bowen, a Joyce scholar who worked on
the music for the Bute film, said that the Irish actors were already in New York
at the time of the filming, performing on Broadway in Brendan Behan's *The
Hostage*. These young actors and actresses, wanting credit for working on a
Joyce film, performed for a small fee. Bowen added that Barnard students were
also willing to work for low rates in exchange for learning about filmmaking
from Bute, a conscientious albeit demanding teacher whom the students loved.[5]
Bute said in an interview with Ann Holmes of the *Houston Chronicle*:

> Beyond the concept of the film itself, the most
> difficult task has been the financing. There were
> endless knockings on doors. The money came in
> spurts. After only a few days on location in Ireland,

the project closed down for lack of funds.[6]

Bute went on to say that she completed the film, which took seven years to make for approximately $250,000, with money from Columbia University, The University of Minnesota, and the Avon Foundation of Minneapolis.[7] She sold the 16mm rights to the University of Minnesota for a minimum guarantee of $36,000.[8]

To minimize costs for the musical score of the film, the entire orchestral part was taped in five hours at a sound studio in New York City. The nineteen-person orchestra added some unusual instruments, such as the Honky-Tonk piano and the accordion. Composer Elliot Kaplan, who had studied with the famous French music teacher Nadia Boulanger after receiving two music degrees from Yale, wrote original background music for Bute's film, fitting into the sound track many musical allusions from the film script. Some of these allusions were already in the track in the form of singing and dancing by the cast.[9] Other allusions were identified by Mabel P. Worthington, who had co-authored with Matthew Hodgart *Song in the Works of James Joyce* (1959), and Zack Bowen, who was a graduate student working on his dissertation later entitled "An Analysis of the Music in James Joyce's *Ulysses* as It Pertains to the Stream of Conscious Thought and Activity of Leopold Bloom" (1967).[10] Worthington and Bowen also supplied music and lyrics for songs referred to in the film script.

The musical appeal of Joyce's words, both in Manning's play and in Joyce's text, combined with creative imagery, suited particularly Bute's long experience synchronizing music and avant-garde images into what she called "seeing sound." Bute had pioneered abstract animation in the United States in her 1934 "Rhythm in Light," a five-minute short synchronizing the music of Grieg's "Anitra's Dance" frame by frame with abstract images fabricated from sculptures, found objects, and lighting effects. She created eleven more prize winning abstract animated films before 1953, including "Abstronic" in 1952, the first film using electronic images from a cathode ray oscilloscope.

The fabrication of the title word "Abstronic" combining "Abstract" and "electronic" was the kind of verbal game that had been used by Joyce. This particular portmanteau word was actually suggested to Bute by her friend Albert Tomkins. Bute said at the time she made "Abstronic":

> For years I have tried to find a method for controlling a source of light to produce images in rhythm. I wanted to manipulate light to produce visual compositions in time continuity much as a musician manipulates sounds to produce music . . . I felt keenly the limitations inherent in the plastic and graphic mediums and determined to find a medium in which movement would be the primary design factor.[11]

Her perceptual goal was close to that of James Joyce, who designed his musical text in the form of circular motion.

Kaplan, commenting on the complexities of the scoring for the film and the unifying role of the music said:

> The project of scoring *Finnegans Wake* was more
> complex than that of scoring most other films in
> several ways. Not only was the film itself more
> diffuse and multi-leveled in narrative terms than other
> films, even those with comparable aspirations (of
> which there are few) but the depth of significance in
> the serious episodes and the humor of the "punny"
> parts are profound. The abrupt transitions between
> these extremes also called for a greater than usual
> emphasis on the structurally clarifying function of the
> music.[12]

Discussing the song allusions in the film script, Kaplan added, "Often, there is
only the rhythm remaining to identify the selection, mentions of titles, of
songs." Characterizing the songs, he said they were "Irish Folk, popular tunes
of Joyce's immediate period, nursery tunes, songs from many other countries
. . . operas and concert works." He pointed out that the lengthiest reference was
taken from Wagner's *Tristan and Isolde*, but that not all the allusions were so
exact since most took the form of fleeting phrases worked in counterpoint to his
own material. He said that some of these allusions became identified with
characters, such as the theme composed by him that is associated with Finnegan,
which emerges in the final resurrection scene as a strident march.[13]
Characteristic of Bute's earlier work synchronizing music and abstract
animation, the music in her *Wake* film coordinated closely with the visual
images and reflected Joyce's musical allusions and even rhythms of words that
united music and image in his text. In a sense both Bute and Joyce created
"seeing sound."

To actualize montage simulated in the written text, Bute juxtaposes
diverse images in rapid sequence, conveying new meaning in the relationship,
a technique pioneered by filmmaker Sergei Eisenstein, whom Joyce admired.[14]
Bute opens the film with an image of water, the river Liffy; cuts to HCE and
ALP in bed, thus linking water and ALP; then to a crumbling wall, which
becomes associated with the fall of civilization and with Humpty Dumpty, an
egg; and finally cuts to the wake. Her rapid pacing builds energy and
excitement, characteristics of both the text and the filmmaker. Bute's extensive
experience with animation helps her transform realistic figures into surrealistic
symbols. Glowing in light and treading an ambiguous space, HCE appears at
the end of the film as the risen Christ greeting a new day.

Bute directs live action as if it were animation, with special effects,
impersonal characterizations, and imaginative juxtapositions. Animation adds
to the film's excitement. The sparkle of the sunrise at the end of the film is
augmented by the use of special filters; pixillation or the broken illusion of
continuous motion characterizes figures in dream sequences; inanimate objects
(like the egg, which becomes the face of HCE in the commercial/bath scene) are
animated. All illustrate film vocabulary at its most dramatic. Moreover,
animation techniques convey an impression of surrealism, appropriate for a
dream.

Bute did not copy Joyce's text but imprinted her own style on the film.
Her quick cuts and dramatic fades, for example, reflect her energy, creativity

and responsiveness to drama. Unfortunately, her sense of decorum robbed the film of the rich sensuality that pervades the text and play. The novel repeatedly hints that there has been sexual activity in the park between HCE and a woman. In Bute's park scene, Shem and Shaun innocently and happily chase their sister Issy. Tristan and Isolde chastely kiss on the beach. The text, however, refers explicitly to their union: "with a queeleetlecree of joysis crisis she renulited their disunited" (*FW* 395.32-33). In the film, ALP performs a striptease act on stage, but she only teases, remaining clothed. Patrick A. McCarthy comments on this teasing quality of the film when he characterizes Bute's approach as "lighthearted and like vaudeville, picking up on the comic rather than the serious." However, he has high praise for her artistic achievement.[15]

Only a small portion of the sensuousness found in *Finnegans Wake* survives in the evolution from written text to screen. In the film, HCE in a nightshirt and ALP in a modest nightgown, asleep in their separate worlds, hardly touch in bed. Awake they tenderly kiss with more suggestion of sentimentality than of the erotic passion alluded to in the text.

Undoubtedly in 1965 censorship limited Bute's choices to some degree, but even Manning's play, produced earlier and in a less permissive milieu, is more sexually explicit than Bute's film. In the play, the girls start to remove their blouses in front of Shem before disappearing.[16] Bute's young girl in a dream sequence removes her skirt to reveal bloomers covering her legs to the knee. Ann Holmes quoted Bute in 1965 as saying that censorship was no problem: "It [the film] does have some tick words, but I don't think people will be shocked by the romantic aspects of '*Finnegan*.'"[17] In contrast only a few years later in the *Ulysses* film, Boylan is shown with his pants off chasing Molly in bed where she wears a much more revealing nightgown than ALP in Bute's film.

Bute's restrained treatment of sexuality reflected her personality and background. Raised in the early part of the century in a socially prominent family in Houston, she was trained in behavior appropriate for a debutante. She learned to converse artfully, to entertain, and not to reveal. Her best friend from Houston and later from New York, Virginia Gibbs Smyth, acknowledged that Mary Ellen said what she wanted others to hear, regardless of the reality of the situation.[18] Zack Bowen said that one layer of her personality was gushing, "so exuberant it couldn't be for real," and that "you had to sort this out."[19]

Many reviews of *Passages from Finnegans Wake* focused on Bute's achievement. Emily Genauer of *Newsday* wrote that "Mary Ellen Bute produced and directed it [*Passages*] with such extraordinary imagination and invention, assisted by the exceptionally beautiful camera work of her husband, Ted Nemeth."[20] Stanley Eichelbaum of the *San Francisco Examiner* described Bute's film as "witty, adroit, and often a beautiful kaleidoscope of surrealist photography" but he added, "there is nonetheless a staginess in several sequences that conflict with the fanciful abstraction of others."[21] Albert Johnson in *Film Quarterly* described the overall effect as "an original, successful assault upon the senses." He went on to focus on Bute's ability to unite image and sound: "Certain moments are extremely moving because of their precise amalgam of image and sound in order to create a sense of timelessness, emotional loss, and nostalgia." He summed up the film as "a hymn in praise of life."[22]

Jane Reilly (ALP) and Martin J. Kelley (HCE)
in *Passages from Finnegans Wake.*

Some reviewers, however, found that the film obscured the plot of the novel and fabricated scenes not in the text. James Blish in *A Wake Newslitter* said, "there is little in the production that I could connect with any particular scene in the novel. . . . The novel itself is often marred by fond irrelevancies—but I do complain that to pile new plot invention upon Joyce's is at best an act of supererogation."[23] Stanley Kauffmann, by contrast, in *New American Review* saw this inventiveness as positive. He described Bute's strong sense of vision, her "loving perception of the novel and her response to it in cinematic imagination." He found her film "in tune with the work it is about."[24]

Bute said that the novel was "primarily visual and it had to be so on the screen." She added, "The film is not a translation of the book but a reaction to it. It represents my point of view."[25] Many critics would agree that Bute succeeded in doing what she attempted.

Sarah Smith criticized the film medium itself as being incapable of double articulation, that is the separation of the object from the word, enabling the cinema image to act in a purely verbal sense like a metaphor.[26] However, she commented that Bute's film "represents probably the closest approach possible to Joyce's book using standard filmic language."[27] She did not mention Bute's use of subtitles, which become film images working as metaphors. Stanley Kauffmann described the Joycean words in the subtitles as "visual objects enriching the picture."[28] Smith also omitted Bute's use of montage, which links images and produces new associations. HCE's fall followed by the crumbling of an historic wall conveys the idea that HCE's fall is a metaphor for the fall of civilization.

Zack Bowen, remarking on the film when it first appeared, put Bute's accomplishment into perspective:

> The opening [of the film] may very well mark a new milestone in bringing the greatest and most difficult writer of modern times a little closer to general understanding and acceptance. . . . That an attempt was made to make any sort of a picture on *Finnegans Wake* is astounding; that the picture is a genuinely successful work of art is, though perhaps unbelievable, wholly true.[29]

Eighteen years later, at a program honoring Mary Ellen Bute at the Museum of Modern Art in New York, Zack Bowen, who had written extensively on music in Joyce's works, said:

> It is fruitless to review the criticism of Joyce scholars who cite all of the differences between the *Wake* and the film. The question is, rather, do things like the vaudeville show and the elevator scene, with its overtones of Bloom's *Ulysses* trial, have any place at all in a film with *Finnegans Wake* in the title. I think they do. The more times I see the Bute film, the better I think it is, though that appreciation does not stem directly from my love of the novel. Perhaps *Finnegans*

Wake should never have been included in the title,
though Ms. Bute would probably have had been
accused of plagiarism if she had not. Rather I think
the vision is less Joyce's than the director's. The film
portrays a world where man does experience a fall, a
division, and a reunification. More importantly it is
a world of sentimentality, and a world so full of love
that the antagonisms are comic rather than tragic or
heroic. It is also a world of unprovoked mirth and
gaiety, not a satiric existentialist depiction but a gay
romp through the TWA building, and tender,
thoughtful, pregnant passages of sadness and
reflection.

Perhaps what I miss most in the film is Joyce's
sense of the ribald, the bizarre, and virtue unrewarded.
What I like most are the imaginative attempts to do
something visually which Joyce could not with mere
words. Bringing together Mutt and Jute vis-a-vis both
sides of the television was a master stroke. The stage
parody of Isolde and the interchangeability of the sons
were all similarly high points in the film for me. Here
were attempts to capture genuine analogy in Joycean
mood and vigor. Some of the spirited hilarity of Joyce
was there, and of course a form of his words. . . .

Finnegans Wake is perhaps the most impossible
book in the world to film, and any attempt to deal
with any segment, any philosophy, any sense of unity
called forth by the novel should be greeted with
warmth and appreciation. *Passages from Finnegans
Wake* is a good film; it stands up under the pressure of
time, it has exuberance and meaning, something that
often is difficult to find in the novel itself, and a sense
of the joy of *Finnegans Wake*.[30]

Passages from Finnegans Wake, a film based on a literary work, set the
pattern for Bute's subsequent films. At James Joyce Society meetings, Bute
became reacquainted with Thorton Wilder, whom she had known through his
sister, Isabel, a classmate at the Yale School of Drama in 1925. Wilder,
impressed with Bute's creativity, gave her the film rights to *The Skin of Our
Teeth*, his innovative play influenced by Joyce. Unfortunately, although Bute
did some preliminary shooting on *Skin*, she was never able to raise the money
necessary for a feature film. Part of the problem was her unwillingness to
compromise artistically for the sake of financial support and her insistence on
complete artistic control. Isabel Wilder said that she and her brother were both
disappointed that Mary Ellen Bute was unable to come up with a team to work
on *The Skin of Our Teeth* although they were sympathetic to her artistic needs
and admired her creative abilities.[31] Essentially an independent filmmaker, Bute
was unhappy with the compromises necessary to produce feature length films
involving large numbers of people with different interests.[32]

Mary Ellen Bute's adaptation of *Finnegans Wake* triumphed artistically, as acknowledged by the Cannes Film festival award, and reflected her energy, love of life, and refinement while at the same time capturing the humor, energy, creativity and newness of Joyce's text. Bute and Joyce met in the metaphor of cinema.

Notes

1. Ted Nemeth, interview with author, Milwaukee, Wisconsin, 22 November 1984.

2. Vincent Canby, "American-Made 'Finnegan's [*sic*] Wake' To Get Joyce-Language Subtitles," *Variety* 239 (August 18, 1965): 15.

3. James Joyce, *Finnegans Wake* (New York: Viking/Penguin, 1976). All further references to *FW* are cited in the text and refer to this edition.

4. Sarah W. R. Smith, "The Word Made Celluloid: On Adapting Joyce's *Wake*," *The English Novel and the Movies*, eds. Michael Klein and Gillian Parker (New York: Frederick Unger, 1981), 311-312.

5. Zack Bowen, interview with author, Milwaukee, Wisconsin, 12 June 1987.

6. Ann Holmes, "There Goes 'Finnegan,'" *Houston Chronicle*, 25 April 1965, 6.

7. Holmes, 6.

8. Canby, 15.

9. Mary Ellen Bute, "Memorandum on the Music Score to *Finnegans Wake*," n.d., Mary Ellen Bute Papers, Yale University Library (hereafter cited as Bute memo).

10. Bowen, 12 June 1987.

11. Mary Ellen Bute, "Abstronics: An Experimental Filmmaker Photographs the Esthetics of the Oscillograph," *Films in Review* (June-July 1954): 263-266.

12. Bute memo.

13. Bute memo.

14. Alan M. Cohn, "Joyce in the Movies," *James Joyce Quarterly* 2 (Summer 1965): 317.

15. Patrick A. McCarthy, interview with author, 25 February 1988.

16. Mary Manning, *Passages from Finnegans Wake* (Cambridge: Harvard University Press, 1957), 58.

17. Holmes, 6.

18. Virginia G. Smyth, interview with author, 17 June 1984.

19. Bowen, 12 June 1987.

20. Emily Genauer, "Pinter, Picasso and Joyce: A Trio for New York," *Newsday* (10 October 1967).

21. Stanley Eichelbaum, "James Joyce on Film-Admirable Experiment," *San Francisco Examiner*, 24 October 1965, section 2: 4.

22. Albert Johnson, "The Dynamic Gesture: New American Independents," *Film Quarterly* 19 (Summer 1966): 8-10.

23. James Blish, "Mary Ellen Bute: Passages from *Finnegans Wake*," *A Wake Newslitter* 2 (December 1965): 29-30.

24. Stanley Kauffmann, "*Ulysses*: Passages from James Joyce's *Finnegans Wake*," *Figures of Light: Film Criticism and Comment* (New York: Harper and Row, 1971): 27-28.

25. Gretchen Weinberg, "An Interview with Mary Ellen Bute," *Film Culture* 25 (Winter 1964-1965): 27.

26. Smith, 305.

27. Smith, 307.

28. Kauffmann, 27.

29. Zack Bowen, "Lots of Fun with *Finnegans Wake*," Mary Ellen Bute Papers, Yale University Library.

30. Zack Bowen, "*Finnegans Wake* and *Ulysses* into Film," (paper delivered at Cineprobe honoring Mary Ellen Bute, Museum of Modern Art, New York, April 4, 1983), Mary Ellen Bute Papers, Yale University Library.

31. Isabel Wilder, interview with author, 28 July 1984.

32. Bute ran into similar financial problems on her Whitman film, *Out of the Cradle Endlessly Rocking*.

Thoughts on Making Music
From the Hundred-Letter Words in *Finnegans Wake*

Margaret Rogers

The great number of musical allusions in *Finnegans Wake* have been well documented by such eminent scholars as Matthew J. C. Hodgart and Mabel P. Worthington,[1] Zack Bowen,[2] and Ruth Bauerle.[3] Their work was augmented by John Cage's statistical analysis in his background for the *Roaratorio*.[4] Such research supports the fact that in *Finnegans Wake* Joyce used more musical allusion of all kinds—songs, instruments, and musical forms than in any of his previous works. *Finnegans Wake* represents a marriage of words and music with allusions, rhythms, and other musical devices employed by the author to extend the dimension of the text. Words read and spoken go as far as they can; words sung extend language further. The strength of the words is heightened by being made audible.

The *Finnegans Wake* chorale, *A Babble of Earwigs or Sinnegan with Finnegan* grew out of ideas generated by a *Finnegans Wake* seminar presented at the University of Wisconsin-Milwaukee. In addition to instructing the eight seminar participants to read twenty pages of text a day (silently or aloud), Professor Janet E. Dunleavy encouraged her students to tap into his or her personal experience and background whether religious, literary, historical, artistic, or political and to allow the text to merge with that experience. What was tapped in me was music . . . my *other mother* tongue. I have sung, conducted choirs and studied music theory and composition. I am a musician and think in a musical context. So when I read *Finnegans Wake*, I not only saw the words, I heard them. I heard the sounds and rhythms as clearly as I perceived their meaning. (More clearly much of the time.) As I read/listened, long forgotten tunes nudged their way into consciousness. Fragments of melodies began to form. I was constantly aware of the clatter and chatter and babble . . . the *sound* of the book. This sound increased to a roar whenever the hundred-letter words appeared. I was drawn to these words like a sailor to the siren's song and increasingly I was intrigued with the idea that they might form the outline for a musical work.

Of all the words and permutations of words in the *Wake*, the hundred-letter words stand out as unique. They cannot be ignored. They demand attention. What are they? Why are they? How do they function in the narrative? Is there a pattern in them?

Roland McHugh's decipherment in *The Annotations to Finnegans Wake* lays to rest the theory that the words are just an inchoate jumble of letters thrown together helter-skelter. The hundred-letter words each have meaning, individual meaning. They also have many patterns, one of which is numerical. There are ten of them. Nine contain 100 letters and the tenth, 101. The total number of letters contained is 1001, a cycle, the year of the new millennium, and possibly an allusion to *The Thousand and One Nights*. Whether spoken, read, or sung, these words are noise. They demand to be heard.

Words 1, 2, and 10 are about thunder,[5] the greatest noise of all. The

189

hundred-letter words signal an intersection in the psyche of the dreamer. They change the narrative direction of the text. Their noise symbolizes chaos, a chaos which demands release and resolution. And they were written by a man who had a lifelong fear of thunder.[6]

Considering Joyce's absorption with musical allusion, the meticulous construction of the words, their place in the text, chronological significance, and apparent importance as a narrative device, I concluded that he may have intended to combine all ten words to form the outline for a musical work. I decided to attempt to shape these marvels of imagination into music. Since they are *words*, contain other *words*, and are part of a text, I dismissed the idea of an instrumental interpretation and chose a form that would focus on words and music. I chose to call it a chorale, a more encompassing music form that not only is sung but can be augmented by spoken poetry or prose.

STEPS

I typed each word on the top of a sheet of paper and noted my ideas and observations beneath the word. Then I scrutinized, spoke, beat, sang, chanted, recorded, and listened to every word. I searched for rhythms, tempos, and pitch possibilities. I studied the text for rhetorical devices, such as alliteration, onomatopoeia, spondaic, trochaic, anapestic stresses, themes, allusions, and the meaning of the word itself.

After I had lifted the ten words from context and arranged them chronologically, I began to perceive a pattern that indicated the outline of a human life span. They appeared to move from youth to age. In the case of the first word, the beginning of the life cycle is announced by thunder (no. 1) ("In the beginning was the word . . . and the word was . . .").[7] The pattern continues in words nos. 2 and 3 which lend themselves to lighthearted tunes and playful themes evoking visions of children cavorting about chasing and tumbling over one another. Next this sequence follows: the whoring years (no. 4), the pastoral, blissful time (no. 5), the loss of innocence brought about by the horror of diaspora (no. 6), the drunken period (no. 7), the babble of confusion (no. 8), the coughing and coffin (no. 9), and finally, the thunderous finale featuring Norse deities bellowing out the end of the cycle. I added a coda of hope based on lines from text: "Ho, Time Timeagen, Wake! For if sciencium (what's what) can mute uns nought, a thought, abought the Great Sommboddy within the Omniboss, perhaps an artsaccord (hoot's hoot) might sing ums tumtim abutt the Little Newbuddies that ring his panch"(*FW* 415.15-19).

I used musical forms that reflected the meaning of a particular passage. As gradually raising the pitch adds to the overall tension and excitement, musical keys (i.e. F, G) were arranged to move the chorale in an upward direction. As there were so many segments to the chorale, I had to find a means of connecting them and did so through the use of a narrator who spoke lines from the text found in immediate proximity to each of the hundred-letter words.

Above all, I took care not to become too serious. *Finnegans Wake* is fun! Hilarious! Full of laughter! But implicit in the "laughtears" (*FW* 15.9) is the idea that when one is laughing, the tear is just behind the eye. Without these opposites, there would be no motion, no energy, no cycle.

I divided each word into sections suggested by observed differences in sound, appearance and meaning. For example, the initial syllables of word no. 1(*ba ba ba dal gar ágh*) to me rhythmically sound like "Here We Go Lóopty Lóo" evoking a major theme in *Finnegans Wake*, the cycle. The following section (*takaminarronkonnbronnerronn*) differs with more rolling thunder sounds underscored by the use of double *rr*'s and *nn*'s. It also contains *arron* and *erronn*, word-like fragments that sound like Erin or the ronns and tronns for "guns and drums" from "Johnny I Hardly Knew Ye." The following three sections, *hounawnskawn, toohoohoor* and *denenthurnuk* (subtly different from each other) are distinguished by vowel sounds within the sections. These sounds shift from *ou* to *aw* to *oo, oo, oo, eh, eh* and *uh* creating with the previous sounds a wonderful long vocalize (a vocal exercise) like the sound of howling wind behind a storm or a banshee keen. When the entire word is pronounced, it sounds like its meaning, thunder, and no wonder, as it is composed of ten phonetically spelled words for thunder in different languages. (See note 5.)

Other examples of the process are found in word no. 3 where the *klikkakakkak* brings to mind the tune of the "Irish Washerwoman" with an implied 6/8 time signature, the rhythm of the Irish reel. The clapping that accompanies such a song is instinctive and underscored here by words within the word such as *klop, appluddy,* and *appladdy.* No. 4 is a word about a whore. Here we get right to it with *blady* (bloody) *ugh, foul, moecklenburg* (Dublin's red-light district) and *whur* and *whor,* and *strumpa* (strumpet). This is obviously not the proper setting for a hymn tune. No. 7 sounds as if it should be "slurred," as if a couple of drunks named *schumm* (Shem) and *summ* (Shaun) were *slumming and bummin' around* and *humpta dumpt, poo foo* (poor fool) fell off the *waul* (wall).

No. 9 is a jewel of trochaic stress pattern. The *hussten, hassten, caffin, coffin* cries out for an accented/unaccented rhythmic pattern which in turn stresses the coughing sound, and dirge rhythm, and even perhaps, the sound of a hammer driving nails into the coffin.

In order for the reader to understand the process involved in composing the chorale, I am including each word, its location in the text and a simplified explanation of its meaning below:

ILLUSTRATION #1
The Hundred-Letter Words

No. 1 (*FW* 3.15-17): a stutter, then ten phonetically spelled words for thunder in different languages
bababadalgharaghtakamminarronnkonnbronntonnerronntuonnthunntrovarrhou nawnskawntoohoohoordenenthurnuk!

No. 2 (*FW* 23.5-7): lightning, stormy skies, and more multilingual thunder words

Perkodhuskurunbarggruauyagokgorlayorgromgremmitghundhurthrumathunara-
didillifaititillibumullunukkunun!

No. 3 (*FW* 44.20-21): clap and clapping in French, German, Italian, Irish,
Russian
klikkaklakkaklaskaklopatzklatschabattacreppycrottygraddaghsemmihsammihno-
uithappluddyappladdypkonpkot!

No. 4 (*FW* 90.31-33): lightning continues amid a polyglot of whores and
whoring
Bladyughfoulmoecklenburgwhurawhorascortastrumpapornanennykocksapastip-
patappatupperstrippuckputtanach, eh?

No. 5 (*FW* 113.9-11): "crookly" and "pasture" suggest "Every Valley Shall Be
Exalted" (Handel's *Messiah*)
Thingcrooklyexineverypasturesixdixlikencehimaroundhersthemaggerbykinkin-
kankanwithdownmindlookingated.

No. 6 (*FW* 257.27-28): doors shut in Irish, Danish, French, Russian, Turkish;
Lucifer and Zeus present
Lukkedoerendunandurraskewdylooshoofermoyportertooryzooysphalnabortansp-
orthaokansakroidverjkapakkapuk

No. 7 (*FW* 314.8-9): amid lots of schummin and summin around, "humpta
dumpta" falls off the wall
Bothallchoractorschumminaroundgansumuminarumdrumstrumtruminahumpta-
dumpwaultopoofooloederamaunsturnup!

No. 8 (*FW* 332.5-7): daddy doodles in English when the moon comes over the
mountain in Irish at the wake
Pappappapparrassannuaragheallachnatullaghmonganmacmacmacwhackfallther-
debblenonthedubblandaddydoodled

No. 9 (*FW* 414.19-20): much multilingual coughing and clearing of the throat
precedes a grim(m?) tale
husstenhasstencaffincoffintussemtossemdamandamnacosaghcusaghhobixhatoux-
peswchbechoscashlcarcarcaract

No. 10 (*FW* 424.20-22): cycle is completed with return of thunder, lightning,
and Norse gods
Ullhodturdenweirmudgaardgringnirurdrmolnirfenrirlukkilokkibaugimandodrr-
erinsurtkrinmgernrackinarockar!

SPECIFIC EXAMPLES OF "WHAT'S IN A WORD"

No. 1 (*FW* 3.15-17): a stutter, then ten phonetically spelled words for thunder
in different languages
bababadalgharaghtakamminarronnkonnbronntonnerronntuonnthunntrovarrhou-
nawnskawntoohoohoordenenthurnuk!

Each word presented its own challenge. What follows is a description of the process used in forming words nos. 1, 2, and 6 into music. After a thorough examination of the word, I divided it into the sections it suggested. The surrounding text is interwoven with allusions to familiar tunes. In word no. 1 "riverrun, past Eve and Adam's, etc." (*FW* 3.1), the first line of *Finnegans Wake*, *takamminarron* translates to "Take him in Erron" (Erin) in the chorale. The chorus sings *arrontronbron* to the tune of "Johnny I Hardly Knew Ye" as "With their *ronns* and *tuons* and *thronns* and *bronns*." (In specific examples italicized words are parts of the hundred-letter words.)

> The song "Mna na heireann" ("Women of Ireland") was chosen for its beauty and haunting quality. It provides a good balance juxtaposed against thunder creating a balance appropriate to Ireland's haunted past and struggle.

> *Bababadalgaragh* is the beginning of the first word. When sounded out rhythmically, it sounds like the song "Here We Go Lóopty Lóo" and underscores the cyclical theme of the *Wake*.

> "I Dreamt I Dwelt Mid Warblers' Walls" is lifted from the adjacent text and is a takeoff on "I Dreamed I Dwelled in Marble Halls." It highlights the dream theme.

> In "The great fall of the offwall, the pftjschute of finnegan" (*FW* 3.18, 19), the narrator announces a major theme—Humpty Dumpty falling off the wall.

> "Whack fall the da, tuck up your part in her" is a revised version of the traditional song "Whack fall the da, dance with your partner . . . lots of fun at Finnegan's wake." This section introduces the title of the book.

> The last two lines include "Hosty" and "Percy," other names for the dreamer, H. C. Earwicker.

Piano and percussion, wind chimes, cymbals, scrapers, slappers, rachets, tympany, tambourines and triangles, plus bass drum, snare drum and other percussion instruments were used to accompany the singers in the performance of the chorale. Voices were chosen for color and quality best able to project the meaning of the text.

(from the chorale) Word One

Chorus: (humming) take him in Erron
             ah, ron, tron, bron . . . eh, ron tuon, thon
Tenor solo: "mna na heireann" (Sung in Irish)

Chorus: bababadalgaragh, bababadalhooroo, bababadagaragh
             Issy he hardly knew yeh

(segue)   I dreamt I dwealth mid warblers' walls

> When throstles and coughs to my si-hie-hied
> But I also dreamt which appeased me most
> That you held me by your si-hie-hied.

Narrator: The great fall of the off-wall, the pfchute of Finnegan.

Solo: Whack fall the tuck up your part-in-her
             Welt the flure his hoddit did shake
             Lots of fun at Finnegan's wake.

Chorus: With their ronns and tuonns and gunds and drums
             huroo, huroo
             With their ronns and tuonns and bronns and tronns, the enemy
             nearly slew ye
             O Hosty my dear, you look so queer
             Percy I hardly knew ye.

No. 2 (*FW* 23.5-7): lightning, stormy skies, and more multilingual thunder words
Perkodhuskurunbarggruauyagokgorlayorgromgremmitghundhurthrumathunara-didillifaititillibumullunukkunun!

Word no. 2—Voices sing different signal colors (*FW* 23.1-2) dissonance, lightning, fire, thunder roll

> —Narrator: "Is it the prank queen?" (*FW* 22.13)
> Voice: "Sea, sea captain." (composer)
> Narrator: "Shtop her, bar the way (*barggruay*) or lay 'er!"
> (*orlayor*).
> —Song to the tune or rhyme of "And he huffed and he puffed" from
> "The Three Little Pigs" (no connection) with syllables from the
> word as part of the text: that is, "ordured delay her *gromgremmit*"
> —(Song continues to words and syllables from the word.) "And thunar it
> didilly, fait and it titilly" (*dillifaititilli*).
> —Narrator asks, "Is this a prank, quean?"   No doubt this is
> Granuwealla, the famous sixteenth/seventeenth-century Irish queen
> of the seas who was notorious for kidnapping the heir to Howth in
> retaliation for a snub she had suffered at the hands of the Earl of
> Howth.[8]
> —Narrator continues, "Stop domb dame, *gromgremmit*. Bring back
> my earring, come back with my Erin!"
> —From this point on in no. 2 there is one long pun on heir, ear,
> earring, Earwicker, Erin.
> —Men sing, "And he clopped his rude hand to his eacy hitch and
> he ordured her in his thick spick spitch" (*FW* 23.3-5).
> —"TIP," which has been intrepreted many ways and may have a
> sexual connotation or indicate a brief moment of consciousness in
> the dreamer, appears throughout *Finnegans Wake* and throughout
> the chorale.
> —Narrator: "Now between you and me . . . flamend floddy flatuous
> word" (*FW* 23.9-10,12-14) sound of "letting of wind" by percussion.

—The composer chose the song tune "I don't wanna walk without you, baby" for "Granuwealla stole away his earring, He no Anna-liv (ALP a.k.a. Anna Livia Plurabelle) without his earrin'."
—Narrator: "Come back! Come Back! Oh bring back my Erin to me, to me." (Based on "My Bonnie Lies Over the Ocean.")
—Song: "Come back with my earrin" based on "Come back to Erin."
—Narrator: "Ach! Big Clap!" (foretelling the events of word no. 3)
—Voice: "He's off the wall" (referring to Earwicker's fall from the magazine wall).

In addition to components of the hundred-letter words, quotations from the text were used throughout the "Chorale." Most often these quotations were found immediately adjacent to the word. Word no. 6 is a good example of the interweaving of surrounding text and the word.

No. 6 (*FW* 257.27-28): doors shut in Irish, Danish, French, Russian, Turkish; Lucifer and Zeus present.
Lukkedoerendunandurraskewdylooshoofermoyportertooryzooysphalnabortansporthaokansakroidverjkapakkapuk

Word no. 6—Shutting the door.

—Narrator: "Come indoor scoffeynosey and shed your swank. Oh, you're well heeled now Missy Cheekspear and your panto's off, oh fie for shame for the prize of a peace of bakin. With a pinch of the ponch and a punch of the haunch was found in the round of the sound of the lound . . ." (*FW* 257.13-15,19,21).
After the narrator speaks, the chorus sings the words to the tune of "D'ye Ken John Peele" which gives the cyclical theme in "the sound of the round."
—Words for conversation are primarily taken from the hundred-letter word concerning shutting the door. "Wanna mango" introduces the "Desperation Tango" adapted from "who, in deesperation of deispiration at the diasporation of his diesparation" (*FW* 257.25) and becomes in the chorale, "and the desperation of the separation of the diasporation of the diesparation."
I decided on the tango rhythm after speaking the words from the text and listening to their pattern. In performance, this could be danced as well as sung. Its lighthearted feeling reflects the carefree innocence of those unaware of the impending disaster of the diaspora which "shut the door" on countless lives.
—Men sing the traditional "Dies Irae" bespeaking the wrath of God while in the background the mindless tango continues.
—Then comes a total change of feeling with the introduction composed of open fifth chords, a prelude to the Gregorian-like chant which tells of the extinguishing of the light (*Lux non eterna est,*) the wrath of God (*Dies Irae*), the plea to the virgin (*Sacroid verja*), *looshoofer* (Lucifer), the fall of the gods (Zeus fall, *zoosphall,* from the word), and the shame of diaspora. All the words in the chant-song are from word no. 6.

—Chorus chants: "Shame, Seamus, Shame on us."
—Solo: "Roisin Duhb" ("dark rose" a synonym for Ireland)[9]

The composition was not realized sequentially. Words were developed as inspiration appeared. No. 5 "little crooklyex," as I affectionately call it, was first. The rise/fall theme was carried out in nos. 4 and 7 with the same tune ascending in no. 4 that when inverted descends in no. 7. Like children, some were tractable, others unruly. No. 8 refused to yield its secrets until we were into rehearsal.

The entire process, including finding and working with the musicians, took about three months. Throughout this period one idea prevailed: to let the words and text tell the story. But since all of us bring to any work our own experiences and knowledge, all such endeavors become a collaboration and after awhile the boundaries blur so that even as I write this, I'm not totally sure who did what to whom or why.[10]

Notes

1. Matthew J. C. Hodgart and Mable P. Worthington, *Song in the Works of James Joyce* (New York: Columbia University Press, 1959).

2. Zack Bowen, *Musical Allusions in the Works of James Joyce* (Albany, N.Y.: State University of New York Press, 1974).

3. Ruth Bauerle, *The James Joyce Songbook* (New York: Garland, 1982).

4. John Cage, *Roaratorio: An Irish Circus on Finnegans Wake* (New York: Athenaum, 1982).

5. Roland McHugh, *Annotations to Finnegans Wake* (Baltimore: Johns Hopkins University Press, 1980), 3.15-18, 23.5-9, 44.20-22, 90.30-35, 113.9-13, 257.25-30, 314.8-9, 332.1-9, 414.18,21, 424.20-22.

6. Richard Ellmann, *James Joyce* (New York: Oxford University Press, 1982), 25.

7. Prologue to the Gospel according to John.

8. Ann Chambers, *Granuaille, The Life and Times of Grace O'Malley* (Dublin: The Wolfhound Press, 1979).

9. James Clarence Mangan, *Mangan's Poems* (New York: Haverty, 1859). The poem "My Dark Rosaleen" was an adaptation of *Roisin Dubh* [Little Black Rose] attributed to Owen Roe MacWard, a poet in the court of Hugh the Red O'Donnell.

10. *A Babble of Earwigs or Sinnegan with Finnegan* was premiered at the Joyce Milwaukee Conference, June 14, 1987, at the Fine Arts Recital Hall, University of Wisconsin-Milwaukee. The chorale based on the ten multilingual portmanteau words of *Finnegans Wake* was performed by ten singers, a pianist percussionist, and narrator. Words and music were written by Margaret Rogers and special jazz arrangements were composed by Sigmund Behan Snopek. The performance was taped live. Cassettes and librettos are available for $12.00 from Margaret Rogers, 207 E. Buffalo, Milwaukee, WI 53202. [Ed.]

Contributors

Kit Basquin, who grew up with Mary Ellen Bute's children in New York, has an M.A. in art history and studied writing at the University of Wisconsin-Milwaukee, at Yale Summer School, and at the Bread Loaf Writers' Conference. She is the curator at the Haggerty Museum of Art at Marquette University.

Bernard Benstock is professor of English, University of Miami, Coral Gables, a past president of the James Joyce Foundation, editor of the *James Joyce Literary Supplement*, author of four books on Joyce, and editor of several books on Joyce.

David Borodin is an art appraiser and vice president of Frisk & Borodin Appraisers, Ltd. of Philadelphia, and is currently writing on an aspect of Joyce and the visual arts. He is a member of the Philadelphia *Wake* Circle, and creator of their internal newsletter, *The Philadelphia Wake Circle Rectangular*.

Sheldon Brivic is associate professor of English at Temple University. He is the author of *Joyce between Freud and Jung*, *Joyce the Creator*, and his forthcoming *The Veil of Signs: Joyce, Lacan, and Perception of Desire* (Illinois). His articles have appeared in *Massachusetts Review*, *Novel*, *James Joyce Quarterly*, and other periodicals.

Vincent J. Cheng is associate professor of English at the University of Southern California. He is the author of *Shakespeare and Joyce: A Study of Finnegans Wake* and *"Le Cid": A Translation in Rhymed Couplets* as well as of numerous articles on Joyce, on Ford Madox Ford, and on modern fiction. He is currently writing *Religion and Passion: The Catholic Ford Madox Ford*.

Kimberly J. Devlin is associate professor of English at the University of California, Riverside. Her work on Joyce has appeared in *PMLA*, the *James Joyce Quarterly*, and in other periodicals and essay collections. She has recently completed a book entitled *Wandering and Return in Finnegans Wake: An Integrative Approach to Joyce's Fiction* (forthcoming Princeton University Press).

John Gordon teaches at Connecticut College in New London, Connecticut. He is the author of *James Joyce's Metamorphoses* and *Finnegans Wake: A Plot Summary*. He has had articles on Joyce published in the *James Joyce Quarterly*, *A Wake Newslitter*, *Modern Fiction Studies*, *Texas Studies in Literature and Language*, and *ELH*. He is currently working on a study of the physiological theories implicit in literature of the modernist period.

John Harty teaches at Northern Michigan University in Marquette, Michigan. He edited this volume and edited *Tom Stoppard: A Casebook*.

David Hayman, professor of Comparative Literature at the University of Wisconsin-Madison, has published widely on Joyce, modern literature, and literary theory. His publications on the *Wake* include several books: *Joyce et Mallarmé* (1956), *A First-Draft Version of Finnegans Wake* (ed.) (1963), the *Wake* volumes of *The James Joyce Archive* (36 vols., ed. with Danis Rose) (1978), and *In the Wake of the Wake* (ed.) (1978). In addition, he has included discussions of the *Wake* in his latest book, *Reforming the Narrative: Toward a Mechanics of Modernist Fiction* (1987). He is currently completing a book-length study of the early notebooks and manuscripts which will show how the *Wake* took shape in Joyce's imagination.

Hugh Kenner is professor of English Literature at The Johns Hopkins University. He has written many distinguished books on modern literature, including two on Ezra Pound, three on Joyce, two on Beckett, and one on T. S. Eliot. Among his other books is a study of Buckminster Fuller's mathematical equations.

Alan Searing Loxterman is associate professor of English at the University of Richmond, Virginia, where he has taught since 1970. His most recent project is "'The More Joyce Knew the More He Could' and 'More Than I Could': Theology and Fictional Technique in Joyce and Beckett," to be published in a forthcoming anthology on Joyce and Beckett (Fordham University Press, 1991).

Colin MacCabe is Professor of English at University of Pittsburgh and Head of Research at the British Film Institute. He is author of *James Joyce and the Revolution of the World* and the editor of *James Joyce: New Perspectives*. He is currently working on the relation between language and literature.

Al Montesi teaches literature at St. Louis University in St. Louis, Missouri. He is the author of three books of poetry, five plays, two children's books—*Peter Bently: The Super-sleuth Cat*, and *Peter Bently: The Case of the 1904 St. Louis World's Fair*—and one critical study, *Radical Conservatism: The Southern Review*, 1935-1942.

David W. Robinson is assistant professor of English at Georgia Southern College. His most recent publication on James Joyce, a study of the opening triad of stories in *Dubliners*, appeared in *Texas Studies in Literature and Language*. His current work apart from Joyce concerns East German fiction.

Margaret Rogers received her musical training at the Elgin Academy, Elgin, Illinois, and at the Chicago Musical College-Roosevelt University in Chicago, Illinois. Ms. Rogers also attended the University of Chicago and the University of Milwaukee-Wisconsin. For seventeen seasons, she was a professional member of the Chicago Symphony Chorus and performed widely in the Chicago area as a soloist. Her most recent publication is "Decoding the Fugue in 'Sirens'" in *James Joyce Literary Supplement* 4.1 (Spring 1990): 15-20.

INDEX